Baltic Yearbook of International Law

Baltic Yearbook of International Law

VOLUME 16, 2016

Editors-in-Chief

Lauri Mälksoo, Ineta Ziemele, Dainius Žalimas

Editorial Board

Egidijus Bieliunas (*Judge at the General Court of the Court of Justice of the EU*) – Tanel Kerikmäe (*LL.M., LL.Lic., Acting Director of Tallinn Law School at the Tallinn University of Technology*) – Egils Levits (*Judge at the Court of Justice of the EU*) – Rein Müllerson, *President of the Tallinn University Law School; Member of the Institut de droit international*) – Lauri Mälksoo (*Professor of International Law, University of Tartu*) – Vilenas Vadapalas (*former Judge of the General Court of the Court of Justice of the EU*) – Dainius Žalimas (*Professor and Head of the Institute of International and European Union Law (Faculty of Law, Vilnius University, President of the Constitutional Court of Lithuania*) – Ineta Ziemele (*President of the Constitutional Court of Latvia*) – Pēteris Zilgalvis, J.D. (*Staff Member at the European Commission*)

Advisory Board

Gudmundur Alfredsson (*Professor, University of Akureyri; Visiting Professor, University of Strasbourg*) – Theo van Boven (*Professor Emeritus of International Law, University of Maastricht*) – James Crawford (*Judge, International Court of Justice, The Hague*) – Andrew Drzemczewski (*Ph.D., Barrister-in-Law, Council of Europe Secretariat*) – John Dugard (*Emeritus Professor of Public International Law, University of Leiden; Emeritus Professor of Law, University of the Witwatersrand, Johannesburg; Member, International Law Commission*) – Asbjørn Eide (*Founder of the Norwegian Institute of Human Rights, University of Oslo*) – Christine Gray (*Ph.D., Professor in International Law, University of Cambridge*) – Mahulena Hofmann (*Professor, SES Chair at the University of Luxembourg*) – Göran Melander (*Professor Emeritus of International Law, University of Lund*) – Allan Rosas (*Professor, Judge at the Court of Justice of the EU*) – Bruno Simma (*Arbitrator, Iran-United States Claims Tribunal; former Judge, International Court of Justice*) – Brigitte Stern (*Professor Emeritus of International Law, University of Paris I*) – Rüdiger Wolfrum (*Professor, Dr. Dr. h. C., former Director, Max Planck Institute for Comparative Public Law and International Law*)

The titles published in this series are listed at *brill.com/balt*

Baltic Yearbook of International Law

BRILL
NIJHOFF

LEIDEN | BOSTON

Typeface for the Latin, Greek, and Cyrillic scripts: "Brill". See and download: brill.com/brill-typeface.

ISSN 1569-6456
E-ISSN 221-5897

ISBN 978-90-04-35977-2 (hardback)

Copyright 2018 by Koninklijke Brill NV, Leiden, The Netherlands.

Koninklijke Brill NV incorporates the imprints Brill, Brill Hes & De Graaf, Brill Nijhoff, Brill Rodopi, Brill Sense and Hotei Publishing.

All rights reserved. No part of this publication may be reproduced, translated, stored in a retrieval system, or transmitted in any form or by any means, electronic, mechanical, photocopying, recording or otherwise, without prior written permission from the publisher.
Authorization to photocopy items for internal or personal use is granted by Koninklijke Brill NV provided that the appropriate fees are paid directly to The Copyright Clearance Center, 222 Rosewood Drive, Suite 910, Danvers, MA 01923, USA. Fees are subject to change.

This book is printed on acid-free paper and produced in a sustainable manner.

Contents

About the Volume	VII
In Memoriam Dr. Kristīne Krūma (1974-2016)	IX
In Memoriam Dr. Kristīne Krūma (1974-2016)	XIII
We Will Always Have International Law: Editorial Note *Martins Paparinskis*	1
Territorial Conflicts and Disputes in Europe: What Role for International Law in the 21st Century? *Enrico Milano*	7
Attribution of Responsibility after the EU Accession to the ECHR and the "Co-Respondent Mechanism" *Przemyslaw Tacik*	29
Republic of Estonia Materials on International Law 2015 *Edited by René Värk*	55
Republic of Latvia Materials on International Law 2015 *Edited by Kristaps Tamužs*	143
Republic of Lithuania Materials on International Law 2015 *Edited by Aiste Augustauskaite and Saulius Katuoka*	187
Information for Authors	259

About the Volume

This volume of the *Baltic Yearbook of International Law* contains articles based on presentations delivered at the Annual Conference of the European Society of International Law which took place in Rīga, Latvia, from 8-10 September 2016. It was organized by the Riga Graduate School of Law in co-operation with the Constitutional Court of Latvia. The Government of Latvia in recognition of the importance of the issues discussed at the conference provided a financial grant to the Constitutional Court.

This was the first time since the ESIL was founded in 2004 that the Society's annual event took place in Eastern Europe which fact may have contributed to a particularly active participation of the young scholars from this region at the conference. Altogether the conference brought to Riga over 400 participants from 43 States. This was the first time in the history of Latvia when so many international lawyers came to Riga to discuss crisis and international law, crisis of international law and different other understandings of crises. Among the many fora and agora, the panel on the Baltic States and International Law solicited a wide audience. The following papers were presented therein.

Gleb Bogush spoke about "Dubious Legacy: Assessing the Contribution of the Eastern European Practice to ICL." Eva Kalnina dealt with the Baltic States and International Dispute Settlement. Maxim Timofeev discussed the Kononov and Vasiliauskas judgments of the European Court on Human Rights, concluded by René Värk's reflection on Russia's misuse of international law.

The agora panel was chaired by Martins Paparinskis, the Reader at the University College London, graduate of Oxford and University of Latvia. The Yearbook invited Martins to organize a selection of papers to be published in volume 16 with a view to transmit the impressions and reflections of the ESIL conference.

The volume also presents the international law practice of all three Baltic States for the year 2015. Over the years the contributors of the state practice reports have consistently noted judgments and decisions of the highest national courts in the three States which are fully engaged with international law. Application of international rules by the domestic courts is a norm and part of methodology of adjudication. At the same time, the Baltic States clearly consider the judgments of international courts and those of the two European courts in particular as part of their international law practice not only because the judgments in respect of each State are binding but also in a broader sense, i.e., they are part of European law that is followed in the Baltic States. It is notable that courts play a role in strengthening common European legal space. The state practice reports also show that there continue to be several international issues at the center of attention of the Baltic States. First, illegal occupation of Crimea and other territories where the Russian Federation exercises undue influence. Second, the effectiveness of the United Nations Security Council. Third, commemoration of the historical events that are important to the statehood of the three States.

2016 was also marked by a particularly sad event since Latvia lost one of its most talented international lawyers – Kristīne Krūma.

Ineta Ziemele
Editor-in-Chief

In Memoriam Dr. Kristīne Krūma (1974-2016)

On 4 July 2016 pro-rector and associate professor of the Riga Graduate School of Law Dr. Kristīne Krūma passed away at the age of 42. Kristīne Krūma had graduated from the University of Latvia in 1996 and following the restoration of the independence of the Republic of Latvia as one of the first Latvian lawyers had pursued her education in several European universities.

Dr. Krūma obtained her doctorate in law (LL.D.) from the Law Faculty of Lund University in 2012 and her master degree in international human rights law from the same University in 1998. She continued to pursue research at several leading academic institutions, such as the Max Planck Institute for Public International and Comparative Law in Heidelberg and the Centre for Migration Studies in Nijmegen, and she participated in several national and multilateral research projects. Her research focused on European integration, freedom of movement and citizenship. She was a true believer in multilateral fora for the solution of international problems and especially the kind of integration that the European Union represented. It is no surprise that her working carrier begun at the Latvian Ministry of Foreign Affairs in the department of international organizations.

For her age Dr. Krūma had a significant list of publications to her name.[1] Her doctoral dissertation, *EU Citizenship, Nationality and Migrant*

---

[1] Among her most notable contributions the following should be mentioned:
   Kruma, K., Latvian Integration Policy: Lost in Translation in A Re-definition of Belonging? Language and Integration Tests in Europe 241–270 (van Oers Ricky, Ersbøll Eva & Kostakopoulou Dora eds, Leiden: Martinus Nijhoff Publishers, 2010).
   Kruma, K., EU Citizenship, Nationality and Migrant Status. An Ongoing challenge (Leiden: Martinus Nijhoff Publishers 2014).
   Kruma, K., Latvia: Comprehensive Citizenship Reform on the Agenda in Parliament and in a Referendum Campaign, 2 Sep. 2012. Available at http://eudo-citizenship.eu/news/citizenship-news/700-latvia-comprehensive-citizenship-reform-on-the-agenda-in-parliament-and-in-a-referendum-campaign-
   Kruma, K., Access to Electoral Rights. Latvia, European University Institute, Florence, Robert Schuman Centre for Advanced Studies (EUDO Citizenship Observatory, June 2013. Available at http://cadmus.eui.eu/bitstream/handle/1814/29816/ER_2013_14-Latvia-FRACIT.pdf?sequence=1),

Status. An Ongoing Challenge, was published by Martinus Nijhoff Publishers/Brill in 2014. Her books and articles, most of them with leading publishing houses and in well-known journals, are characterized by thorough research and clear, well-organized and well-written texts. Her last book co-authored with Ms Dita Plepa on Constitutional Law in Latvia with the Wolters Kluwer publishing house came out already after her untimely death.[2]

In addition to her academic research and the long list of publications, Dr. Krūma taught a series of courses at the Riga Graduate School of Law (RGSL) and the University of Latvia. She supervised the research work and writings of several master students. Despite her own young age she was an authority and inspiration for her students and was really appreciated for always having the time to help the students and provide her advise.

Furthermore, Dr. Krūma engaged in many other scholarly and professional activities that are relevant to her having established a good name and name recognition in academic circles well beyond Latvia. Just to mention examples, she was a member of the Scientific Committee and the EU Fundamental Rights Agency (FRA) and of the Council of Europe Commission against Racism and Intolerance (ECRI).

She was one of the youngest judges to have served on the Constitutional Court of Latvia from 2007 to 2015. Her term of office was marked soon after her arrival in the Court by a landmark dissenting opinion in the case on the Border Agreement between Latvia and the Russian Federation.[3] The Court found the Agreement to be compatible with the Constitution even if it resulted in Latvia giving up part of its territory to the Russian Federation which during the illegal Soviet occupation of Latvia was given to the Russian Federation due to administrative re-drawing of the borders.

In all of these activities, from Lund to Strasbourg and in Riga, Dr. Krūma left people with the impression of an intelligent, articulate, ana-

---

Kruma, K., Statkus, S., Country Report in the Volume *National Constitutions in European and Global Governance: Democracy, Rights, the Rule of Law* by T.M.C. Asser Press in 2017 (edited by Anneli Albi and Samo Bardutzky). Available at https://www.kent.ac.uk/roleofconstitutions/network-of-experts.html.

2 See Krūma, K. and Plepa, D., *Constitutional Law in Latvia*, The Netherlands, Kluwer Law International B.V., 2016.

3 Constitutional Court of the Republic of Latvia, Separate Opinion of Judge *Kristīne Krūma* in Case No 2007-10-0102, 29.11.2007 (05.12.2007).

lytical, serious and hard-working academic. Her record was indeed one of quality and productivity.

It is a great loss to the Latvian and European legal communities to part with Kristīne Krūma so early in her career as a lawyer and academic. She will be remembered for her independent views, often reflected in her dissenting opinions at the Constitutional Court of Latvia which have already gone down in the history of legal thought in Latvia, as well as for her commitment to democratic and liberal values and human rights as well as her hard work. She will remain among the generation of those Latvian post-independence lawyers who among the first embraced Western values and legal thought.

Ineta Ziemele
Editor-in-Chief

Gudmundur Alfredsson
Member of the Advisory Board

In Memoriam Dr. Kristīne Krūma (1974-2016)

It is with deep sadness that I am writing to inform readers that Dr Kristīne Kruma, Associate Professor and Prorector of the Riga Graduate School of Law and former justice at the Constitutional Court of Latvia, passed away on 4 July 2016 after a serious illness.

I have been enormously impressed with Kristīne's work both in her capacity as a constitutional court judge and as a scholar, and I remember her as a very kind and warm colleague. I have been particularly impressed by how Kristīne on the one hand was a strong champion of European and international law and co-operation, and emphasised the need to redefine classic national concepts such as sovereignty. At the same time, especially in her role as the judge rapporteur in the IMF austerity cases at the Constitutional Court of Latvia, she sought to ensure a fairer balance between the exigencies of tackling the economic crisis and the impact of the drastic cuts on those affected, including pensioners, children, disabled persons and parents of newborn children.

Kristīne's scholarly research has been highly esteemed internationally and she was a frequent invited speaker at academic conferences and a member of numerous collaborative projects. The pre-eminent European constitutional law professor Leonard Besselink (University of Amsterdam) asked me to add the following note: 'I will remember her gentle character, and acute sense and awareness of where rule of law, discrimination and fundamental rights could be involved where social or other policies seemed to ignore them'.

On my part, I invited Kristīne to join – as a constitutional law expert for Latvia – the Network of Constitutional Experts which was established in the framework of the large-scale ERC funded research project 'The Role of National Constitutions in European and Global Governance', co-ordinated at the University of Kent. Kristine, in co-operation with Sandijs Statkus, prepared a highly interesting national report 'The Constitution of Latvia – A Bridge Between Traditions and Modernity', which is forthcoming in a two-volume edited book *National Constitutions in European and Global Governance: Democracy, Rights, the Rule of Law*, to be published by TMC Asser Press in 2017. In the comparative report that I have prepared, it emerges that the Latvian Constitutional Court, along with the German and Portuguese Constitutional Courts, seem to be the only courts in Europe that have been taking a more proactive approach in seeking to find a better balance and uphold fundamental rights and constitutional values in the context of the IMF and EU crisis measures and austerity programmes. In addition to the more well-known stance in protecting the legitimate expectations of individuals in the context of the austerity measures, the Latvian Constitutional Court notably underlined that taking international loans is an important matter of state and public life which must be decided by the legislator on the basis of the principle of separation of powers, and furthermore that the government cannot restrict fundamental rights by assuming international obligations. In so doing, the Court protected an important continental European constitutional tradition that dates back to the 19th century but that has increasingly come under strain in EU and global governance.

In my view, Kristīne has left an enormous legacy to the legal thinking about constitutional values and the rule of law based state in the context of transnational governance.

Everyone who knew Kristīne will be deeply saddened by her death. Our sincere condolences go to Kristīne's husband Ivars and daughter Zane. According to Kristīne's last will, her ashes were scattered into the Baltic Sea.

Anneli Albi
Professor of European Law
University of Kent

We Will Always Have International Law: Editorial Note

Martins Paparinskis [*]

Casablanca opens with a shot of a revolving globe.[1] The intention, as the producer of the movie explained, was 'to have a spinning globe – an unusual, interesting shot, sketchily lighted', 'immediately preceding the montage of the refugees'.[2] Before the camera zooms in to the refugee trail starting in Paris, it shows the political map of Europe, which – as a careful eye might spot – also includes the boundaries of Estonia, Latvia, and Lithuania. Baltic States do not play a major (or indeed any) role in the movie, but a watcher familiar with the history of international relations might pause and wonder about the cartographic solution. The demarcated presence of the three Baltic States on the world map of December 1941 – when the story of *Casablanca* unfolds – is not an obvious choice. These States had been effectively annexed by the Soviet Union in 1940,[3] and in 1941 were under the effective control of the German Reich. Why, then, are they still on the map?

An international lawyer, if one were available to discuss the pedantic minutiae, would likely explain the presence of the Baltic States as an application of the more general proposition that illegal annexation does not affect the existence of the State under international law[4] (or, to use the modern State responsibility parlance, third States are under an obli-

---

[*] Reader in Public International Law, University College London, Faculty of Laws.
[1] *Casablanca* (Warner Bros., 23 January 1943), <http://www.imdb.com/title/tt0034583/> accessed 1 September 2017.
[2] N Isenberg, *We'll Always Have Casablanca: The Life, Legend, and Afterlife of Hollywood's Most Beloved Movie* (2017) 131.
[3] J Crawford, *The Creation of States in International Law* (2nd ed 2007) 703.
[4] Ibid, 689-90. I am not arguing that the map of *Casablanca* was crafted with such a legal proposition in mind: my (admittedly superficial) research of the issue suggests that the key political point was the Nazi threat across the globe, Isenberg (n 2) 101-2, 129-133 (the director of the opening montage does not mention it in his autobiography, D Siegel, *Don Siegel: A Siegel Film* (1993) 75). It would be interesting to explore, still, whether the US public position on non-recognition of annexation of Baltic States, <http://digitalarchive.wilsoncenter.org/collection/279/united-states-non-recognition-policy> accessed 1 September 2017, had any trickle-down effect here.

gation not to recognize as lawful a situation created by the breach of a *jus cogens* rule[5]. In short, it does not matter that all or nearly all manifestations of the Baltic States disappeared:[6] the pristine legal proposition is unaffected by the mundane unlawfulness of everyday practice. In *Casablanca*, the substance of this point is articulated by Viktor Lazlo: when Major Strasser remarks to him that 'You were a Czechoslovakian. Now you are a subject of the German Reich!', Lazlo responds that 'I've never accepted that privilege'.

The Lazlo approach of speaking the truth (of international law) to power is an attractive and powerful way of conceiving the professional role of international lawyers.[7] It is often accompanied by anecdotes of how international law shapes and directs international power(s)[8] –speaking the truth may be its own reward, but it does feel nice if, in addition, it also matters in that elusive place 'the real world'. Judge James Crawford, one of the participants in the opening discussion of the 2016 European Society of International Law Riga Conference, points to East Timor as an example of a case where international law contributed to persistence of disputes and their eventual resolution against the interests of the powerful.[9] With a nod to the possibility of projection, this framing of international law, as both important and benign, has a powerful influence on Baltic international lawyers, with the recent example of restoration of statehood before their eyes.[10] Upon this reading, international law did

---

5   2001 ILC Articles on State responsibility art 41(2); *Jurisdictional Immunities of the State (Germany v Italy: Greece intervening)* [2012] ICJ Rep 99, para 93.
6   Crawford (n 3), 690.
7   Cf. D Kennedy, 'Speaking Law to Power: International Law and Foreign Policy: Closing Remarks' (2005) 23 Wisconsin International Law Journal 173; J Crawford, 'International Law as Discipline and Profession' (2012) 106 ASIL Proceedings 471, 485.
8   E.g. the effect of the *Alabama* arbitration on the conflict between the US and Great Britain was somewhat exaggerated, leading to unrealistic expectations about the potential of international dispute settlement in, D Caron, 'War and International Adjudication: Reflections on the 1899 Peace Conference' (2000) 94 AJIL 4, 9; VV Veeder, 'The Historical Keystone to International Arbitration: The Party-Appointed Arbitrator—From Miami to Geneva' in D Caron et al (eds), *Practicing Virtue: Inside International Arbitration* (2015) 127, 147-9; see (1872) 29 RIAA 125.
9   J Crawford, 'Chance, Order, Change: The Course of International Law' (2013) 365 Hague Recueil 9, 43-6.
10 It is also plausible to expect that this perception will become stronger with the passage of time, as the new generations of international lawyers increasingly view the restoration as necessity, rather than contingency; on the concepts see S Marks, 'False Contingency' (2009) 62 Current Legal Problems 1.

(eventually) deliver on its promise, perhaps even more impressively than for East Timor, since the effective control of Baltic States by other States was twice as lengthy as for East Timor, and practice of non-recognition could not be anchored within the structure of the United Nations. (Some will say that this success was due to the almost complete lack of practical effect to the question of whether the post-1991 Baltic States continued the identity of the pre-1940 Baltic States[11] – unlike the case of East Timor[12] – but that is a discussion for another day.)

The Lazlo effect on the Baltic States' practice is less clear cut in the more contemporary regimes of international law. One school of thought in policy-making, perhaps somewhat influenced by the normative considerations sketched above, suggests that serious engagement with international law and institutions is the right thing *and* the smart thing for States like Baltic States. For example, weaker participants in international dispute settlement will generally benefit from having access to more formalised dispute settlement through arbitration and judicial settlement, which would have direct influence on the type of arguments that have relevance in dispute settlement and also indirectly influence less formal dispute settlement mechanism by throwing the shadow of law. More generally, Baltic States could have a strategic interest in promotion of (in various jargons) greater institutionalisation of international rule of law and normative power.

Another way of reading Baltic States' engagement with international law by reference to *Casablanca* would, if tongue in cheek, rather emphasise the pursuit of goals of various degrees of merit through imperfect institutions: here, Captain Louis Renault is a better metaphor, with Baltic States acting not worse than others but certainly not better (whether normatively or in terms of competence) either. A superficial look cast by some at decisions in relation to Baltic States that emerge from various judicial and quasi-judicial bodies would not find any obvious differences in the attitude by these States to, and involvement with international law, if compared to other States in this and other regions. Indeed, contemporary refugee trails do not appear to have put the Baltic States at the

---

11   J Crawford and A Boyle, 'Opinion: Referendum on the Independence of Scotland – International Law Aspects' (10 December 2012) <https://www.gov.uk/government/uploads/system/uploads/attachment_data/file/79408/Annex_A.pdf> accessed 1 September 2017 para 103.

12   See various disputes between East Timor and Australia in the Permanent Court of Arbitration, <https://pcacases.com/web/allcases/> accessed 1 September 2017.

forefront of humanitarian engagement. Perhaps inescapably, it is harder to maintain the purity of the principled argument when one has carry out the job of governance and expertise.[13]

There is one particular point, though, on which the international law practice of Baltic States (or at least of Latvia, with which I am more familiar) is markedly more enlightened than is commonly the case, and it relates to gender diversity in international courts and tribunals. Within contemporary international law, international judges and other comparable decision-makers play an increasingly important role, and gender diversity has been identified as one element of their institutional legitimacy (*Casablanca* provides a useful contrast here of deeply problematic assumptions about female agency; Ilsa Lunde's role is basically that of a helpmate to a great man, and the movie's real question is: which great man?[14]). The law and policy of gender diversity in international adjudication has been the subject to sophisticated debates in recent years, in relation to institutionalised courts, *ad hoc* dispute settlers, as well as monitoring institutions. In Latvian practice, gender-diverse nominations and appointments have been made to the International Criminal Court, the Human Rights Committee, the Working Group on Arbitrary Detention, the Permanent Court of Arbitration, ICSID Panel of Arbitrators, the General Court of the European Union, the European Court of Human Rights, the European Committee of Social Rights, the European Commission against Racism and Intolerance, and in investor-State treaty arbitration (indeed, the only obvious gap so far is the Court of Justice of the European Union). It may be of interest to explore the institutional and normative reasons for why Latvia has become a positive outlier in this field, and the extent to which Latvian experience is transposable elsewhere.

Is there a common and consistent thread to these observations? Perhaps not --- but the ambiguity itself is a useful frame of reference for reading (Baltic/European) perspectives of international law, where broader normative idealism intersects with strategic promotion of (particular institutions of) the rule of law, mundane compromises and shortcuts, and unexpected glimpses of enlightenment. That is exactly how interna-

---

13 D Kennedy, *A World of Struggle: How Power, Law and Expertise Shape Global Political Economy* (2016).

14 R Ebert, 'Casablanca' (1996) <http://www.rogerebert.com/reviews/great-movie-casablanca-1942> accessed 1 September 2017. Cf. *Barcelona Traction, Light and Power Company, Limited (Belgium v Spain)* (*New Application: 1962*) [1970] ICJ Rep 3, Separate Opinion of Judge Sir Gerald Fitzmaurice 64 fn 23.

tional law works. The papers in this symposium quite fittingly consider European challenges to two classic general international law questions. Enrico Milano picks one of the great topics of general international law and analyses the role that international law in the 21st century can play regarding territorial conflicts and disputes in Europe. While noting the undoubted importance of international law in this area, Milano calls for (what one might describe as) enlightened modesty about the role of law, and proposes a sophisticated analytical framework that distinguishes between resistance and stability; adaptation and change; and silence and neutrality. Przemyslaw Tacik addresses another classic topic – the law of international responsibility – and situates it within the framework of relationship between the European Union and the European Court of Human Rights, where he identifies genuinely new contributions to law of responsibility. To conclude, perhaps the modest broader point of the editorial note, reflected in the contributions to the symposium, is this: not everything in the world turns upon international law (nor should it![15]) – but the role of law in setting the broader systemic assumptions and providing the vocabulary for articulating the small(er) print should not be understated either.[16]

---

15   V Lowe, 'The Limits of the Law' (2016) 379 Hague Recueil 21.
16   F Berman, 'Why Do We Need a Law of Treaties' (2017) 385 Hague Recueil 17.

Territorial Conflicts and Disputes in Europe: What Role for International Law in the 21st Century?

Enrico Milano*

1   Introduction

The main purpose of the present article is to provide a useful analytical and explanatory framework in order to understand how international law works in times of territorial crises and conflicts, with special regard for the European region. In general, the task of reflecting upon the role of international law in contributing to the settlement and termination of territorial disputes is one that should not be taken too lightly. On the one hand, international law and third-party international adjudication has been traditionally considered as the main solution to territorial conflicts and disputes. Several of the proposals made during the Interwar Period for a compulsory system of international adjudication were exactly tailored to contain and resolve territorial conflicts in Europe, which endangered the objective of peaceful coexistence.[1] In general, international law can be employed in order to give effect to diplomatic means of dispute settlement, such as mediation and fact-finding. On the other hand, the lessons of history have shown the risk of overestimating the role of international law in that respect and of excessively blaming international law for its impotence towards intractable territorial conflicts. Also, a further dimension of the role of international law has hardly been considered in the literature; namely that associated with the risk that international law may contribute to exacerbating certain territorial conflicts.[2] It will

---

*   Associate Professor of International Law, University of Verona. The present article elaborates on the presentation made in Riga on 8 September 2016 at the Forum "Territorial Disputes in Europe" of the 12th Annual Conference of the European Society of International Law.

1   C.J. Tams, "World Courts as Guardians of Peace?", *Global Cooperation Research Papers*, n. 15, 2016, 5, at 13-15; J. von Bernstorff, "Hans Kelsen on Judicial Law-Making by International Courts and Tribunals: A Theory of Global Judicial Imperialism?", *The Law & Practice of International Courts and Tribunals*, 2015, 35.

2   E. Milano, M. Nicolini, F. Palermo (eds.), *Law, Territory and Conflict Resolution. Law as a Problem and Law as a Solution,* Brill, 2016.

be submitted that a more sophisticated analytical framework is needed in order to tackle the issue. Namely one that construes the relationship of international law with territorial disputes along three main dynamics, which are inherent in the function performed by international law in international crises: resistance and stability; adaptation and change; and silence and neutrality.

2   Setting the Context

Border disputes, namely disputes over the course of an international boundary, are relatively few in Europe, as compared to other regions, such as Africa, Asia and Latin America, and generally they are well managed and settled.[3] In very few cases, the need to submit the dispute to arbitration or judicial settlement has arisen, as it was the case with the Gulf of Piran dispute between Slovenia and Croatia currently pending before the PCA.[4] This is an important contextual element, as border disputes, if submitted to international adjudication, are certainly amenable to a settlement primarily dictated by international law rules and principles.

Instead most territorial disputes in Europe nowadays can be qualified as disputes over governance and sovereignty. From Kosovo to Crimea, but including also secessionist claims in Georgia, Spain, Moldova, Cyprus, what is at stake is often a claim to exercise a right of self-determination by way of separation from the parent State: the latter parent State normally puts forward a counter-claim to territorial integrity. The matter of controversy is not where exactly the boundary should run, but who should rule over a certain territory – the central government or some local authorities – and under which title – as sovereign ruler or as autonomous region. That is the most recurrent form of territorial disputes in Europe and it is in that respect that we must measure the role of international law in managing, settling and terminating them, or, else, in exacerbating them.

With regard to this latter type of disputes international law tends to be characterised by the application of norms and principles of general international law, which, by definition, are unwritten, relatively undefined

---

3   For an example of a well managed border dispute in Europe see H.G. Post, "Dutch-German Boundary Relations in the Eems-Dollard (Ems-Dollart) Estuary: An Implicit Condominium", in *Law, Territory and Conflict Resolution*, cit., 346.
4   *Arbitration between the Republic of Croatia and the Republic of Slovenia*, available at https://pcacases.com/web/view/3 (last accessed 29 May 2017).

and, more than treaty law, have to be "mobilised" and invoked by the relevant parties and actors in order to find application. That also means that the "political" dimension of those international law principles and norms is enhanced; territorial conflicts hardly reach the like of an international tribunal, and even in those few cases where that occurs, the "political" element is like an "elephant in the room". The *Kosovo* Advisory Opinion rendered by the International Court of Justice (ICJ) is a good case in point: for all the twisting and interpretive creativity the Court has engaged in avoiding the conflicting accounts provided by States during the proceedings on crucial principles, such as territorial integrity and self-determination, the laconic and parsimonious opinion issued by the Court was a powerful "push" for Kosovo's claim to independence (in contrast to the political intentions underlying the General Assembly's initiative).[5]

Another important contextual element is that Europe in the 21st century is characterized by the high density of regional organizations, one may mention the European Union (EU), the Council of Europe and the Organization for Security and Cooperation in Europe (OSCE), most of them dedicated to the promotion of democracy, human and minority rights in the continent. One would expect that in this institutional and normative *milieu*, political conflicts over territory, normally associated with contesting claims by sovereign entities, were reduced in numbers and gravity. If that is true for classic border disputes, the same cannot be said for disputes concerning self-government and self-determination: one may wonder whether it is probably the contrary and namely that the link between democratic legitimation, governance and territorial ownership enhances the possibility of contesting claims among States as well as non-State actors. Certainly what is not a matter of contention is that those regional organizations are an important element in the containment of territorial conflicts and management of their most perilous consequences.

---

5 *Accordance with International Law of the Unilateral Declaration of Independence in Respect of Kosovo*, Advisory Opinion of 22 July 2010, *ICJ Reports 2010*, 403. Resolution 63/3 of 8 October 2008 was approved with 77 in favour, 74 abstained and 6 against. The resolution was sponsored by the Serbian delegation and it was clearly instrumental to reasserting its sovereign claim to Kosovo on the basis of international law.

3 Resistance and stability

By capturing the dynamics of "resistance and stability", I am referring to the phenomenon by which international law opposes certain claims or situations as illegal, resists illegal change and reaffirms the stability of territorial situations. That is the case, for instance, when territorial integrity is mobilised in order to counter an unlawful territorial *status quo* and is guaranteed by certain legal means and institutions, the most typical being enforcement through collective non-recognition. Russia's annexation of Crimea is the latest example in this respect; with few exceptions, the international community has countered the unilateral change of status through legal means and techniques, including non-recognition and countermeasures.

Key to the understanding of the dynamics of resistance and stability is the principle of territorial integrity. It is common knowledge that the principle finds normative expression in Article 2, paragraph 4, of the UN Charter protecting States from forcible annexations and uses or threats of force directed against their territorial integrity. The principle is also enshrined in important international instruments, such as the 1960 General Assembly (GA) Declaration on the Granting of Independence to Colonial Countries and Peoples, the 1970 GA Declaration on Friendly Relations, the 1975 Helsinki Final Act and the 1993 Vienna Declaration;[6] in the 2010 Kosovo Advisory Opinion the ICJ has maintained that the principle is "an important part of the international legal order", implicitly pointing to its customary international law nature.[7] In the European context, territorial integrity has been mobilised to counter unilateral territorial changes, whether imposed through the use or threat of force from another State or group of States or brought about by non-State actors acting from within the State without the consent of the central government.

---

[6] Declaration on the Granting of Independence to Colonial Countries and Peoples, UN doc. A/RES/15/1514, 14 December 1960; Declaration on the Principles of International Law Concerning Friendly Relations and Cooperation Among States in Accordance with the Charter of the United Nations, UN doc. A/RES/25/2625, 24 October 1970; Final Act of the Conference on Security and Cooperation in Europe, Helsinki, 1 August 1975, 1292; Vienna Declaration and Programme of Action, Vienna, 25 June 1993, *International Legal Materials*, 1993, 1661.

[7] *Accordance with International Law of the Unilateral Declaration of Independence*, cit., para. 80.

For instance, in Bosnia and Herzegovina, despite the many attempts to carve out mono-ethnic State entities from within, the UN Security Council already during the war passed resolution 787 reaffirming the territorial integrity of the Republic of Bosnia and Herzegovina and declaring that "any entities or arrangements in contravention thereof will not be accepted".[8] Annex 4 of the Dayton Peace Agreement, which established the new Constitution of Bosnia and Herzegovina, provided that the latter would "continue its legal existence under international law as a state, with its internal structure modified as provided herein and with its present internationally recognised borders".[9] In 2008 the Steering Board of the Peace Implementation Council – the *ad hoc* international setting supervising the application of the Dayton Peace Agreements in Bosnia and Herzegovina – condemned the attempts made by political leaders of the Republika Srpska to put into motion a process for the organization of a referendum on self-determination of the Bosnian Serbs and "strongly emphasized that under the Dayton Peace Agreement an entity has no right to secede from Bosnia and Herzegovina".[10] Similarly, with regard to Abkhazia's secessionist claims in Georgia, the UN Security Council and regional organizations in Europe since the 1990s have promoted a political settlement within Georgia, respecting the territorial integrity of the latter country. In resolution 1096, adopted in January 1997, the Security Council has "reaffirm[ed] its commitment to the sovereignty and territorial integrity of Georgia, within its internationally recognised borders, and to the necessity of defining the status of Abkhazia in strict accordance with these principles, and underlines the unacceptability of any action by the Abkhaz leadership in contravention of these principles, in particular the holding on 23 November 1996 and 7 December 1996 of illegitimate and self-styled parliamentary elections in Abkhazia, Georgia".[11] A similar commitment to the principle of territorial integrity as an antidote to unilateral territorial changes can be seen in other territorial conflicts, including Crimea, Northern Cyprus and Nagorno-Karabakh.

---

8   UN doc. S/RES/787 (1992), 16 November 1992, para. 3.
9   General Framework Agreement for Peace in Bosnia and Herzegovina, Annex 4, art. I, para. 1, available at http://www.ohr.int/dpa/default.asp?content_id=380 (last accessed 29 May 2017).
10 Declaration by the Steering Board of the Peace Implementation Council, 27 February 2008, available at http://www.ohr.int/pic/default.asp?content_id=41352 (last accessed 29 May 2017).
11 UN doc. S/RES/1096 (1997), 30 January 1997, para. 3.

In all these cases, we see that the principle is mobilised by the central government with the active support of relevant international actors, including universal and regional organisations, in the presence of two recurrent factors, namely the grave or deteriorating human rights situations in the affected regions and the sponsoring and support (including military support) of the secessionist entities by external actors, including neighbouring countries. One must here note that the ICJ in the Kosovo Advisory Opinion has somewhat muddied the waters of the scope of application of the principle in point, by stating that it "is confined to the sphere of relations between States", hence excluding its application to the relations between a central government and a seceding entity.[12]

As for the doctrine of non-recognition, it represents, since its very inception during the Manchurian crisis in the 1930s, an attempt to legally resist the effects and consequences of a violation of international law, inducing a change in territorial status. The doctrine gives normative expression to the Latin maxim *ex iniuria ius non oritur*. Nowadays, the doctrine has been codified by the International Law Commission (ILC), at Article 41 of the ILC Draft Article on State Responsibility, which concerns the obligations deriving from a grave violation of a peremptory norm. Article 41 also provides for the duty of third States to refrain from aid or assisting in maintaining the illegal territorial situation and for the duty to cooperate through lawful means to bring to an end the situation. One of the inherent weaknesses of the regime of aggravated responsibility envisaged by the ILC is the determination of illegality; in other words, international law is not endowed with a mechanism of third-party, impartial determination. The latter determination is mainly effected by States, individually and jointly, within the framework of international organisations and non-institutional mechanisms of international cooperation.

Non-recognition practice concerning the recent situation in Crimea has been quite significant, especially with regard to the non-recognition of the referendum held on 16 March 2014 and of the ensuing annexation by Russia. In a statement issued on 12 March 2014, the G-7 leaders declared that "[...] such referendum would have no legal effect. Given the lack of adequate preparation and the intimidating presence of Russian troops, it would also be a deeply flawed process, which would have no

---

[12] *Accordance with International Law of the Unilateral Declaration of Independence*, cit., para. 80.

moral force. For all these reasons, we would not recognize the outcome".[13] The President of European Commission, José Barroso, and the President of the European Council, Herman Van Rompuy, on 16 March 2014 jointly stated that "the European Union considers the holding of the referendum on the future status of the territory of Crimea as contrary to the Ukrainian Constitution and international law. The referendum is illegal and illegitimate and its outcome will not be recognised".[14] On the same day and on a similar tone, the White House declared that "[the] referendum is contrary to Ukraine's constitution, and the international community will not recognize the results of a poll administered under threats of violence and intimidation from a Russian military intervention that violates international law".[15] NATO's Secretary-General, Anders Rasmussen, on 19 March 2014, stated that "Crimea's annexation is illegal and illegitimate and NATO Allies will not recognize it".[16]

At the level of the United Nations, the draft resolution concerning the referendum in Crimea and presented by 41 countries (predominantly Western countries) for approval by the Security Council at the meeting of 15 March 2014 was vetoed by Russia, with only China abstaining in the vote.[17] The resolution reaffirmed in the preamble that "no acquisition of territory resulting from the threat or use of force shall be recognised as legal"; it declared that the referendum could "not have legal validity" and could "not form the basis for any alteration of the status of Crimea";

---

13   Statement of G-7 Leaders on Ukraine (12 March 2014), http://www.whitehouse.gov/thepress-office/2014/03/12/statementg7leadersukraine accessed 29 April 2014.

14   Joint Statement on Crimea by the President of the European Council, Herman Van Rompuy, and the President of the European Commission, José Manuel Barroso (16 March 2014), http://ec.europa.eu/commission_2010-2014/president/news/archives/2014/03/20140317_1_en.htm accessed 29 April 2014.

15   White House, Statement by the Press Secretary on Ukraine (16 March 2014), http://www.whitehouse.gov/the-press-office/2014/03/16/statement-press-secretary-ukraine accessed 29 April 2014.

16   "NATO Secretary General condemns moves to incorporate Crimea into Russian Federation", (18 March 2014), http://www.nato.int/cps/en/natolive/news_108100.htm accessed 29 April 2014.

17   UNSC Draft Resolution, UN Doc S/2014/189; UNSC Verbatim Record (15 March 2014) UN Doc S/PV.7138. On the question of the applicability of the obligation to abstain under the last sentence of Article 27, paragraph 3 of the UN Charter, to the draft resolution vetoed by Russia See E. Milano, "Russia's Veto in the Security Council: Whither the Duty to Abstain under Art. 27(3) of the UN Charter?" 75(1) Zeitschrift für ausländisches öffentliches Recht und Völkerrecht 215 (2015).

and it "call[ed] upon all States, international organizations and specialized agencies not to recognize any alteration of the status of Crimea on the basis of this referendum and to refrain from any action or dealing that might be interpreted as recognizing such altered status." During the meetings of the Security Council of 15 and 19 March calls for the non-recognition of the results of the referendum and of the prospective annexation by Russia were voiced by the delegations of France, the United Kingdom, Lithuania, Australia, Jordan, Ukraine and Luxembourg.

On 24 March 2014, the UN General Assembly approved a draft resolution proposed by Poland, Lithuania, Germany, Canada, Ukraine and Costa Rica, with 100 votes in favour, 11 against and 58 abstentions, titled "Territorial integrity of Ukraine". Paragraphs 5 and 6 of the operative part of the resolution reiterate, in almost identical words, the determinations made in the draft Security Council resolution vetoed by Russia a few days earlier; it includes the call for non-recognition of "any alteration of the status of the Autonomous Republic of Crimea and of the city of Sevastopol" and to avoid "any action or dealing that might be interpreted as recognizing such altered status".[18] The delegations of the EU, Norway, Georgia, Turkey, Liechtenstein in their statements expressly referred to the need for non-recognition of the outcome of the referendum and of Russia's annexation of Crimea.[19]

As specifically recalled in GA Res. 68/262, a comprehensive approach to non-recognition is not limited to the formal recognition of the legality of the situation as such, such as an act of annexation, but it also extends to all relations, of an economic, political, diplomatic, commercial nature, which imply recognition of the illegal situation. For instance, as a reaction to the annexation of Crimea, the European Union has adopted successive regulations prohibiting the import into its territory of goods originating in the territory of Crimea and of Sevastopol, unless certified

---

18 UN Doc A/RES/68/262(24 March 2014).
19 UN Doc. GA Verbatim Record (24 March 2014) UN Doc A/68/PV.80.

by Ukrainian authorities.[20] Similar legislation has been adopted by countries, such as the United States, Australia, Canada and Japan.[21]

As already anticipated, among the obligations laid down in Article 41, one must also mention the duty to "cooperate to bring to an end through lawful means any serious breach within the meaning of Article 40".[22] Of the three obligations envisaged in Article 41, the latter is the only positive obligation. And yet according to the commentary "[b]ecause of the di-

---

20 Council Decision 2014/386/CFSP and Council Regulation (EU) No 692/2014 prohibit the import into the European Union of goods originating in Crimea and Sevastopol, unless they are accompanied by a certificate of preferential origin issued by the Ukrainian authorities. Financial services, such as provision of financing, financial assistance, insurance and re-insurance services, related to the import of goods subject to the prohibition are equally forbidden. On 30 July 2014, the Council adopted a Decision (2014/507/CFSP) and a Regulation (EU) No 825/2014 amending Council Decision 2014/386/CFSP and Council Regulation (EU) No 692/2014 to prohibit investment in Crimea and Sevastopol in specific sectors and to prohibit trade in certain goods with Crimea and Sevastopol in specific sectors.

21 On 29 April 2014, Japan decided to temporarily suspend issuing visas to enter Japan to 23 individuals who are considered to have contributed to the violation of Ukraine's sovereignty and territorial integrity. On 28 July, Japan decided to adopt, as soon as the required internal procedures are completed, the following sanctions: the freezing of assets in Japan of the individuals and organizations considered to have been directly involved in the annexation of Crimea and the introduction of restrictive measures with regard to imports from Crimea and Sevastopol. On 5 August, Japan implemented the above-mentioned measures against the individuals with a restriction on payments, a restriction on capital transactions and, in addition, a restriction on importation (on all goods originating from the Autonomous Republic of Crimea or the city of Sevastopol).

On 17 June 2014, the Australian government imposed sanctions, in relation to the Russian threat to Ukraine's sovereignty, which placed targeted financial sanctions and travel bans on designated persons and entities.

U.S. sanctions have been implemented through the Office of Foreign Assets Control, U.S. Department of the Treasury, which has issued a series of directives and established a new list of persons subject to OFAC restrictions; U.S. Department of Commerce has issued amendments to the Export Administration Regulations to impose new export licensing requirements and policies in connection with certain items exported to and end users in Russia. In addition, the U.S. has announced that certain items imported into the U.S. from Russia would no longer benefit from duty-free status.

22 Draft Articles on the Responsibility of States for Internationally Wrongful Acts, *Yearbook of the International Law Commission* (2001), Vol. II (Part 2) and corrigendum, 112-116.

versity of circumstances which could possibly be involved, the provision does not prescribe in detail what form this cooperation should take. Co-operation could be organised in the framework of a competent international organization, in particular the United Nations. However, paragraph 1 also envisages the possibility of non-institutionalised cooperation".[23] In *Legality of the Wall*, dealing with the legal consequences of the construction of a wall by Israel in the Palestinian occupied territories, the ICJ determined that "the United Nations, and especially the General Assembly and the Security Council, should consider what further action is required to bring to an end the illegal situation resulting from the construction of the wall and the associated régime, taking due account of the present Advisory Opinion".[24] However, the ILC concedes that that "[i]t may be open to question whether general international law at present prescribes a positive duty of cooperation, and paragraph 1 in that respect may reflect the progressive development of international law".[25]

Be that as it may, the practice concerning Crimea has seen States and international organizations engaging in numerous efforts of multilateral cooperation aiming at addressing the crisis in Crimea, and Ukraine in general, through international organizations and *fora*, including the United Nations, the Organization for Security and Cooperation in Europe, the Council of Europe, the G-7, the European Union and NATO. It is quite significant that most of the non-recognition and sanctioning measures against Russia have been adopted in the framework of these multilateral efforts and the insertion of the obligation in point before those of non-recognition and non-assistance seems to indicate that cooperation is the preferred course of action in performing a policy of non-recognition and non-assistance. The practice concerning Crimea, but also similar situations such as Northern Cyprus and Nagorno-Karabakh, points to an increasing awareness in the European region of the importance of multilateral cooperation to "resist" the effects of grave violations of international law, albeit not necessary indicating a belief that cooperation is obligatory under international law.

---

[23] Ibidem.
[24] *Legal Consequences of the Construction of a Wall in the Occupied Palestinian Territory*, Advisory Opinion of 9 July 2004, *ICJ Reports 2004*, 202.
[25] ILC Articles on State Responsibility with Commentary, cit., p. 114, para. 3.

4 Adaptation and change

By adaptation and change, I am referring to the phenomenon by which international law adapts itself to social reality, namely to the social changes produced by territorial disputes, and to a certain extent it strives to regulate and lead those social changes through means such as mediation, arbitration and judicial settlement, intervention by legitimating, external actors. Despite the centrality of the prohibition of the use of force in the contemporary international legal system, international law still knows of situations in which an unlawful *status quo* produced by the use of force may come to be accommodated over time.

The case of Kosovo is quite instructive in this latter respect. There is a strong argument to be made that NATO's bombing of 1999 was illegal under international law and that KFOR's presence – together with the simultaneous withdrawal of the Serbian administration from its former province – were directly linked to that illegal military intervention. However, the new *status quo* was gradually legitimised as a result of Security Council Resolution 1244, which authorised the deployment of a UN administration backed by KFOR's military presence, and the new attitude of the Serbian institution post-Milosevic.[26] It is also quite evident that Kosovo's successful secession from Serbia would have been quite unlikely had it not been for Serbia's total loss of factual control over its former province.

The so-called "EU-facilitated dialogue" which has been initiated by the UN General Assembly in 2010, after the ICJ declared Kosovo's declaration of independence to be "not in violation of international law", is another example of the way in which international law may provide the instruments and techniques by which territorial disputes are managed and channelled towards certain desired outcomes.[27] The 2013 Agreement of Principles on Normalization of Relations is the main fruit of the mediation undertaken by the EU High Representative for Foreign Affairs and it is in fact made of two parallel instruments of identical content concluded

---

26   UN doc. S/RES/1244 (1999), 10 June 1999, para. 7. Declaration on Kosovo and Metohia, 27 August 2003, reproduced in Material Relating to the Establishment of UNMIK Administration of Kosovo – Actions by Kosovo institutions (Part II-H), available at http://www.icj-cij.org/docket/files/141/15038.pdf.

27   Request for an advisory opinion of the International Court of Justice on whether the unilateral declaration of independence of Kosovo is in accordance with international law, UN doc. A/RES/64/298, 9 September 2010.

between the EU, on the one hand, and Kosovo and Serbia, separately, on the other hand.[28] While the conclusion of Serbia's Constitutional Court to the effect that the agreement is only a political deal, and not an international treaty, seems correct from the point of view of international law, one must though underline that both parallel instruments contain binding unilateral undertakings by the authorities of both States.[29] The

[28] First Agreement of Principles Governing the Normalization of Relations (Brussels: 19 April 2013). The text of the agreement is attached to the law of ratification passed by the Parliament of Kosovo in June 2013. See Law on Ratification of the First International Agreement of Principles Governing the Normalization of Relations between the Republic of Kosovo and the Republic of Serbia, Law 04/L-199 (27 May 2017), http://www.kuvendikosoves.org/common/docs/ligjet/Law%20on%20 ratification%20of%20agreement%20-normalization%20of%20relations%20between%20Kosovo%20and%20Serbia.pdf (accessed 20 June 2015). A copy of the original text signed by the EU High Representative and the Prime Minister of Serbia is available at http://euobserver.com/media/src/0807580ad8281aefa2a89e38c4 9689f9.pdf (accessed 27 May 2017).

[29] The Court rejected a referral made by a group of Serbia's members of parliament (MPs) seeking a declaration of the BA's unconstitutionality. According to those MPs, the agreement would constitute a form of *de jure* recognition of Kosovo's statehood and independence and, to that extent; it would be in breach of Article 182 (2) of the Constitution, which provides for the autonomy of the province of Kosovo and Metohija to be regulated by special constitutional legislation. After an extensive analysis, the Court reached the conclusion that the BA is a political compact only, having no legal relevance and effect in Serbia's legal order and, to that extent, it could not be reviewed by the Court, which, according to Article 167 of the Constitution, can only review legal acts. More specifically, according to the Court, the agreement is not a treaty in accordance with the definition given by the VCLT, as Kosovo is not a sovereign entity having *jus contrahendi*, and Serbia has consistently protested its unilateral separation and has never recognised Kosovo as a new State. The ICJ Advisory Opinion rendered on 22 July 2010 is legally untenable and, in any case, Kosovo's recognition by numerous countries produces effects in bilateral relations between Kosovo and those countries only. While implied recognition is indeed possible when an unambiguous intention to that effect is established – and the 1996 agreements of the Federal Republic of Yugoslavia on normalisation of relations with Croatia and cooperation with Macedonia, according to the Court, are two examples of that possibility – the BA cannot be considered a form of implied recognition of Kosovo's independence, as no indication of the 'Republic of Kosovo' can be found in the text of the agreement, and the negotiating mandate approved by the Parliament on 13 January 2013 specifically stated that such negotiations and the results thereof should not be construed as recognition of the unilateral declaration of independence. The Court also notes that the BA has not been sent to the UN Secretariat for registration in accordance with Article 102 UN

agreement and its ancillary instruments have allowed Serbia to maintain its claim to territorial integrity, on the one hand; on the other hand, to pursue concrete results on matters of cooperation between Belgrade and Pristina, to consolidate further Kosovo's authority over its territory, including the Serb-inhabited north, and to ensure progress by both countries in the path towards accession to the EU.

International law may also have an important role in setting the conditions upon which territorial change occurs: one may consider the dismemberment of the Former Yugoslavia or the dissolution of the Soviet Union in which the *uti possidetis* principle guided the creation of new sovereign entities by freezing the administrative boundaries of former constituent republics and transforming them in international boundaries. In the former dissolution, the Badinter Commission, having found that the process of collapse of the former Yugoslavia was irreversible, already in Opinion n. 2, when called to adjudicate upon the claim to self-determination of Serb minorities in Croatia and Bosnia and Herzegovina, stated that the "[...] the right to self-determination must not involve changes to existing frontiers at the time of independence (*uti possidetis juris*) except where the states concerned agree otherwise".[30] In subsequent Opinion n. 3 the Commission established that the *uti possidetis* is a "general principle, which is logically connected with the phenomenon of obtaining independence, wherever it occurs. Its obvious purpose is to prevent the independence and stability of new states being endangered by fratricidal struggles".[31] *Uti possidetis* has indeed been employed by the international community as a principle of general international law, previously applied in the decolonization context, in order to channel territorial changes and mitigate their potential for instability and conflict.[32]

Charter. The Court finally points to the fact that the ordinary procedures required for the implementation of international treaties in Serbia's legal order were not followed, and that further substantiates the conclusion that the agreement is not an international treaty, but a political compact only. Decision 247/2013 was issued on 10 December 2014 and published on 2 February 2015, see Official Gazette of the Republic of Serbia, n. 13/2015, 2 February 2015, 9.

30 Badinter Arbitration Committee, Opinion n. 2, *International Legal Materials*, 1992, 1488, at 1497.
31 *Ibidem*, Opinion n. 3, 1499.
32 A. Tancredi, "In Search of a Fair Balance between the Inviolability of Borders, Self-Determination and Secession in International Law", *Law, Territory and Conflict Resolution*, cit., 90, at 102-103.

As for the doctrine of non-recognition, in the *Namibia* advisory opinion, the ICJ introduced an element of flexibility in the doctrine of non-recognition, by stating that "the non-recognition of South Africa's administration of the Territory should not result in the depriving the people of Namibia of any advantages derived from international co-operation. In particular, while official acts performed by the Government of South Africa after the termination of the Mandate are illegal and invalid, this invalidity cannot be extended to those acts, such as, for instance, the registration of births, deaths and marriages, the effects of which can be ignored only to the detriment of the inhabitants of the Territory".[33] We shall refer to this qualification made by the Court as the "Namibia exception". What is interesting in our respect is that the effects of illegal territorial situations are not completely voided and international law, even when applying the doctrine of non-recognition, does take into account certain acts and facts produced by the wrongdoer, especially when such recognition is made to the benefit of the local population. Furthermore, the contours of the "Namibia exception" are somewhat blurred and that may broaden the room for manoeuvre of relevant decision-makers.

For instance, in the 2001 decision in the inter-State proceedings in *Cyprus v. Turkey*, concerning the treatment of Greek-Cypriots in Northern Cyprus, the European Court of Human Rights (hereinafter "ECtHR") found no violation of Article 6 by reason of an alleged practice of denying to the Greek-Cypriot population a fair hearing by an independent and impartial tribunal in the determination of their civil rights and obligations. The ECtHR held that, for the settlement of disputes relating to civil rights and obligations defined in domestic law, there was a functioning court system in the Turkish Republic of Northern Cyprus (hereinafter "TRNC") which was available to the Greek-Cypriot population, and such system had no flaws in its legal framework with regard to independency and impartiality.[34] Moreover, the Court affirmed that the illegality of the TRNC under international law and the policy of non-recognition adopted by the international community were irrelevant for the purpose of iden-

---

33 *Legal Consequences for States of the Continued Presence of South Africa in Namibia (Southwest Africa) notwithstanding Security Council Resolution 276*, Advisory Opinion of 21 June 1971, *ICJ Reports 1971*, 16, at 55.

34 European Court of Human Rights, *Case of Cyprus v. Turkey*, Application no. 25781/94, Judgment of 10 May 2001, paras. 236-240, available at http://hudoc.echr.coe.int/eng#{"itemid":["001-59454"]} (last accessed 31 May 2017).

tifying the existence of domestic remedies available to private parties in the framework of the European Convention of Human Rights.[35]

One must also note that following the pilot judgment issued by the ECtHR in in *Xenides-Arestis v. Turkey*, the TRNC authorities have enacted a new compensation Law for Greek-Cypriots deprived of their properties, namely Law no. 67/2005.[36] The Immovable Property Commission that was established under this Law for the purpose of examining applications made in respect of properties has been composed of seven members, two of whom foreign members, Mr Hans-Christian Krüger (former Secretary to the European Commission of Human rights and former Deputy Secretary General of the Council of Europe) and Mr Daniel Tarschys (former Secretary General of the Council of Europe), and has the competence to decide on the restitution, exchange of properties or payment of compensation. A right of appeal is provided before the TRNC High Administrative Court.[37] What is interesting is that the scheme was promoted by the Council of Europe within the framework of the European Convention of Human Rights, regardless of any obligation of non-recognition under international law, exactly due to the purpose of finding practical solutions aimed at the effective protection of individual human rights.

Much more controversial is the possibility of coming to terms with the *fait accompli* over time and recognising partly or *in toto* its effects with regard to the change in territorial status. If one was to identify possibly the most important feature of the obligation of non-recognition, the choice would likely fall on the latter's ability to counter the passing of time and implicit recognition of the factual situation. On the other hand, consolidation of an illegal situation is likely in the long run to lead to formal or informal ways of legitimation as a way to further the best interest of the local population and of the States in dispute. With regard, for example, to the situation in Crimea, one could envisage a situation in which in the future to come the international community may seek to promote a deal between Ukraine and Russia, in which the Crimean population is called to vote on its future status in the framework of an internationally-supervised referendum, including the option of retaining the *status quo*.

---

35   *Ibidem*, paras. 89-98.
36   European Court of Human Rights, *Case of Xenides-Arestis v. Turkey*, Application no. 46347/99, Judgment of 22 December 2005, available at http://hudoc.echr.coe.int/eng#{"appno":["46347/99"],"itemid":["001-71800"]} (last accessed 31 May 2017).
37   For the activities and composition of the Immovable Property Commission see the official website at http://www.tamk.gov.ct.tr (last accessed 31 May 2017).

That is not tantamount to arguing that such possible legitimation of the *status quo* could occur without endorsement or consent by the Ukrainian government; on the contrary, a proper settlement including all relevant parties would be a pre-requisite for legitimation of the territorial situation of Crimea. For instance, the 2007 Treaty between Latvia and the Russian Federation on the State Border between Latvia and Russia is a lawful adaption to the *de facto* situation produced by the Soviet transfer of certain territories from the Latvian Soviet Socialist Republic to the Russian Soviet Federalist Socialist Republic which took place in 1944, a few years after the USSR unlawful annexation of Latvia: one must concur with Latvia's Constitutional Court that such means of adaptation are in line with international law and do not contradict Latvia's claim to State continuity with the pre-1940 independent Republic of Latvia.[38]

---

38   "The Constitutional Court has no doubts that the State of Latvia, by means of the Border Treaty, has not disclaimed its State continuity, but just on the contrary – it has repeatedly expressed its opinion regarding this issue and the Cabinet of Ministers has signed the Border Treaty based on the Law on Authorization that established a clear framework of action for it. Since the representative of the Russian Federation, when signing the Border Treaty, had to be aware of the content of the mandate of the Latvian representative and he did not object against the fact that the Prime Minister of the Republic of Latvia signed the Border Treaty by observing the State continuity doctrine of Latvia, one can consider that the State of Latvia has acted in accordance with the requirements of this doctrine.
Moreover, as the Constitutional Court has already established, territorial changes made by means of the Border Treaty have been carried out according to the order established by the Satversme. The State continuity doctrine prohibits neither changing the State territory in accordance with the order established in the Satversme, nor the Saeima authorizing the Cabinet of Ministers to sign a respective treaty. The international law doctrine also expresses the view that change of the State borders does not affect continuity of this State. Under the general international law, a State as a legal person remains unaffected also in the case if it changes its territory. State continuity is not affected by minor territorial changes or loss of separate territories [...]. "Latvia is entitled to cede Abrene to Russia like France is entitled to cede Alsace to Germany, and neither Latvia, nor France would loose their Statal identity as a result" (Paparinskis M. Maisot tiesisko „spageti bļodu": Robežlīgums, Satversme un starptautiskās tiesības // Jurista Vārds, January 30, 2007, No. 5)". *Border Treaty, Re, Kariņš and ors v Parliament of Latvia and Cabinet of Ministers of Latvia*, Constitutional Review, Case No 2007-10-0102, *International Law in Domestic Courts* 884 (LV 2007), 29 November 2007, Constitutional Court, para. 69.2, full translation available at http://www.satv.tiesa.gov.lv/wp-content/uploads/2007/04/2007-10-0102_Spriedums_ENG.pdf

5 Neutrality and Silence

By silence and neutrality, I am referring to those situations in which international law remains neutral to a certain conflict, simply as a result of its rules being non-applicable to the case at hand or, as it most frequently occurs, as a result of its rules not being "mobilised" by the actors involved in order to regulate a certain situation. There is a discrete tendency among international lawyers nowadays to assume that the reach of international law is so wide that hardly any situation can escape its normative grip. And yet such proposition does not stand at a deeper analysis, including that of territorial conflicts in Europe.

For instance, traditionally the prevailing paradigm over the phenomenon of secession was that international would be neutral. International would neither provide for a right of secession for minorities and territorial entities within the State, nor would it prohibit secession. In other words, international law would simply take cognition of the formation of a new State on the part of the territory of the parent State, once it was effectively established and it had acquired full independence. The rationale underlying the neutrality paradigm is both that secessionist movements are an internal affair of the State; and that any foreign intervention – instrumental to enforcement of an alleged right to secession or prohibition thereof – would be contrary to the self-determination of the people as it may shift the balance in favour of the secessionist movement or in favour of the central government.[39] Also, neutrality affords a compromise between the needs of stability and the possibility of adapting to an effective and stable territorial change.[40] The neutrality paradigm has been put under considerable pressure during the second part of the XX century by the emergence of *jus cogens* rules and the frequent affirmation of the principle of territorial integrity in the Post Cold War Period, however it is still the case that *secession as such* is not regulated by international law. Where the process of attempted secession does not produce an internal conflict, where it does not produce trans-boundary effects in terms of destabilisation of neighbouring countries and where the debate remains within the realm of internal political conflict and negotiation, international law still remains neutral. That is, for instance, the case with

---

39 Institut de droit international, Le principe de non-intervention dans la guerre civile, 1975, available at http://www.justitiaetpace.org/idiF/resolutionsF/1975_wies_03_fr.pdf.

40 Tancredi, "In Search of a Fair Balance...", cit., 99.

Catalunya and Scotland, where the latters' claims to independence from Spain and the United Kingdom, respectively, have not triggered (yet) any rule of international law to come into play.

An illustrative example of silence is that of the 2010 ICJ *Kosovo* advisory opinion. According to the ICJ, international law was simply "silent" on the declaration of independence of Kosovo, hence it could declare it as being not in violation of international law (which, as we have argued elsewhere, was something different from the question posed by the General Assembly referring to the *conformity with international law* of the declaration).[41] According to the Court, the declaration of independence (*nota bene*, not the secession) was not prohibited by any rule of general international law, as the scope of application of the principle of territorial integrity is confined to relations between and among States and declarations of independence are condemned by the international community only when associated with grave violations of peremptory norms.[42] As for the 2001 UNMIK Provisional Constitutional Framework, while the Court conceded that it was part of the body of international law potentially relevant to the question posed by the General Assembly, it concluded that it was not applicable to the extent that the authors of the declaration willingly acted outside and beyond that framework and could not be identified – as erroneously done by the General Assembly – with the Provisional Institutions of Self-Government created within that constitutional framework.[43] Despite its reference to territorial integrity of Serbia, according to the Court not even UNSC Resolution 1244 was applicable to the declaration of independence: neither the text nor the object and purpose of the resolution indicated a prohibition imposed by the Security Council upon local representatives to issue a declaration of independence.[44] In general, one cannot but agree with the Judge Simma, when he expressed strong reservations about the legal method employed in the Court's reasoning. In the Declaration attached to the advisory opinion, he opined that "in a contemporary legal order which is strongly influenced by ideas of public law, the Court's reasoning on this point is obsolete. [...] First, by unduly limiting the scope of its analysis, the Court has not answered the question before it in a satisfactory manner. To do so would

---

41 *Accordance with International Law of the Unilateral Declaration of Independence,* cit., *dispositif.*
42 *Ibidem*, paras. 79-83.
43 *Ibidem*, paras. 104-109.
44 *Ibidem*, paras. 115-119.

require a fuller treatment of both prohibitive and permissive rules of international law as regards declarations of independence and attempted acts of secession than what was essayed in the Court's Opinion".[45] Be that as it may, what is interesting for our purposes is that the Court has refrained from "mobilising" international law rules and principles, despite the enormous normative potential inherent in some of those principles and rules, and adopted an attitude of restraint. One can easily see the parallel with the official attitude maintained by the UN themselves and other important regional organizations, such as the EU, which today continue to characterise their formal position with regard to the final status of Kosovo as one of *status-neutrality*. It is arguable that the latter formal position has been coupled with a substantial attitude of more or less explicit support towards the accomplished facts of Kosovo's independence; the legitimising effect of the *Kosovo* advisory opinion with regard to those accomplished facts is hard to contest.

In sum, neutrality and silence are an important part of the puzzle representing international law in relation to territorial conflicts. Most of the times silence and neutrality are not so much and only the result of a manifest inability of international law to affect territorial conflicts rather of a deliberate choice of policy-makers and judicial authorities to render it irrelevant to the management and settlement of territorial disputes.

Concluding Remarks

The three "dynamics" of relationship between international law and territorial conflicts may of course co-exist and each of these three dynamics should be tested on a case-by-case basis in terms of efficiency and pursuit of societal goals, be it stability, peace and realization of justice. While principles such as *uti possidetis* and territorial integrity will be generally instrumental to legitimate demands of stability and peace, whereas principles such as self-determination and the doctrine of non-recognition are in the abstract instrumental to the realization of justice, a definite evaluation must be made with regard to each and every specific territorial conflict and in view of the possible interrelation between the three dynamics. As shown above, even legal neutrality may reveal important policy and political implications, no less important than those underlying dynamics of resistance or dynamics of adaptation.

---

45   *Ibidem*, Declaration of Judge Simma, para. 3.

For instance, the affirmation of the principle of *uti possidetis* in different processes of State formation in Europe in the 1990s was mainly inspired by the need of avoiding resort to the use of force as the means by which new boundaries are carved out: to that extent, *uti possidetis* has been applied with a view to furthering an idea of justice. As already shown, its gist was that of ordering territorial change and adapting international law to a new state of affairs, rather than simply upholding stability. As far as "efficiency" is concerned the assessment must be a different one: it requires an evaluation of inner coherence in the application of the principle and a cost-benefit analysis related thereto. In the case of the application of the *uti possidetis* to the conflict in the Former Yugoslavia, coherence was generally upheld (possibly with the exception of Kosovo) and there is little indication that the bloodshed produced by the conflict in the Former Yugoslavia would have been reduced had territory been "up for grabs" irrespective of administrative boundaries.

Finally, one must observe that in Europe the occasional apparent "silences" of international law have been partially compensated by the development of soft law standards and by resort to comparative constitutional law and to human rights law. One can think not only of the case law of the European Court of Human Rights in many of the territorial conflicts still present in Europe, but of the work of the Venice Commission on the holding of territorial referenda and the work of the OSCE High Commissioner on National Minorities on minority/kin-State relations.[46] For instance, in the former case the Venice Commission has established that the minimal international standards for a territorial referendum are the following: a) free and universal suffrage; b) the authorities must provide objective information; c) the public media have to be neutral, in particular in news coverage; d) the authorities must not influence the outcome of the vote by excessive, one-side campaign; e) the use of public funds for campaigning purposes must be restricted; f) respect for fundamental human rights; g) presence of international observers; h) availability of an effective appeal system.[47] Whether the "moral and normative

---

46 See V. Bilkova, "Territorial (Se)cession in Light of Recent Events in Crimea", in *Law, Territory and Conflict Resolution*, cit., 194; F. Palermo, N. Sabanadze (eds.), *National Minorities in Inter-State Relations*, 2011.

47 European Commission for Democracy through Law, Opinion on the Compatibility of the Existing Legislation in Montenegro concerning the Organization of Referendum with Applicable International Standards, Opinion no. 343/2005 of 19 December 2005, CDL-AD(2005)041, para. 12.

suasion" inherent in the development of these soft law standards can be considered as adequate in managing, settling and terminating territorial disputes and conflicts is a matter of contention as it is a matter of contention whether these normative prescriptions already represent binding international law. What is undoubtedly positive is that these soft law instruments are instrumental to the consolidation of normative principles that may become part of an emerging regional international law of Europe, in which regional organizations play a crucial role as standard-setters and "guardians" in their application. There is hope that international law will continue to play a decisive role in preventing, containing, settling and terminating territorial disputes and conflicts in the decades to come.

Attribution of Responsibility after the EU Accession to the ECHR and the "Co-Respondent Mechanism"

Przemyslaw Tacik

1   Introduction

Whether the European Union accedes to the European Convention on Human Rights is not a foregone conclusion, or at least not to the extent that it used to be in the period 2010-2014. Even though the accession remains a self-imposed obligation of the EU (Art. 6 (2) TUE), difficulties with gearing the Convention system to the EU's specificity, especially after the convoluted Opinion 2/13 of the CJEU,[1] might finally turn out too overwhelming for the Union – which currently needs to address much more urgent issues. Yet apart from the symbolic dimension of the accession (which still might rekindle some pro-European enthusiasm), this act, even viewed only from the theoretical point of view, offers a surprisingly innovative perspective of relations between international organisations and control systems of international human rights conventions. Among these relations issues related to international responsibility – and shared responsibility in particular – come to the fore.

Attributing responsibility to the EU and/or its Member States after the accession is something of an uncharted territory. There exist general rules of law of international responsibility, there is case law of the ECtHR (and of the EComHR), but the exact norms governing attributing responsibility and co-responsibility in the case of the EU are not yet fully determined. Nevertheless, they might be of considerable importance for future development of law of international responsibility of IOs.

This article attempts to outline basic characteristics of future EU responsibility for violations of the ECHR. First it sketches out the specificity of the accession in the context of international responsibility. Then it proceeds to analysing successive sets of rules which may determine the boundaries of responsibility of the EU and its Member States before the ECtHR. Finally, it proposes a theoretical enquiry into the nature and status of the so-called co-respondent mechanism – which, parenthetically,

---

1   *Opinion 2/13* (2014), ECLI:EU:C:2014:2454.

will be one of the most intriguing novelties of the accession – in the light of general rules of international responsibility and previous case law of the ECtHR.

2 EU Accession to the ECHR

The accession of the European Union to the European Convention on Human Rights – since the 70s a recurring pet subject for legal scholars[2]

---

2 The accession process and its relation to autonomy of EU law have been broadly dealt with in literature. Among the most important see: 'Adhésion des Communautés à la Convention européenne des droits de l'homme. Mémorandum de la Commission', Bulletin des Communautés européennes – Supplément 2/79 in Walter Jean Ganshof van der Meersch (ed.), *L'adhésion des Communautés européennes à la Convention européenne des droits de l'homme*, Brussels, Bruylant & Vander, 1981; José Rafael Aìs Marìn, 'La adhesión de la Unión Europea al Convenio de Roma. El cumplimiento de las obligaciones derivadas del Convenio Europeo de Derechos Humanos en el ordenamiento jurídico de la UE', *Revista de Derecho Comunitario Europeo*, núm. 44, 2013; Patrick Auvret, 'L'adhésion de l'Union à la Convention européenne des droits de l'homme' in Joël Rideau (ed.), *Les droits fondamentaux dans l'Union européenne. Dans le sillage de la Constitution européenne*, Brussels, Bruylant, 2009; Roberto Baratta, 'Accession of the EU to the ECHR: The Rationale for the ECJ's Prior Involvement Mechanism', *Common Market Law Review*, Vol. 50, 2013; Florence Benoît-Rohmer, 'L'adhésion de l'Union à la CEDH', *Revue universelle des droits de l'homme*, vol. 12, no. 1-2, 2000; Susana Sanz Caballero, 'Crónica de una adhesión anunciada: algunas notas sobre la negociación de la adhesión de la Unión Europea al Convenio europea de derechos humanos', *Revista de Derecho Comunitario Europeo*, núm. 38, 2011; Gérard Cohen-Jonathan, 'L'adhésion de l'Union Européenne à la Convention européenne des droits de l'homme' in Allain Brun, Gérard Cohen-Jonathan (eds.), *Quelle justice pour l'Europe? La Charte Européenne des Droits Fondamentaux et la Convention pour l'Avenir de l'Europe*, Brussels, Bruylant, 2004; José Manuel Cortés Martìn, 'Sur l'adhésion à la CEDH et la sauvegarde de l'autonomie de l'ordre juridique de l'Union dans l'identification du défendeur pertinent : le mécanisme du codéfendeur', *Revue du Droit de l'Union européenne*, 2011, no. 4; Vasiliki Kosta, Nikos Skoutaris, Vassilis P. Tzevelekos, *The EU Accession to the ECHR*, Oxford and Portland OR, Hart Publishing, 2014; Christina Eckes, 'EU Accession to the ECHR: Between Autonomy and Adaptation', *The Modern Law Review*, Vol. 76, Issue 2, 2013; Heribert Golsong, 'Nochmals: zur Frage des Beitritts der Europäischen Gemeinschaften zur Europäischen Menschenrechtskonvention', *Europäische Grundrechte Zeitschrift*, Vol. 6, 1979; Andrea Huber, *Der Beitritt der Europäischen Union zur Europäischen Menschenrechtskonvention. Art. 6 Abs. 2 S. 1 EUV*, Hamburg, Verlag Dr. Kovač, 2008; Jean-Paul Jacqué, 'L'adhésion de l'Union européenne à la Convention européenne des droits de l'homme', *Revue trimestrielle de droit européen*, no. 1, 2011;

and now a legal obligation of the EU under Article 6 (2) TEU – had been perceived for a long time as a fairly simple method of elevating human rights protection in the Union to a satisfying level. When the idea of accession of the European Communities was originally proposed (first by Pierre Pescatore in the 60s,[3] in a limited institutional context, and then – in its current sense – in the 70s[4]), human rights protection in the Communities was only budding. The accession seemed a fast and relatively easy option to equip these organisations with a written catalogue of hu-

---

Jean-Paul Jacqué, 'The Accession of the European Union to the European Convention on Human Rights and Fundamental Freedoms', *Common Market Law Review*, Vol. 48, 2011; Fisnik Korenica, *The EU Accession to the ECHR. Between Luxembourg's Search for Autonomy and Strasbourg's Credibility on Human Rights Protection*, Heidelberg-New York-Dordrecht-London, Springer 2015; Tobias Lock, 'EU Accession to the ECHR: Implications for Judicial Review in Strasbourg', *European Law Review*, Vol. 35, no. 6, 2010; Tobias Lock, 'Walking on a Tightrope: the Draft ECHR Accession Agreement and the Autonomy of the EU Legal Order', *Common Market Law Review*, Vol. 48, 2011; Georg Minichmayr, *Der Beitritt der Europäischen Gemeinschaft zur Konvention zum Schutze der Menschenrechte und Grundfreiheiten*, Wien, Euro-Jus Schriftenreihe, MANZ'sche Verlag, 1999; Walter Obwexer, 'Der Beitritt der EU zur EMRK: Rechtsgrundlagen, Rechtsfragen und Rechtsfolgen', *Europarecht*, Vol. 47, 2012; Theodor Schilling, 'Der Beitritt der EU zur EMRK-Verhandlungen und Modalitäten', *Humboldt Forum Recht*, no. 8, 2011; Olivier de Schutter, 'L'adhésion de l'Union européenne à la CEDH: feuille de route de la négociation', *Revue trimestrielle des droits de l'homme*, Vol. 83, 2010; Susanne Stock, *Der Beitritt der Europäischen Union zur Europäischen Menschenrechtskonvention als Gemischtes Abkommen?*, Hamburg, Verlag Dr. Kovač, 2010; Antonio Tizzano, 'Quelques réflexions sur les rapports entre les cours européennes dans la perspective de l'adhésion de l'Union à la Convention EDH', *Revue trimestrielle de droit européen*, no. 1, 2011; Françoise Tulkens, 'La protection des droits fondamentaux en Europe et l'adhésion de l'Union européenne à la Convention européenne des droits de l'homme', *Kritische Vierteljahresschrift für Gesetzgebung und Rechtsprechung*, Vol. 95, no. 1, 2012; Wolfgang Weiß, 'Human Rights in the EU: Rethinking the Role of the European Convention on Human Rights After Lisbon', *European Constitutional Law Review*, no. 7, 2011; Sebastian Winkler, *Der Beitritt der Europäischen Gemeinschaften zur Europäischen Menschenrechtskonvention*, Baden-Baden, Nomos 2000; Julie Vondung, *Die Architektur des europäischen Grundrechtsschutzes nach dem Beitritt der EU zur EMRK*, Tübingen, Mohr Siebeck 2012.

3   Pierre Pescatore, 'Compte rendu de la discussion sur le rapport de M. Waelbroeck' in *Droit communautaire et droit national. Community Law and National Law*, Bruges, De Tempel-Tempelhof, 1965, p. 319.

4   'Adhésion des Communautés...', *supra* note 2, p. 140; cf. also Kim Economides, Joseph H. H. Weiler, 'Accession of the Communities to the European Convention on Human Rights: Commission Memorandum', *The Modern Law Review*, Vol. 42, no. 6, 1979, p. 683.

man rights, an obligation to respect and protect them, as well as an external legal remedy allowing of control of their actions and omissions. What might be surprising in the current circumstances is that the Commission once perceived the accession to the ECHR as a much more feasible option than preparing a new catalogue of human (or fundamental, as they are called in the context of the Communities/EU following BVerfG's example) rights.[5] Obviously, 25 years after introducing references to the ECHR in the Treaties, 17 years after the adoption of the Charter of Fundamental Rights, 8 years after it was granted binding force, and with the accession still far on the horizon, this claim seems ironic at best.

Throughout these approximately 40 years when the accession has been considered, planned and scrutinised, the legal context significantly changed. The EU no longer needs a human rights catalogue on its internal plane. Despite limitations of access to the CJEU for individuals under the so-called Plaumann test,[6] it cannot be denied that the Luxembourg Court together with national courts of Member States provides an advanced (even if somewhat convoluted) system of human rights protection. Through the so-called "horizontal clause" (Article 52 (3)) and the explanations to the CFR the Charter is now linked both to the ECHR and to case law of the ECtHR.[7] Given that the ECHR has been already materially incorporated into EU law (albeit indirectly), is there any lacuna to speak of that the accession could remove?

Apart from its symbolic dimension and consequences on EU law as such, the accession will impose on the Union an international obligation to respect and protect human rights enshrined in the Convention. Moreover, the compliance with this obligation will be safeguarded by the control mechanism of the ECHR. Arguably it will be the greatest advantage of the accession, but simultaneously the most problematic one for at least a few reasons.

Firstly, never has an international organisation been a party to the ECHR. The Convention was dovetailed for states, not for organisations. Apart from rather minor inconveniences stemming from the inadequacy of the ECHR's language (using for example terms like "national security" or "territory") to international organisations, this fact will demand thorough reconsideration of principles of responsibility attributed by the ECtHR. Even though the Strasbourg Court has had quite a few opportuni-

---

5 'Adhésion des Communautés...', *supra* note 2, p. 137.
6 Julie Vondung, *supra* note 2, pp. 36-38.
7 Jean-Paul Jacqué, 'The Accession of the European Union...', *supra* note 2, pp. 999-1000.

ties to refer to shared responsibility of international organisations and states,[8] its case law never had an actual bearing on ECHR-related responsibility of IOs, as none of them has ever been a party to the Convention. On the contrary, when the accession becomes a fact, the ECtHR will be obliged to adjudicate on potential international responsibility of the EU. To this purpose it will have to remould its principles concerning attribution, content and consequences of responsibility first formulated in relation to states. Alternatively, it will have to recall its previous case law regarding the attribution of conduct to international organisations and draw from these rather incoherent rulings some pertinent conclusions. In the latter case, however, the rules of attribution of conduct would have to be supplemented by a wide range of further norms so that the regime of responsibility be complete.

Secondly, if the EU were simply a new party to the ECHR, of a special kind, but acting exclusively on its own, the complications still would not be immense. The Union, however, more often than not carries out its actions in close cooperation with its Member States. As a consequence, applications brought against the EU in Strasbourg will usually concern alleged violations in which some or all the Member States have participated. Multiple attribution of conduct or of responsibility, as well as generally construed shared responsibility might become a rule rather than an exception as far as the EU is concerned. Yet it would be wrong to suppose that the problem of shared responsibility will arise only in relation to the Union as party to the Convention. On the contrary, the accession will significantly transform the whole functioning of the ECHR control mechanism in relation to EU Member States, that is 27 out of 47 current parties to the Convention. Each application brought against them will have to be vetted in search of a possible "EU element" and, if such an element is found, the need for the EU's joining the proceedings will have to be considered.

Apart from the increase of purely administrative work that will affect the ECtHR, the Court will have to address a wide range of questions that have not been so far elucidated either in international jurisprudence or in scholarly research. Shared and joint responsibility, albeit always ritually mentioned as a theoretical by-product of principles of international

---

[8] See Maarten den Heijer, 'Procedural Aspects of Shared Responsibility in the European Court of Human Rights', *Journal of International Dispute Settlement*, no. 2, 2013, pp. 361-383; 'Shared Responsibility Before the European Court of Human Rights', *Netherlands International Law Review*, no. 3, 2013, pp. 411-440.

responsibility, backed up by scarce examples, had not become a subject of thorough consideration until quite recently.[9] The ECtHR will have to formulate a new set of rules and standards of attribution with limited help from its previous case law and fairly general ILC's Articles on Responsibility of States for Internationally Wrongful Acts[10] (later as: ARS) and Articles on Responsibility of International Organisations[11] (ARIO).

Thirdly, the relations between the EU as party to the Convention and its Member States are governed by unique rules, determined by the principle of loyalty. The Union will accede to the ECHR only on condition of appropriate safeguards for its autonomy and special features of its law.[12] The overall length of the accession process, currently put on hold by the CJEU's Opinion 2/13, stems mostly from the difficulty of finding an acceptable balance of interests between the EU and the Council of Europe (and some of the extra-EU parties to the Convention). The CoE naturally tends towards preserving the effectiveness of the ECHR in relation to all its parties; the EU, however, seems more concerned about safeguarding its unique position. Whatever the final compromise will be (if there will be one), the modalities of responsibility of the EU for violating the Convention will be laid down in a set of special rules, incorporated into the future Accession Agreement (later as: AA). To all complications caused by specificity of an international organisation being a party to the Convention and its extensive cooperation with Member States, also ECHR-parties, the need for safeguarding the autonomy of EU law will add further demands. The rules of attribution that the ECtHR will have to lay down eventually will have to respect the norms of the AA, but also – in all probability – the specificity of EU law in its relation to Member States.

The current stage of the accession process allows of outlining basic modalities of responsibility of the EU for violating the Convention. The final (so far) Draft Accession Agreement (later as: DAA), agreed upon in

---

9   At least as far as the ECtHR is concerned, the key rulings that fuelled debates on the attribution of conduct were delivered in the last two decades. In-depth and comprehensive scholarly analyses of shared responsibility had not been undertaken until the SHARES Project, which was carried out in the years 2010-2015.

10 'Draft Articles on the Responsibility of International Organizations', *Yearbook of the International Law Commission*, Vol. II (2), 2011, pp. 19-25.

11 'Draft Articles on the Responsibility of States for Internationally Wrongful Acts', *Yearbook of the International Law Commission*, Vol. II (2), 2011, pp. 26-30.

12 On the issue of EU autonomy in relation to the Union's accession to the ECHR, see generally: Paul Gragl, *The Accession of the European Union to the European Convention on Human Rights*, Oxford and Portland OR, Hart Publishing, 2013.

2013,[13] attests to a general compromise as to general rules of attribution of conduct and of responsibility to the EU and its Member States. This compromise includes the so-called "co-respondent mechanism" (later as: CRM), a special legal institution designed to address the necessity of attributing joint responsibility of the EU and its Member States. Naturally, the DAA was found incompatible with the Treaties by the CJEU in Opinion 2/13; however, the Court's objections in the domain of responsibility concerned only three detailed regulations, not the CRM itself. Therefore, although the DAA cannot be an unquestionable starting point for predicting how the attribution of responsibility to the EU and/or its Member States will look like after the accession, it is highly probable that the model of the CRM envisaged in the DAA, reshaped in application of the CJEU's demands, will make its way to the future AA. The Court's conclusions do not demand thorough transformation of the CRM which would require a new debate to be opened. On the contrary, the necessary modifications, although not inconsequential, can be introduced without reconsidering the very idea of the CRM. It should be emphasised, however, that the need to prepare a new draft of the AA might provide a good opportunity to reconsider the DAA's rules, especially in the areas in which they are most vague.

3 Legal Context of Attribution of Responsibility to the EU and/or Its Member States After the Accession

Undoubtedly, predicting the future modalities of responsibility of the EU and/or its Member States, especially if they are yet to be determined by the ECtHR, is – to a certain degree – nothing but walking on thin ice. If the accession finally takes place, the CRM will provide a fascinating legal laboratory in which new rules concerning shared/joint responsibility will be minted. They cannot be predicted, but their uncharted territory might be at least delimited.

The attribution of responsibility to the EU and/or its Member States under the ECHR after the accession will be governed by a few sets of rules of different kind. Some of them are expressed explicitly in normative acts

---

13   Council of Europe, 'Fifth Negotiation Meeting Between the CDDH Ad Hoc Negotiation Group and the European Commission on the Accession of the European Union to the European Convention on Human Rights. Final report to the CDDH' [2013] 47+1(2013)008rev2.

(for example rules determined by EU Treaties) or are presumed to be thus expressed in the future (e.g. in the case of the AA). Their scope and content must be deciphered in the context of the CJEU's jurisprudence, especially Opinion 2/13. Other rules belong to general international law and are codified in both ILC's Articles; although they have not yet made their way to a regular international convention, according to the prevalent (albeit not unanimous[14]) opinion they have acquired binding status as customary rules. Finally, some of them are derived by the ECtHR from the Convention and – to a lesser degree – international law; their significance is, however, limited due to their vagueness and dependence on circumstances of particular cases.

Even though it might be rightly claimed that all these rules will not suffice to determine fully the modalities of adjudicating on responsibility, they circumscribe a field which needs to be reconstructed before further analysis is conducted. In this article I will concentrate on rules provided by EU law and the DAA, given that they are most specifically addressing the key question. I will make references, however, to both ILC's codifications and case law of the ECtHR in order to put them in a broader perspective.

3.1   EU Law

In the domain of attribution of ECHR-related responsibility EU law is fairly laconic. In this regard only Art. 6 (2) TEU and Protocol No. 8 to the Treaty of Lisbon provide any regulations. Although they belong to a legal order of only one of the future parties to the ECHR, they will significantly influence attribution of responsibility. The first channel of influence is obvious: the future AA must respect the boundary conditions set out by the Treaties (their compliance falls under the control of the CJEU). Nevertheless, there will be yet another, unobvious channel of influence. If the ECtHR after the accession resorts to ARIO, it should take into account the *lex specialis* clause in Art. 64, whose scope encompasses among others constitutive instruments, decisions and other acts of international organisations.[15] This broad understanding of *leges speciales*, partly adopted

---

14   Kenneth Keith, 'The Process of Law-making: the Law Relating to International Organizations as an Example' in Maurizio Ragazzi (ed.), *Responsibility of international organizations. Essays in Memory of Sir Ian Brownlie*, Leiden – Boston, Nijhoff, 2013, pp. 15-27.

15   Commentary to the Draft Articles on Responsibility of International Organizations, Art. 2, § 16.

in response to specific features of some organisations (chiefly the EU[16]), opens the general regime of responsibility to modifications stemming from internal norms of IOs. Consequently, the ECtHR cannot reckon without the fact that the ARIO might paradoxically become a vehicle for EU law in the ECHR regime. Finally, the rules formally derived from EU law might (and probably should, in light of Art. 32 VCLT) be viewed as a context of interpretation for more concrete norms of the (D)AA, whose objective lies in safeguarding some characteristic features of EU law.

As to the material content of responsibility-related provisions, Art. 6(2) TEU contains two norms: the first one states that the EU accedes to the ECHR and the second one safeguards that the accession should not modify the division of competences as established by the Treaties. As to the first of these norms, its significance by far exceeds simple granting to the EU the competence for accession. Art. 6 (2) TEU not only obliges the EU to accede, but also – according to some[17] – highlights the urgency of the accession through its original wording in the present tense. It might be argued that this provision acknowledges the general compatibility between EU law and the demands of the ECHR control system. The accession should not be viewed as a long-term goal, requiring vast adaptations of the Convention to the EU. The wording of Art. 6 (2) TEU suggests that the Treaty-makers perceived the accession as an act for which all main obstacles had been cleared and only minor technical arrangements appeared necessary.[18] Consequently, it might be argued that they recognised the EU's capability to bear responsibility for violating the Convention within the current institutional and procedural framework of the ECHR.

For this reason Art. 6 (2) TEU should have attracted more of the CJEU's attention in its Opinion 2/13.[19] It could have provided a counterweight to the need of safeguarding autonomy of EU law and might have even tipped the balance in favour of the DAA's compatibility with the Treaties. Nevertheless, apart from this already out-of-date criticism of Opin-

---

16   José Manuel Cortés Martín, 'European Exceptionalism in International Law? The European Union and the System of International Responsibility' in *Responsibility of international organizations, supra* note 14, p. 197.
17   Andrea Huber, *supra* note 2, pp. 33-34.
18   Cf. Johan Callewaert, *The Accession of the European Union to the European Convention on Human Rights*, Strasbourg, Council of Europe Publishing, 2014, p. 48.
19   Cf. 'The EU's Accession to the ECHR – a "NO" from the ECJ!', CMLR Editorial Comments, *Common Market Law Review*, Vol. 52, 2015, p. 13.

ion 2/13, Article 6 (2) TEU should be taken into account in the context of attribution of responsibility. It might be interpreted as an expression of general readiness of the EU to bear responsibility for violating the ECHR and, consequently, as an imperative to minimise amendments of the current rules governing attribution of responsibility. As such, it should be viewed as a general rule to which particular demands of Protocol No. 8 to the Treaty of Lisbon are exceptions.

Art. 6 (2) TEU *in fine* shields the division of competences between the EU and its Member States after the accession. As far as attribution of responsibility is concerned, this provision has at least three consequences. Firstly, it excludes that the accession could impose on the EU an obligation which the Union would not be able to carry out within its competences already granted by the Treaties. This prohibition is particularly relevant in the domain of positive obligations of parties to the ECHR. In this area the Convention no longer limits execution of public authority, but prescribes actions that need to be undertaken by the parties.[20] In case of the EU, which, unlike state parties, does not dispose of sovereignty-backed full public authority, but relies on competences acquired from its Member States, positive obligations derived both from the Convention and the AA must be limited precisely at the point at which EU competences end. Consequently, the division of competences cannot be breached even in the case of shared responsibility.

Secondly, Art. 6 (2) TEU *in fine* requires appropriate mechanisms of attributing joint responsibility to the EU and its Member States. If the division of competences is to be preserved, the ECHR system must recognise the EU and the Member States as mutually coordinated actors which often carry out the same tasks but at different levels. For this reason the AA should establish necessary mediation between the demands of attribution of responsibility and the division of competences, prohibiting the ECtHR from adjudication on the latter. Nevertheless, the exact content of this mediation is unclear. The compromise reached in the DAA reserves for the EU and its Member States the right to attribute particular obligations to each of them in the aftermath of the ECtHR's rulings declaring joint responsibility. As it will be demonstrated further, it is not obvious how the ECtHR should conduct its reasoning in order to satisfy this de-

---

20   On relation between the accession and positive obligations under the ECHR see: Catherine Stubberfield, 'Lifting the Organisational Veil: Positive Obligations of the European Union Following Accession to the European Convention on Human Rights', *Australian International Law Journal*, Vol. 7, 2012, p. 121f.

mand. As far as Art. 6 (2) TEU *in fine* is concerned, it might be argued that any declaration that even potentially touches upon the division of competences may involve creating international obligations under the ECHR to carry out specific tasks which would not match the EU division of competences. The demands of EU law go far in this regard, so it is sensible to assume that if the ECtHR might technically adjudicate on an alleged violation without any reference to the division of competence, it should do so.

Moreover, the need to safeguard EU competences might determine the possibility of adjudicating on joint responsibility of the EU and its Member States if the conduct in question cannot be attributed directly to the EU. Theoretically speaking, joint responsibility might be declared even if the respondent(s) and the co-respondent(s) take part in proceedings as one *sui generis* subject of responsibility and the conduct in question is attributable to only one of them. Even if the co-respondent mechanism allowed of adjudicating joint responsibility in such cases, Art. 6 (2) TEU might preclude it, because the EU would in such cases bear joint responsibility for acts which lay outside of its competences.

In this regard the CRM must strike a balance between two divergent imperatives. On the one hand, joint responsibility is supposed to shield the division of competences from the purview of the ECtHR. On the other hand, declaration of joint responsibility might entail – from the point of view of international law – imposing on the EU an obligation to remove consequences of a violation even if the EU has no competences to remove them. Although in this case the declared responsibility is technically attributed to a "joint subject" (the EU and its Member State(s)), it is unclear how such an attribution affects international responsibility of the EU itself. Certainly, to be responsible as part of the joint subject is not equivalent to be responsible individually, yet it might be argued that if consequences of declaring responsibility, as stipulated in the ARS and in the ARIO, do not distinguish between "individual" subjects and "joint subjects", they apply equally to both. If so, then from the point of view of international law, declaring joint responsibility of the EU and its Member State(s) would impose on the EU itself obligations to cease the violation, guarantee non-repetition and offer reparation (art. 30-31 ARIO). It is in this respect that the future AA will have to establish special rules governing the content and consequences of joint responsibility, which will be *leges speciales* in the meaning of art. 64 ARIO. Without them joint responsibility will run the risk of being effectively meaningless, because the specificity of this institution will not be reflected in particular modalities.

Neither the general regime of responsibility nor case law of the ECtHR – being adapted rather to separate than joint responsibility – provides any detailed regulations of the latter.[21] EU law in itself, however, is not a sufficient ground for determining the exact scope and consequences of declaring joint responsibility.

Therefore it is only the AA that may stipulate relations between the responsibility of a joint subject and of its "parts", determining, in particular, whether and how obligations stemming from joint responsibility may be transferred to individual subjects. The model of tacit regulation, preferred in the DAA, may not be satisfying because it assumes that the attribution of particular obligations can take place only between the EU and its Member State(s) and will always be a harmonious process. Even if such an assumption is backed up by the principle of loyalty and the very construction of EU law, legal norms must be flexible enough to remain applicable also in situations of conflict between the EU and its Member State(s) as "parts" of the joint subject. The AA might – in the very interest of the EU – regulate the possibility of invocation of responsibility of the EU or its Member State(s) if joint responsibility is not attributed to them individually on a friendly basis. Without such a safety valve, the EU runs the risk of having the veil of joint responsibility disregarded. The position of the applicant should be given priority in these rules, so that in case of lack of understanding as to attribution of responsibility her rights, as declared in the ECtHR's judgment, would be respected. The rules in question should also decide whether in a situation where the joint subject does not fulfill its obligations imposed by a ruling of the ECtHR, the responsibility for such a new violation must still be attributed to this joint subject or, contrariwise, might (or should) be attributed separately. For these reasons it seems possible that the need to safeguard the division of competences may be, to a certain extent, incompatible with joint responsibility if the exact content and consequences of the latter are not fully regulated.

Thirdly, specific rules need to be established on the attribution of responsibility in case when joint responsibility is not declared, but it is either the EU or a Member State(s) that are responsible for the alleged violation (regardless of whether the CRM was or was not triggered). In

---

21   Cf. James D. Fry, 'Attribution of Responsibility', SHARES Research Paper no. 37, 2014, p. 14; Christiane Ahlborn, 'To Share or Not to Share? The Allocation of Responsibility between International Organizations and their Member States', SHARES Research Paper no. 28, 2013, p. 12.

this regard Art. 6 (2) TEU, as far as it demands that EU competences be respected, might be interpreted as requiring that all obligations which may be imposed on the EU as a result of a Strasbourg ruling should square with its competences. This may be particularly difficult if the applicant brings an application against a wrong subject (for example against the EU and not its Member State), the CRM is not triggered, and the EU might be found responsible for violations that it cannot remove. In this regard the future AA must contain norms which will strictly link the scope of the ECtHR's adjudication to EU competences.

When it comes to Protocol No. 8 to the Treaty of Lisbon,[22] there are two provisions that concern attribution of responsibility. Firstly, Art. 1 of the Protocol provides for a special agreement relating to the accession, which need to preserve the specific characteristics of the EU and EU law, particularly in relation to (a) the specific arrangements for the Union's possible participation in the control bodies of the European Convention and (b) the mechanisms necessary to ensure that proceedings by non-Member States and individual applications are correctly addressed to Member States and/or the Union as appropriate. This article develops the aforementioned norms of Art. 6 (2) TEU and explicitly requires establishing a procedural aspect of the CRM (as a special modality of EU's participation in proceedings before the ECtHR). Moreover, it demands introducing a mechanism which will ensure that applications are addressed to correct parties. Even though during the accession negotiations it was agreed upon, rather tacitly, that the CRM fulfills this demand, such a conclusion is not obvious (even if Opinion 2/13 did not find any flaws in this regard, the CJEU's verdict does not preclude that this point cannot be raised in the future).[23] The CRM allows of co-opting additional party to the proceedings, but it does not mean that, for example, an application launched incorrectly against a Member State, if only the EU is responsible, can be subsequently modified. Evidently, the need to safeguard the correct selection of a party does not go hand in hand with the main motivation justifying joint responsibility, that is preclusion of the ECtHR from adjudicating on the division of competences. For this rea-

---

22   Protocol (No 8) Relating To Article 6(2) of the Treaty on European Union on the Accession of the Union to the European Convention on the Protection of Human Rights and Fundamental Freedoms, OJEU C 326/1, 26.10.2012.

23   Cf. also Martin Kuijer, 'The Accession of the European Union to the ECHR: A Gift for the ECHR's 60th Anniversary or an Unwelcome Intruder at the Party?', *Amsterdam Law Forum*, Vol. 3, no. 4, 2011, p. 26; Julie Vondung, *supra* note 2, p. 182.

son the mechanism of correction should not resort to using conditions of admissibility of applications. Nevertheless, the facultative co-optation of another party, envisaged in the DAA, does not satisfy fully the demands of Art. 1 of Protocol No. 8.[24]

Art. 2 of Protocol No. 8, except for reiterating the demand to preserve competences of the EU and its institutions, requires that the AA should ensure respect of the situation of Member States in relation to the ECHR (particularly the scope of ratified protocols, derogations and reservations). As far as responsibility is concerned, this provision might be interpreted twofold. A narrower interpretation would focus on the three explicitly listed factors determining a situation of a Member States in relation to the ECHR. Consequently, it would require precluding even joint responsibility of a Member State if, in a given case, it is not bound by a particular Convention norm due to the above-mentioned three conditions. It seems plausible that such a view is shared by the CJEU, which in Opinion 2/13 challenged the CRM regulations in the DAA because they allowed of declaring joint responsibility even if a Member State made a reservation as to a norm relevant in a given case.[25]

Nevertheless, a broader interpretation would also be possible. It would take these three factors only as particular examples of "a situation of a Member State in relation to the ECHR", which, however, do not determine this situation entirely. It might be understood as encompassing the rules of attribution of responsibility and, among them, rules determining the attribution of conduct. In other words, Art. 2 of Protocol No. 8 could be understood as demanding that responsibility might be attributed to a Member State only if a conduct is attributable to this state. If so, establishing joint responsibility under the CRM might be problematic, because it can be attributed to a joint subject (the EU and its Member States altogether) regardless of attribution of conduct and responsibility to each of the parties. For this reason the narrow interpretation should be adopted; otherwise joint responsibility – although demanded by other provisions of EU law – would not be compatible with the Treaties.

3.2 Draft Accession Agreement and Opinion 2/13

The above-mentioned demands laid down in EU primary law had to be confronted with requirements of the Council of Europe and non-EU parties to the Convention. The result of a two-stage negotiation process was

---

24 Cf. Julie Vondung, *supra* note 2, p. 181.
25 Opinion 2/13, §§ 226-228.

the Draft Accession Agreement, agreed upon in June 2013. As far as attribution of responsibility is concerned, its provisions might be divided into two groups: (1) material norms, determining some procedures of attributing conduct and responsibility (although not fully), (2) procedural norms, governing the model of co-participation of the EU and its Member State(s) in proceedings before the ECtHR. Nevertheless, this division is not neat, because procedural norms are not fully subsidiary to material ones; especially the model of facultative co-respondent significantly modifies practical effects of the co-respondent mechanism.

Material norms concerning responsibility are contained in the following three provisions of the DAA:

> Article 1.
> 3. Accession to the Convention and the protocols thereto shall impose on the European Union obligations with regard only to acts, measures or omissions of its institutions, bodies, offices or agencies, or of persons acting on their behalf. Nothing in the Convention or the protocols thereto shall require the European Union to perform an act or adopt a measure for which it has no competence under European Union law.
> 4. For the purposes of the Convention, of the protocols thereto and of this Agreement, an act, measure or omission of organs of a member State of the European Union or of persons acting on its behalf shall be attributed to that State, even if such act, measure or omission occurs when the State implements the law of the European Union, including decisions taken under the Treaty on European Union and under the Treaty on the Functioning of the European Union. This shall not preclude the European Union from being responsible as a co-respondent for a violation resulting from such an act, measure or omission, in accordance with Article 36, paragraph 4, of the Convention and Article 3 of this Agreement.
> Article 3.
> 7. If the violation in respect of which a High Contracting Party is a co-respondent to the proceedings is established, the respondent and the co-respondent shall be jointly responsible for that violation, unless the Court, on the basis of the reasons given by the respondent and the co-respondent, and having sought the views of the applicant, decides that only one of them be held responsible.

Art. 1 (3) is explicitly designed to shield the division of competences between the EU and its Member States,[26] particularly in the area of positive obligations. It curbs the scope of obligations imposed by the Convention, which must match the scope of competences of the EU. It is worth noting that although both ILC's codifications establish a logical order of attributing responsibility – in which attributing conduct and determining the scope of international obligations that bind the responsible subject (except for so-called indirect responsibility[27]) precede the attribution of responsibility – the practice of the ECtHR is carried out in a reverse order: it is the ruling that effectively determines the exact content of an ECHR-based obligation. And in this determination Art. 1 (3) requires the ECtHR to take into account an additional factor, namely the scope of competence of the EU (although, as it was mentioned earlier, EU law is deemed to preclude adjudicating on this competence by any other organ than the CJEU). In other words, the DAA seems to demand that the ECtHR consider each of the obligations derived from the Convention (especially positive ones) in the light of EU competences.

Even though Art. 1 (3) DAA seems to be aimed at safeguarding the division of competences between the EU and its Member States, it was effectively formulated in a manner which determines the scope of attribution of conduct to the EU.[28] Here the conceptual framework of the DAA diverges from general principles of international responsibility. The latter clearly separates attribution of conduct, specifying a list of actors whose acts may be considered acts of a state or of an organisation, from international obligations, which bind a state or an international organisation as such. In the language of ARS or ARIO, first an act must be attributed to a state or IO (for example if it was carried out by its organ or agent), then the conduct may be assessed in relation to obligations binding the state/IO.

Art. 1 (3) DAA, however, mixes obligations with rules of attribution of conduct. On literal reading it seems to delimit only the scope of ECHR-derived obligations of the EU; yet in truth it does so in relation to the

---

26 Draft explanatory report to the Agreement on the Accession of the European Union to the Convention for the Protection of Human Rights and Fundamental Freedoms, § 22.
27 James D. Fry, *supra* note 21, p. 1.
28 Cf. Maarten den Heijer, André Nollkaemper, 'A New Framework for Allocating International Responsibility: the EU Accession to the European Convention on Human Rights', SHARES Briefing Paper 2014, pp. 3-4.

listed agents. Theoretically, it would be possible to read this provision as pertaining only to obligations, with rules of attribution of conduct excluded. Nevertheless, even apart from the negotiators' goal, Art. 1 (3) DAA limits effectively the scope of attributable responsibility, making the general rules of attribution of conduct irrelevant if they do not match these specific norms governing the scope of obligations. For this reason the provision in question might seem dubious from the point of view of legislative technique, because it reaches its goal through dismantling the well-established tradition of distinguishing obligations from attribution of conduct – and by assuming, even if inadvertently, that it is not the EU that is bound by international obligations but its institutions, bodies etc.

As far as the list of agents is concerned, it contains no novelty both from the point of ECHR law and ARIO. "Institutions, bodies, offices, agencies, and persons acting on their behalf" generally add up to the notion of an organ or agent in the meaning of Art. 6 (1) ARIO. Nevertheless, as far as the ARIO is concerned, Art. 1 (3) DAA may not envisage attribution of conduct of an organ of a state or of an IO placed at the disposal of the EU (since it will neither be "its" organ nor a person acting on its behalf). This lack might be particularly important in the case of extraterritorial responsibility for foreign missions. In turn, from the point of view of ECHR law, the list from Art. 1 (3) DAA roughly corresponds to the defining formula used by the EComHR in the *Ireland v. The United Kingdom* case:

> The responsibility of a State under the Convention may arise for acts of all its organs, agents and servants. As in connection with responsibility under international law generally, their rank is immaterial in the sense that in any case their acts are imputed to the state. It is true that there are further conditions for responsibility (breach of a norm, a victim, sometimes fault, and damage), and for the jurisdiction of the Commission (Exhaustion of remedies and other formal requirements). The Commission is of the opinion that although the state can only incur new obligations through acts "at the level of the State" by persons duly authorised to bind it (e.g. to conclude a treaty), its existing obligations can be violated also by a person exercising an official function vested in him at any, even the lowest level, without express authorisation and even outside or against instructions.[29]

---

29 *Ireland v. The United Kingdom*, Case No. 5310/71 (1976), Report of the Commission, p. 383.

Art. 1 (3) DAA might be effortlessly interpreted to encompass the demand that parties to the ECHR be responsible for acts or omissions of all its organs, regardless of whether they belong to the legislative, the executive or to the judiciary (although this division is not easily applicable to the EU).[30] It might be dubious, however, whether this provision fits all possible situations of potential responsibility of the EU – for example in case of extraterritorial responsibility.[31] Naturally, responsibility of the EU would be usually incurred through its legislative acts, as the Union has scarce capabilities of using its own institutions and forces. Nevertheless, it seems sensible to supplement the vague formula of Art. 1 (3) DAA with a reference to the concept of some kind of control so that it could match the ECtHR's concept of extraterritorial responsibility.

When it comes to Art. 1 (4) DAA, the negotiators decided to safeguard that, as principle, EU Member States will incur responsibility for the acts or omissions of its organs or persons acting on their behalf even if they act or abstain from acting in application of EU law. This provision preserves to a large degree the *status quo* of ECHR responsibility, guaranteeing that after the accession the basic possibility of applying against a Member State for its violations of the ECHR will not be inoperative due to its relation to the EU. Nonetheless, Art. 1 (4) DAA does not exclude that responsibility for an act of a Member State cannot be attributed to the European Union if the co-respondent mechanism is triggered. Yet as far as the ground principles are concerned, the EU and its Member State(s) are to be responsible separately and individually for committed violations. Consequently, if the-corespondent mechanism is not triggered, each application which is directed simultaneously against the EU and its Member State(s) might result in four configurations: (1) both parties are declared responsible, (2) only the EU is declared responsible, (3) only a Member State is declared responsible (or, in case of multiple states taking part in proceedings, any number or all of them may be deemed responsible), (4) both the EU and its Member State(s) are declared responsible.

More importantly from the doctrinal point of view, in each case the ECtHR will have to undertake separate reasoning pertaining to the act

---

30   *Young, James and Webster* v. *United Kingdom*, Case No. 7601/76, 7806/77 (1981), A44. Cf. also Maarten den Heijer, André Nollkaemper, *supra* note 28, pp. 4-5.

31   The explanatory report seems to allow such responsibility, disregarding the problem of the scope of Art. 1 (3) DAA. Cf. Draft explanatory report to the Agreement on the Accession of the European Union to the Convention for the Protection of Human Rights and Fundamental Freedoms, § 23.

which violated the Convention, its attribution to the EU or a Member State and, finally, the legal assessment of the act in question. Therefore, if the CRM is not set off, both proceedings and judgment of the Strasbourg Court will look, to all instants and purposes, similar to current cases in which more than one party to the ECHR is involved. It must be noted that in each of the above-mentioned configurations the responsibility of a given party will be assessed in relation to its own act and omission, because the possibility of derivative responsibility of the EU for its Member States' acts, mentioned in Art. 1 (4) DAA *in fine*, applies only to situations in which the co-respondent mechanism is active. Nonetheless, given that general rules of attribution of conduct under the ECHR will be still applicable, multiple attribution of the same conduct of the same agent is not excluded. Such a path was famously opened by the ECtHR in the *Al-Jedda* case,[32] which modified the previously applied principles from *Behrami and Saramati* case[33] and allowed of concurrent attribution of conduct to a state and an IO (even if the UN, not being a party to the Convention, could not incur responsibility in *Al-Jedda*).[34] Sufficient level of "normative control" of the EU over a given conduct might therefore entail parallel attribution both to the Union and to a Member State.[35] Even if, from theoretical point of view, such a possibility will not be a novelty, it is worth noting that the EU will be the first international organisation which, in cases like *Al-Jedda*, will effectively incur responsibility. Abstract findings of the Strasbourg Court will thus be filled out with flesh.

Finally, Art. 3 (7) DAA, if preserved in the final AA, will bring a true novelty not only to rules of attribution of conduct and of responsibility under the Convention, but also to general regime of responsibility under the ARS and the ARIO. This provision allows of declaring joint responsibility of the EU and its Member State(s) if the co-respondent mechanism is active. Before we proceed to analysing joint responsibility, a few remarks need to be made on the construction of the CRM as agreed upon in the DAA.

---

[32] *Al-Jedda* v. *The United Kingdom*, Case No. 27021/08 (2011), RJD 2011-IV. Cf. also Christiane Ahlborn, *supra* note 21, p. 10.

[33] *Behrami and Behrami* v. *France* and *Saramati* v. *France, Germany and Norway*, Case No. 71412/01, 78166/01 (2007).

[34] Francesco Messineo, "Things Could Only Get Better: *Al-Jedda* Beyond *Behrami*", *Military Law and the Law of War Review*, Vol. 50, 2011, no. 3-4, pp. 337-338.

[35] Francesco Messineo, 'Attribution of Conduct', SHARES Research Paper no. 32, 2014, pp. 13-15.

The final version of the CRM does not, in fact, constitute a full method of correcting applications inappropriately addressed against the EU and/or its Member States. In particular, it cannot make the EU solely responsible for a violation whose allegation was erroneously addressed to a Member State only. The CRM allows, first, to extend the scope of parties to the EU or its Member States and, second, to treat them as one, joint subject for the purpose of attributing responsibility. Both elements of the CRM are, to a certain degree, independent: the first one is redundant if the application was already directed (correctly) against both the EU and its Member State(s).

As it was already mentioned, the final model of the CRM agreed upon during the negotiation process is fully facultative, albeit moderated by a unilateral declaration of the EU to join the proceedings if conditions of the CRM are met. Apart from obvious shortcomings of this option (from the point of view of individual applicant, the CRM will not be a method of correcting applications), it means that joint responsibility might be declared only if the parties concerned approve such a ruling. From the theoretical point of view, it gives the parties a considerable margin of appreciation as to what kind of responsibility is to be adjudicated. According to their own needs, they may either demand being considered as a joint subject of responsibility or be treated as separate subjects. In the former option, the joint subject is composed not of ordinary respondents, but of a respondent (the party originally mentioned in the application) and a co-respondent (the party which joins the proceedings). The difference between the usual respondent and the co-respondent lies in two features of the latter: (1) domestic remedies do not need to be exhausted against the co-respondent and (2) responsibility of the co-respondent is determined only in conjunction with the responsibility of the respondent.

This voluntary aspect was even strengthened by the Court of Justice in Opinion 2/13. The DAA envisaged two possible moments of intervention of the ECtHR into triggering the CRM. First, the mechanism was to be set off only on condition of acceptance the joining party, but it was the ECtHR's final decision either to invite this party or to approve its new status (Art. 3 (5) DAA) after assessing whether the condition of the CRM is met (namely if the allegation calls into question compatibility with the Convention of a norm of EU law[36]). Second, if in the light of the pro-

---

36 Here the details differed depending on whether it was the EU or its Member States that joined the proceedings – cf. Art. 3 (2) and (3) DAA.

ceedings joint responsibility was not applicable despite triggering the CRM, the ECtHR was entitled to terminate it, having assessed the reasons given by the respondent and the co-respondent (and having sought the views of the applicant). Yet any possibility of the ECtHR's deciding on the launching or terminating the CRM were found incompatible with the Treaties by the CJEU.[37] If the current model of the CRM is to be reused in the future AA, these two elements of the ECtHR's discretion will have to be eliminated. Consequently, the decision to set off the CRM (or to terminate it, if this is at all allowed by Opinion 2/13) will fall entirely into the hands of the EU and its Member State(s). Given that there will be no external body to assess whether the conditions for launching the CRM are met, the parties' demand will effectively conflate with the premise of the CRM. Consequently, it will depend on the EU and its Member States whether in each case in which EU law is involved responsibility should be declared individually or jointly.

Returning to the analysis of Art. 3 (7) DAA, it needs to be noted that the regulation of the joint responsibility is fairly laconic. The provision in question stipulates only that it can be declared if "the violation in respect of which a High Contracting Party is a co-respondent to the proceedings is established". The explanatory report suggests that typically the co-respondent's act will consist in enacting either a norm of secondary EU law (if the EU is the co-respondent) or a norm of primary law (if the Member States are co-respondents).[38] Yet it is not clear how the attribution of responsibility for a violation is to be carried out. The DAA uses a singular form, suggesting that under the CRM there is only one violation. In other words, the respondent and the co-respondent do not incur joint responsibility for their individual acts, but for one effect that violates the Convention. They should be treated as one joint subject that committed a violation.

The joint subject of responsibility may be, under the CRM, made independent from its "parts", according to the negotiators' needs. It is quite obvious that in order to safeguard the execution of judgments in which an EU element is involved, the CRM must primarily envisage independence of the joint subject from the EU and its Member State(s), so that the ruling which declares its responsibility does not create direct obli-

---

37 Opinion 2/13, §§ 218-225, 229-235.
38 Draft explanatory report to the Agreement on the Accession of the European Union to the Convention for the Protection of Human Rights and Fundamental Freedoms, § 62.

gations for the EU and the Member State(s) independently (which does not mean that it cannot impose an obligation to undertake attribution of obligations among these subjects). Yet the CRM is not confined only to the execution of judgments. It may equally detach rules of attribution of conduct and of responsibility applied to the joint subject from those which concern parties independently.

In the latter respect the regulation of Art. 3 (7) DAA does not seem perfect. It is a provision of very general character which leaves open the questions of attribution of conduct and of responsibility.[39] The aforementioned norms of EU law – Art. 6 (2) TUE and Protocol No. 8 – should lead to extending the scope of joint responsibility, so that the ECtHR would never have the actual opportunity to assess the division of competences.

4 The Co-respondent Mechanism Between Joint and Individual Responsibility

The co-respondent mechanism is one of the most intriguing institutions recently proposed in the field of international responsibility. In its both limbs, procedural and material, it allows of investigating, declaring and executing shared responsibility of multiple parties to the ECHR. Nevertheless, the CRM in itself might be linked to different modes of adjudicating on shared responsibility. In particular, it might be closer to the model of full joint responsibility or include elements of individual responsibility. Between these two poles of the continuum various options are possible.

The CRM involving full joint responsibility would produce a complete organisational veil which shields individual parties from attribution (and execution) of responsibility separately. Fused into a joint subject, not only there would be declared jointly responsible, but also this kind of responsibility would be extended both to the assessment of premises of finding a violation and to execution of judgments. As far as the former is concerned, the ECtHR would not be entitled to first establishing violations of each of the parties and, subsequently, to produce a "sum of individual responsibilities". What the Strasbourg Court would be entitled to do would be determining the act and its relation to the Convention. Attribution of conduct, however, would have to be supplemented by the request of both (or more) parties to trigger the CRM. Since they would be

---

39   Cf. Maarten den Heijer, André Nollkaemper, *supra* note 28, p. 7.

willing to incur responsibility jointly, there would be no need of individual attribution of conduct.[40] Afterwards, the ECtHR would have to enquire into the Convention-related scope of obligations of the respondent and the co-respondent(s) and, if they were identical in relation to the violation in question, could declare joint responsibility. In turn, execution of judgments could never lead to holding a party responsible for a singular obligation. In other words, carrying out of obligations declared in a judgment could be assessed only globally, that is in relation to the respondent and the co-respondent(s) jointly. If they fail to distribute obligations in relations between themselves, or if one of them does not abide by the adopted agreement, any further violations of the ECHR could be declared still only in relation to the whole joint subject, not its "parts".

The other pole of the continuum is occupied by the CRM consisting in a limited form of joint responsibility, which is declared only as a sum of individual attributions of conduct and of responsibility. When it comes to the execution of judgments, such a CRM could assume that although responsibility may be declared only jointly, there still might be situations which justify piercing of the veil of responsibility and assessing individual input into fulfillment of the ECtHR's demands.

Between these two poles there might be various models of the CRM. Against this theoretical background the model selected by the negotiators may appear ambiguous. It does not specify the exact meaning and content of joint responsibility. Sure enough, it imposes on the ECtHR an obligation to declare joint responsibility if the mechanism was set off. Yet both the reasoning that leads up to such a ruling and its execution were not well determined. Consequently, the CRM as proposed in the DAA may be adaptable to both poles of the above-outlined continuum.

Such a laconic regulation might be interpreted twofold. Either the negotiators wanted to leave some questions open, so that they could be answered by the EU with its Member States and the ECtHR in its judicial practice, or they wanted to give green light to the vastest form of joint responsibility. In both cases, however, the main onus of developing more detailed rules would lie upon the Strasbourg Court. Formally, the DAA demands only that if the CRM is launched, the ECtHR should attribute joint responsibility to the EU and its Member State(s) which therefore, as Walter Obwexer put it, "melt into one".[41] But the main goal of the CRM de-

---

40   The ECtHR could refer to Art. 9 ARIO in this regard, taking the demand to trigger the CRM as an acknowledgment of conduct.
41   Walter Obwexer, *supra* note 2, p. 129.

mands that the ECtHR should tend towards the joint responsibility pole of the continuum rather than the other. The main point of the Court's reasoning should be the assessment of the alleged conduct in the light of its conformity with the Convention. As far as the attribution of conduct is concerned, the reasoning should be much more restrained. It should be sufficient to demonstrate that a member state undertook a certain action or omission and that this action or omission was generally determined by EU law. Any further investigation into the substantial link before the norm of EU law in question and the action or omission should be suspended. In this regard the request of the EU or of its Member State(s) to join the proceedings should be perceived as acceptance of responsibility insofar as the attribution of conduct is concerned.

The safest way to guarantee the safe form of attribution of responsibility would be to assume a negative presumption. Responsibility could be therefore attributed to the joint subject if the following conditions would be met: (1) the conduct in question infringes the Convention, (2) the EU and its member state(s), taking part in proceedings, request that joint responsibility be adjudicated, (3) the conduct in question cannot be causally linked to any other party to the Convention. Thus it would be safeguarded that the conduct could be attributed only to the Member State and the EU, but it would be done in a negative way, by elimination of any other causal links.

As far as the execution of judgments is concerned, the DAA does not contain any clues as to whether the veil of responsibility may be pierced or not, especially in order to safeguard the applicant's rights if the EU and its Member State(s) do not cooperate harmoniously. It needs to be noted that joint responsibility is an institution generally foreign to the ARS, ARIO although it is not inconsistent with them. For this reason the demands of Art. 6 (2) TUE and Protocol No. 8 must be translated into the precise terms of the AA much more diligently than it was done in the DAA. Naturally, distribution of particular obligations was rightly left in the hands of the EU and its Member States; yet this need cannot justify the fact that no relation between joint responsibility and individual responsibility of the respondent and the co-respondent(s) was established by the DAA. In particular, it is unclear how the declaration of joint responsibility relates to the payment of just satisfaction. Can the applicant demand the payment only from the respondent and the co-respondent jointly? Or only from one of them? These questions should be answered precisely in the future AA.[42]

5   Conclusion

After the EU accession to the ECHR, attribution of responsibility under the Convention will be enriched with a new institution: the co-respondent mechanism. So far little can we know about its nature and functioning. What we do know, however, is that the CRM in the DAA version diverges from the general framework of attributing responsibility under the ARS and the ARIO.[43]

The CRM blurs the distinction between attribution of conduct and of responsibility. The DAA assumes that there is only one joint violation, but in truth, apart from the CRM, both a Member State and the EU commit a violation of their own. The EU infringes the ECHR by enacting a norm which does not comply with the Convention,[44] while Member States undertake measures to apply this norm. From the point of view of the ILC's codifications, in both cases they incur direct responsibility. The CRM, however, not only allows of declaring them jointly responsible, but also breaks the chain between conduct, obligation and responsibility. It focuses on the result that violates the Convention, but abstracts from causal links that relate it to acts and omissions of the EU and its Member State(s). It supplements the relation between the conduct and attribution of responsibility with a demand of the parties to trigger the CRM.

As a result, the CRM will provide a real novelty for rules of international responsibility. It only remains to be hoped that in the best interests of

---

42   Cf. Maarten den Heijer, André Nollkaemper, *supra* note 28, p. 17.

43   Cf. Pieter Jan Kuijper, 'Attribution – Responsibility – Remedy. Some comments on the EU in different international regimes', SHARES Research Paper no. 30, 2014.

44   Art. 17 ARIO allows of attributing (indirect) responsibility to an IO if it adopts a decision that obliges a member state to commit an act which violates its obligations. At first sight it may appear plausible that the CRM is built upon this rule (see Maarten den Heijer, André Nollkaemper, *supra* note 28, p. 5). But under the ECHR even adopting a legislative act discordant with the Convention is a violation (apart from the fact if there is a victim of such a violation). For this reason any kind of "normative control" of the EU over its Member States will not require resorting to Art. 17 ARIO. The EU will commit its own violation, irrespective of its influence on the Member States.

the EU its regulation in the future AA will be closer to the model of joint responsibility rather than individual responsibility.

Republic of Estonia Materials on International Law 2015

*Edited by René Värk**

[*Editorial Notes:*

1. Republic of Estonia Materials on International Law 2015 (REMIL 2015) have been classified according to the Recommendation (97)11 of 12 June 1997 of the Committee of Ministers of Council of Europe, as applied by the British Yearbook of International Law from the year 1997, with certain minor amendments.

2. The REMIL mostly concern the opinions made by the institutions and officials of Estonia. In case it has not been expressly stated otherwise, the institutions and officials mentioned in the REMIL are those of Estonia. Often, different officials expressed views on same issues. In order to prevent unduly repetion, the editor has selected materials from the highest possible level. Some materials are quoted in length due to their importance or because they provide useful insight to the relevant aspects of Estonian history, politics and geopolitical concerns.

3. There were several recurring topics in the speeches given and statements made by officials, for example, cyber issues, human rights, online freedom of expression. In many cases, nothing new was added compared to previous speeches and statements, and therefore the editor has not included them or has limited their inclusion in the materials. Not surprisingly, the conflict in Ukraine received continued attention from several perspectives due to its extraordinary nature and Estonia's concerns over aggressive Russia.

4. The European Court of Human Rights handed down five judgments on the merits against Estonia and found violations in three cases. Violations

---

* Dr iur; Associate Professor of International Law and Deputy Head of the Department of Public Law at the School of Law, University of Tartu, Estonia; Associate Professor of Constitutional and International Law at the Estonian National Defence College.

concerned Articles 6, 8 and 13, and Article 1 of Protocol No. 1. 181 applications were declared inadmissible or struck out.]

Index**

Part One: International Law in general
I. Nature, basis, purpose
    A. In general
    B. *Jus cogens*
    C. Soft law
II. History

Part Two: Sources and Codification of International Law
I. Sources of international law
    A. Treaties
    B. Custom
    C. General principles of law
    D. Unilateral acts, including acts and decisions of international organisations and conferences
    E. Judicial decisions
    F. Opinions of writers
    G. Equity
    H. Comity (*comitas gentium*)
II. Codification and progressive development of international law

Part Three: The Law of Treaties
I. Definition, conclusion and entry into force of treaties
    A. Definition
    B. Conclusion, including signature, ratification, and accession

---

** The Baltic Yearbook provides the Index for State practice reports only in front of the first State report – Ed.

    C. Reservations, declarations, and objections
    D. Provisional application, and entry into force
II. Observance, application, and interpretation of treaties
    A. Observance of treaties
    B. Application of treaties
    C. Interpretation of treaties
    D. Treaties and third States
III. Amendment and modification, derogation
IV. Invalidity, termination and suspension of the operation
    A. General rules
    B. Invalidity
    C. Termination and suspension of operation, denunciation, and withdrawal
    D. Procedure
    E. Consequences of invalidity, termination, or suspension of operation
V. State succession in respect of treaties (see Part Five)
VI. Depositaries, notifications, corrections, and registration
VII. Consensual arrangements other than treaties

Part Four: Relationship between International Law and Internal Law
I.   In General
II. Application and implementation of international law in internal law
III. Remedies under internal law for violations of international law

Part Five: Subjects of International Law
I. States
    A. Status and powers
        1. Personality
        2. Sovereignty and independence
        3. Non-intervention
        4. Domestic jurisdiction
        5. Equality of States
        6. State immunity
        7. Other powers, including treaty-making power
    B. Recognition
        1. Recognition of States
        2. Recognition of governments
        3. Types of recognition

(a) *de facto/de jure*
(b) conditional/unconditional
4. Acts of recognition
   (a) implied/express
   (b) collective/unilateral
5. Effects of recognition
6. Non-recognition (including non-recognition of governments) and its effects
7. Withdrawal of recognition

C. Types of States
   1. Unitary states
   2. Personal and real unions
   3. Protected States

D. Formation, identity, continuity, extinction, and succession of States
   1. Conditions for statehood
   2. Formation
   3. Identity and continuity
   4. Extinction
   5. Succession
      (a) Situations of State succession
         (i) Union with or without the demise of the predecessor State
         (ii) Dismemberment
         (iii) Separation
         (iv) Newly independent States
      (b) Effects of State succession
         (i) Territory and other areas under national jurisdiction
         (ii) Nationality
         (iii) Succession in respect of treaties
         (iv) Archives
         (v) Debts
         (vi) Property
         (vii) Responsibility
         (viii) Other rights and obligations

II. International organisations
   A. In general
      1. Status and powers
         (a) Personality

            (b) Privileges and immunities of the organisation
            (c) Powers, including treaty-making power
        2. Participation of States and international organisations in international organisations and in their activities
            (a) Admission
            (b) Suspension, withdrawal, expulsion, and deportation
            (c) Obligations of membership
            (d) Representation of States and international organisations to international organisations, including privileges and immunities
        3. Legal effect of the acts of international organisations
        4. Personnel of international organisations
        5. Responsibility of international organisations (see Part Thirteen)
        6. Succession of international organisations
    B. Particular types
        1. Universal organisations
        2. Regional organisations
        3. Organisations constituting integrated (e.g. economic) communities
        4. Other types
III. The Holy See
IV. Other subjects of international law and other entities or groups
    A. Mandated and trust territories
    B. Dependent territories
    C. Special regimes
    D. Insurgents
    E. Belligerents
    F. Others (indigenous people, minorities, national liberation movements, etc.)

Part Six: The Position of the Individual (including the Corporation) in International Law

I. Nationality
II. Diplomatic and consular protection (see Part Thirteen)
III. Aliens
IV. Members of minorities
V. Stateless persons
VI. Refugees
VII. Immigration and emigration, extradition, expulsion, asylum

- A. Immigration and emigration
- B. Extradition
- C. Expulsion
- D. Asylum

VIII. Human rights and fundamental freedoms
- A. General concept
- B. Under United Nations treaty system
- C. Under Council of Europe treaty system
- D. Other aspects of human rights and fundamental freedoms

IX. Crimes under international law

X. Responsibility of the individual (see Part Thirteen)

Part Seven: Organs of the State and their Status
I. Heads of State
II. Ministers
III. Other organs of the State
IV. Diplomatic missions and their members
V. Consulates and their members
VI. Special missions
VII. Trade and information offices, trade delegations, etc.
VIII. Armed forces
IX. Protecting powers

Part Eight: Jurisdiction of the State
I. Bases of jurisdiction
- A. Territorial principle
- B. Personal principle
- C. Protective principle
- D. Universality principle
- E. Other bases

II. Types of jurisdiction
- A. Jurisdiction to prescribe
- B. Jurisdiction to adjudicate
- C. Jurisdiction to enforce

III. Extra-territorial exercise of jurisdiction
- A. General
- B. Consular jurisdiction
- C. Jurisdiction over military personnel abroad
- D. Other (artificial islands, *terrae nullius*, etc.)

IV. Limitations upon jurisdiction (servitudes, leases, etc.)

V. Concurrent jurisdiction

Part Nine: State Territory
I. Territory
    A. Elements of territory
        1. Land, internal waters, lakes, rivers, and land-locked seas (see also Parts Ten and Eleven)
        2. Sub-soil
        3. Territorial sea (see Part Eleven)
        4. Airspace (see Part Twelve)
    B. Good neighbourliness
II. Boundaries and frontiers
    A. Delimitation
    B. Demarcation
    C. Stability
III. Acquisition and transfer of territory
    A. Acquisition
    B. Transfer

Part Ten: International Watercourses
I. Rivers and lakes
    A. Definition
    B. Navigation
    C. Uses for purposes other than navigation
    D. Protection of the environment
    E. Institutional aspects
II. Groundwaters
III. Canals

Part Eleven: Seas and Vessels
I. Internal waters, including ports and bays
II. Territorial sea
III. Straits
IV. Archipelagic waters
V. Contiguous zone
VI. Exclusive economic zone, exclusive or preferential fisheries zones
VII. Continental shelf
VIII. High seas
    A. Freedoms of the high seas, including overflight
    B. Visit and search
    C. Hot pursuit

  D. Piracy
  E. Conservation of living resources
IX. Islands, rocks and low-tide elevations
X. Enclosed and semi-enclosed seas
XI. International sea bed area
XII. Land-locked and geographically disadvantaged States
XIII. Protection of the marine environment
XIV. Marine scientific research
XV. Cables and pipelines
XVI. Artificial islands, installations, and structures
XVII. Tunnels
XVIII. Vessels
  A. Legal regime
    1. Warships
    2. Public vessels other than warships
    3. Merchant vessels
  B. Nationality
  C. Jurisdiction over vessels
    1. Flag State
    2. Coastal State
    3. Port State
    4. Other exercises of jurisdiction

Part Twelve: Airspace, Outer Space, and Antarctica
I. Airspace
  A. Status
  B. Uses
  C. Legal regime of aircraft
II. Outer space and celestial bodies
  A. Status and limits
  B. Uses
  C. Legal regime of spacecraft
III. Antarctica
  A. Limits and status
  B. Uses
  C. Protection of the environment

Part Thirteen: International Responsibility
I. General concept
II. General issues of international responsibility

A. The elements of responsibility (such as wrongfulness of the act, imputability)
B. Factors excluding responsibility (self-defence, necessity, reprisals)
C. Procedure
   1. Diplomatic protection
      (a) Nationality of claims
      (b) Exhaustion of local remedies
   2. Consular protection
   3. Peaceful settlement of disputes (see Part Fourteen)
D. Consequences of responsibility (*restitutio in integrum*, damages, satisfaction, guarantees)

III. Responsible entities
A. States
B. International organisations
C. Entities other than States and international organisations
D. Individuals and groups of individuals (including corporations)

Part Fourteen: Peaceful Settlement of Disputes
I. The concept of an international dispute
II. Means of settlement
   A. Negotiations and consultations
   B. Good offices
   C. Enquiry (fact-finding)
   D. Mediation
   E. Conciliation
   F. Arbitration
      1. Arbitral tribunals and commissions
      2. Permanent Court of Arbitration
   G. Judicial settlement
      1. International Court of Justice
      2. Other courts and tribunals
   H. Settlement within international organisations
      1. United Nations
      2. Other organisations
   I. Other means of settlement

Part Fifteen: Coercive Measures Short of the Use of Force
I. Unilateral measures

  A. Retorsion
  B. Counter-measures
  C. Pacific blockade
  D. Intervention (see also Part Five)
  E. Other unilateral measures
II. Collective measures
  A. United Nations
  B. Outside the United Nations

Part Sixteen: Use of Force
I. Prohibition of the use of force
II. Legitimate use of force
  A. Self-defence
  B. Collective measures
    1. United Nations
    2. Outside the United Nations
  C. Others
III. Use of disarmament and arms control

Part Seventeen: The Law of Armed Conflict and International Humanitarian Law
I. International armed conflict
  A. Definition
  B. The law of international armed conflict
    1. Sources
    2. The commencement of international armed conflict and its effects (e.g. diplomatic and consular relations, treaties, private property, nationality, trading with the enemy, *locus standi personae in judicio*)
    3. Land warfare
    4. Sea warfare
    5. Air warfare
    6. Distinction between combatants and non-combatants
    7. International humanitarian law
    8. Belligerent occupation
    9. Conventional, nuclear, bacteriological, and chemical weapons
    10. Treaty relations between combatants (cartels, armistices, etc.)

11. Termination of international armed conflict, treaties of peace
II. Non-international armed conflict

Part Eighteen: Neutrality and Non-Belligerency
I. The laws of neutrality
   A. Land warfare
   B. Sea warfare
   C. Air warfare
II. Permanent neutrality
III. Neutrality in the light of the United Nations Charter
IV. Policy of neutrality and non-alignment
V. Non-belligerency

Part Nineteen: Legal Aspects of International Relations and Co-operation in Particular Matters
I. General economic and financial matters
   A. Trade
   B. Loans
   C. Investments
   D. Taxes
   E. Monetary matters
   F. Development
II. Transport and communications
III. Environment
IV. Natural resources
V. Technology
VI. Social and health matters
VII. Cultural matters
VIII. Legal matters (e.g. judicial assistance, crime control, etc.)
IX. Military and security matters

Part One: I. B. International Law in general – Nature, basis, purpose – History

1/1

On 23 July, Foreign Minister Marina Kaljurand spoke at the symposium dedicated to the 75th anniversary of the Sumner Welles declaration and unveiled a memorial plaque to acknowledge the role of the United States non-recognition policy in the restoration of Estonian independence.

> Today, 75 years ago, the United States made a crucial decision regarding the recognition of the continuing existence of Estonia and the other Baltic states.
>
> As we know, the 1939 Molotov-Ribbentrop Pact contained a secret protocol by which the states of Northern and Eastern Europe were divided between Germany and Soviet Union.
>
> As a result of this, Estonia was occupied on June 17, 1940, by the Soviet Army and was forcibly incorporated into the Soviet Union on August 6, 1940. The United States never recognized the illegal occupation and annexation of the Baltic states, in accordance with the principles of the Stimson Doctrine and U.S. Undersecretary of State Sumner Welles' Declaration of July 23, 1940. More than 50 countries followed this position.
>
> The forcible annexation of Estonia to the Soviet Union was an illegal act under both customary and conventional international law. The legal recognition of Baltic incorporation on the part of the U.S. and other Western countries was withheld, based on the fundamental legal principle of ex injuria jus non oritur, since the annexation of the Baltic states by force was found to be illegal. And the continued recognition, and ultimately the restoration of the Baltic States' de facto independence, has in itself confirmed the relevance of the international law.
>
> As a consequence of the U.S. policy of non-recognition of the Soviet seizure of Estonia, Latvia and Lithuania, combined with the resistance of our peoples to the Soviet regime and the uninterrupted functioning of our diplomatic missions in exile, the Baltic states continued to exist as subjects of international law, and remained

de jure independent states under illegal occupation throughout the period from 1940 to 1991.

The principled U.S. non-recognition policy was of invaluable help to the Estonian people during our fight for restoring our independence. On March 30, 1990, the Estonian Supreme Council adopted the resolution on the state status of Estonia. The resolution announced that the independence of Estonia de jure had never been suspended, because of the illegal occupation since 1940. A resolution of the restoration of the Republic of Estonia was adopted on August 20, 1991, confirming the restoration of Estonia's independence on the basis of legal continuity.

Today, we face the situation in Europe, that for the first time since the Second World War, one country has illegally occupied and annexed the territory of another state. I'm referring to the Russian occupation and illegal annexation of the internationally recognized Ukrainian territory of Crimea in March of 2014.

This act, not recognized by the international community, reminds us that the need to uphold the principles of international law and to resist power politics and spheres of influence logic is as important today, as it was 75 years ago.

It is necessary, as was stated in the Sumner Welles declaration, to continue to oppose "predatory activities, whether they are carried out by the use of force or by the threat of force".

It is important to continue to reiterate our collective condemnation of the illegal annexation of Crimea and to forcefully implement the non-recognition policy. The EU's Crimea-related sanctions are in place. We also remain concerned about the continuing fragile situation in eastern Ukraine.

Ukraine should be able to regain control of its internationally recognized borders. We welcome the message from the G7, that any further escalation by Russia will bring further consequences.

To conclude, we in Estonia will always remember that by virtue of the Sumner Welles' declaration, the U.S. continued to recognize our independence and the exiled Estonian diplomatic mission, accredited our diplomats and flew the Estonian flag in the State Department's Hall of Flags. And today, we commemorate this principled U.S. stance of upholding the principles of international law, which as I pointed out, has as great a relevance in our present day, as it had 75 years ago.

The U.S. non-recognition policy has laid the foundation for a cooperative relationship between our countries based on mutual trust. As partners, Estonia and the U.S. work together to uphold and develop international law. And as allies in NATO, we cooperate to enhance the security of the transatlantic area. And as an EU member, Estonia contributes to developing the relationship between the EU and U.S., including the conclusion of the Transatlantic Trade and Investment Partnership.

(Available at the website of the Ministry of Foreign Affairs, <www.vm.ee/en/news/address-foreign-minister-marina-kaljurand-occasion-75th-anniversary-welles-declaration>, visited on 30 November 2016)

Part Five: I. A. 7. Subjects of International Law – States – Status and powers – Other powers, including treaty-making power

5/1

On 18 March, Foreign Minister Keit Pentus-Rosimannus condemned the signing of the so-called "Treaty on Alliance and Integration" between Russia and the de facto authorities of South Ossetia in Moscow today. She said that this is yet another step, which violates the sovereignty and territorial integrity of Georgia. Also, the signing of the given agreement confirms Russia's aggressive attitude and desire to annex South Ossetia.

The signed agreement is a violation of international law and the obligations assumed by Russia. The signing of this agreement damages the Geneva negotiations process and thus threatens the security and stability of the entire region."

(Available at the website of the Ministry of Foreign Affairs, <www.vm.ee/en/news/foreign-minister-pentus-rosimannus-agreement-signed-moscow-today-confirms-russias-aggressive>, visited on 30 November 2016)

Part Five: I. B. 6. Subjects of International Law – States – Recognition – Non-recognition (including non-recognition of governments) and its effects

5/2

On 5 May, Foreign Minister Keit Pentus-Rosimannus declared that Estonia does not recognize the independence of Nagorno-Karabakh and therefore does not consider the results of the so-called parliamentary election held on May 3 to be legitimate or valid. She said that the Nagorno-Karabakh conflict must be resolved and security and stability in the entire region must be achieved as a result of international negotiations.

Negotiations must determine the future of Nagorno-Karabakh. The region's status cannot be influenced by holding illegal elections."

(Available at the website of the Ministry of Foreign Affairs, <www.vm.ee/en/news/estonia-considers-so-called-parliamentary-elections-nagorno-karabakh-illegal>, visited on 30 November 2016)

Part Five: II. A. 2. c. Subjects of International Law – International organisations – In general – Participation of States and international organisations in international organisations and in their activities – Obligations of membership

5/3

On 2 October, Foreign Minister Marina Kaljurand said at the United Nations Security Council meeting, focusing on limiting the use of the veto, that all countries have a role to play in changing the behaviour of the Security Council in responding to crimes against humanity. Voluntary renunciation of the right of veto would give a clear message that perpetrators of crimes against humanity will be prosecuted.

Estonia is an active member in the United Nations Security Council's working methods pressure group ACT (Accountability, Coherence, Transparency) Group, which has prepared a code of conduct governing the exercise of the right of veto for voting in the Security Council in the case of crimes against humanity.

> Its adoption would give a clear message, that impunity will not be tolerated and would also help to prevent potential crimes in the future.

Nearly 60 members of the United Nations have expressed their support for the regulatory code of conduct for the Security Council vote, prepared by the ACT Group. According to Foreign Minister Kaljurand, the Security Council has a crucial role to play in the prevention, halting and investigating of crimes against humanity, if countries are not able to do so on their own.

> The current use of a rigid veto by permanent members of the UN Security Council puts obstacles on substantive activities and does not allow for finding solutions to conflicts, or dealing with investigating crimes against humanity."

(Available at the website of the Ministry of Foreign Affairs, <www.vm.ee/en/news/foreign-minister-kaljurand-no-country-un-security-council-should-have-right-veto-action-against>, visited on 30 November 2016)

Part Five: II. A. 2. d. Subjects of International Law – International organisations – In general – Participation of States and international organisations in international organisations and in their activities – Representation of States and international organisations to international organisations, including privileges and immunities

5/4

On 10 June, Foreign Minister Keit Pentus-Rosimannus met with the United Nations Deputy Secretary-General Jan Eliasson and said that Estonia supports reforming the United Nations Security Council in order for it to reflect the current, not the 1945 world order.

We consider it important to reach a better representation of UN membership in the Security Council in terms of improving the involvement of small and developing countries and various regions, as well as in reforming the Council's working methods. [...] We support the initiative of France to restrict the right to veto in the Security Council, so that in the case of serious crimes against humanity, permanent members of the Security Council would collectively forgo using the veto.

(Available at the website of the Ministry of Foreign Affairs, <www.vm.ee/en/news/estonian-foreign-minister-deputy-secretary-general-united-nations-estonia-supports-un-reform>, visited on 30 November 2016)

5/5
On 17 September, Estonia was elected Vice President of the United Nations Economic and Social Council (ECOSOC). The Estonian Ambassador to the United Nations, Sven Jürgenson, said that membership in and holding the vice presidency of the ECOSOC provides Estonia with an opportunity to significantly increase its international influence and visibility and to intensify relations with developing countries.

Furthermore, Estonia can continue to be actively involved in the promotion of human rights, including women's and children's rights, the rule of law, good governance, the rights of indigenous people and internet freedom."

(Available at the website of the Ministry of Foreign Affairs, <www.vm.ee/en/news/estonia-was-elected-vice-president-un-economic-and-social-council>, visited on 30 November 2016)

Part Six: VII. A. Immigration and emigration, extradition, expulsion, asylum – Immigration and emigration

6/1
On 16 July, Prime Minister Taavi Rõivas delivered a political statement addressing several pressing issues. Among others, he addressed the migrant crisis in Europe, which has resulted in polarised debates in Estonia:

Article 14 of the UN Universal Declaration of Human Rights, which was approved in 1945, says that "Everyone has the right to seek and to enjoy in other countries asylum from persecution." In Estonia we probably do not have to explain to anybody how important this right was and is for the Estonians who were deprived of their homes, lands and country several generations ago because of war and occupation. Mentally speaking, it was not easier for them to cope with their lives than the people who stayed in Estonia and it is very likely that most of these refugees would have exchanged life in a foreign country for a ticket back home. [...]

The right that is secured by the Universal Declaration of Human Rights has also been confirmed by the EU Charter of Fundamental Rights (Article 18). A right for asylum on equal grounds is of vital importance for exercising the fundamental freedoms of Schengen area and Europe. So that people can move and work freely inside Europe without internal border controls. Current European legislation imposes liability primarily on the countries linked to the people. It means that the biggest responsibility lies with the border states.

This requirement might be reasonable up to a certain limit, but in a serious crisis situation the burden is too heavy for the countries at the forefront. It is not enough to send more border guards, when we cannot send back the people.

For that reason, the European Commission proposed that all the European countries should take a fraction of these people under their wings. This helps also to avoid demands to restore border controls and reverse freedoms in Europe. It is also an expression of solidarity to the countries which have direct borders with the Mediterranean Sea.

However, I have repeatedly stressed that the mechanical quota offered by the Commission is disproportionate for Estonia. The basis for the solution that is currently lying on the table of the Ministers of Interior is a model proposed by Estonia and unanimously approved by all the fractions of the *Riigikogu* [the Parliament] at the European Union Affairs Committee, i.e. a proportional division according to the sizes of countries. I believe that Estonia is able to receive these couple of hundred people within a year without any kind of hysteria and panic.

(Available at the website of the Government, <www.valitsus.ee/en/news/political-statement-prime-minister-taavi-roivas-riigikogu-16-july-2015>, visited on 30 November 2016)

Part Six: VII. D. Immigration and emigration, extradition, expulsion, asylum – Asylum

6/2

On 14 January, a person released from the Guantanamo Bay detention camp arrived in Estonia yesterday afternoon and applied for asylum. He was received based on the Government's decision to meet a United States request in order to support the goal of the United States to shut down the Guantanamo Bay detention camp.

> People released from Guantanamo Bay often cannot return to their homelands, as it would mean a great risk to their safety. The person who arrived in Estonia has not been convicted of a crime; he arrived here at his own free will and he wishes to stay here.
>
> Estonia aims to guarantee a smooth acclimatization to the individual in order to ensure his independent subsistence in our society in the future. At present, the person has applied for asylum in Estonia, i.e. international protection on the basis of the Act on Granting International Protection to Aliens, administered by the Police and Border Guard Board. As an applicant for international protection, the person has the right to social support services from the state, which are administrated by the Ministry of Social Affairs as stipulated in legislation.
>
> A person to whom international protection is granted, will receive a temporary residence permit and subsistence support according to the law, an opportunity to learn Estonian is guaranteed to make acclimation easier and, if needed, translation services are provided in communicating with the authorities and health institutions."

(Available at the website of the Government, <www.valitsus.ee/en/news/estonia-accepted-person-released-guantanamo-bay>, visited on 30 November 2016)

Part Six: VIII. C. The Position of the Individual (including the Corporation) in International Law – Human rights and fundamental freedoms – Under Council of Europe treaty system

6/3

On 15 January, the European Court of Human Rights gave a judgment in the case of *Rummi* v. *Estonia*, where the applicant complained that her right of access to court had been violated (Article 6 § 1), she had been deprived of the possessions which had belonged to her husband and which had become her possessions through succession (Article 1 of Protocol No. 1), that the length of the proceedings in which her civil rights were determined had been excessive (Article 6 § 1), and had had no effective remedy in respect of her complaint of excessive length of civil proceedings (Article 13). The Chamber found the following:

I. Alleged Violation of Article 6 § 1 of the Convention in respect of the Complaints Concerning Access to Court and Fairness of the Proceeding

[...]

(a) Access to court

79. As regards the question whether the applicant's right of access to court was breached, the Court notes that the property in question was confiscated by the Viru County Court's decision of 24 March 2009. An appeal by the applicant against this decision was dismissed by the Tartu Court of Appeal on 25 May 2009. The Court has taken note, in this context, of the emphasis placed by the applicant on the Court of Appeal's position, namely that the applicant was not a party to the proceedings and that the County Court had not been required to involve her in the proceedings. However, the Court notes that the Court of Appeal nevertheless decided to examine the applicant's appeal in view of her allegation that her rights

had been violated by the confiscation of the property. The Court considers that in these circumstances it cannot be said that the applicant had no access to court. The Court reiterates in this context that it is not its task to rule on national law and practice *in abstracto*. Instead, it must confine itself to an examination of the specific facts of the cases before it (see, for example, *Findlay v. the United Kingdom*, 25 February 1997, § 67, *Reports of Judgments and Decisions* 1997-I; *B. and P. v. the United Kingdom*, nos. 36337/97 and 35974/97, § 35, ECHR 2001-III; and *Olujić v. Croatia*, no. 22330/05, § 69, 5 February 2009). Furthermore, the Court has also taken note of the Government's argument according to which the applicant could have had recourse to a civil or administrative court which would have constituted further avenues for the applicant to exercise her right of access to court. For this reason too the Court is unable to conclude that the applicant had no access to court.

(b) Fair trial

(*i*) *Recapitulation of the applicant's complaint*

80. The Court notes that the applicant in substance also complained that the confiscation proceedings had not been fair. She mainly argued in this connection that there had been no oral hearing and that the domestic courts' decisions had lacked sufficient reasoning.

(*ii*) *General principles*

81. The Court reiterates that an oral, and public, hearing constitutes a fundamental principle enshrined in Article 6 § 1 of the Convention. That said, the obligation to hold a hearing is not absolute. There may be proceedings in which an oral hearing may not be required, for example where there are no issues of credibility or contested facts which necessitate a hearing, and the courts may fairly and reasonably decide the case on the basis of the parties' submissions and other written materials. The Court has clarified that the nature of the circumstances that may justify dispensing with an oral hearing essentially comes down to the nature of the issues to be decided by the competent national court. The overarching principle of fairness embodied in Article 6 is the key consideration (see

Jussila v. Finland [GC], no. 73053/01, §§ 40-42, ECHR 2006XIV, with further references).

82. Furthermore, according to its established case-law reflecting a principle linked to the proper administration of justice, judgments of courts and tribunals should give an adequate statement of the reasons on which they are based. The extent to which this duty to give reasons applies may vary according to the nature of the decision, and must be determined in the light of the circumstances of the case. Although Article 6 § 1 obliges courts to give reasons for their decisions, it cannot be understood as requiring a detailed answer to every argument. Thus, in dismissing an appeal, an appellate court may, in principle, simply endorse the reasons for the lower court's decision (see, for example, *Garcia Ruiz v. Spain* [GC], no. 30544/96, § 26, ECHR 1999I, with further references). A lower court or authority in turn must give such reasons as to enable the parties to make effective use of any existing right of appeal (see *Hirvisaari v. Finland*, no. 49684/99, § 30, 27 September 2001).

(iii) Application of the principles to the present case

83. In the present case, the Court observes that the Viru County Court in its decision of 24 March 2009 (see paragraph 31 above) referred to the legal provision according to which property received as a result of a criminal offence and whose legal owner could not be identified, was to become State property. It then, "having examined the materials of the criminal case", concluded that the property in question in the present case was to be confiscated and transferred to the State. The County Court did not specify on which materials of the criminal case it had based its decision, or what led it to the conclusion that the property had been received as a result of a criminal offence or that its legal owner could not be identified. The Court considers that such brief reasoning, which amounts to a lack of reasoning, in addition to raising in itself an issue of lack of a fair trial, made it virtually impossible for the applicant to meaningfully challenge the County Court's position. The Court observes that in her appeal against the County Court's decision the applicant argued that the decision lacked reasoning and stated that in her view the material of the criminal case did not allow a conclusion to be drawn that the property had been obtained through crime, but merely that

it had been in R.'s possession. She also complained that she had not been heard, and asked for the case to be remitted to the first-instance court for a fresh examination.

84. The Court observes that the Tartu Court of Appeal's decision of 25 May 2009 (see paragraph 36 above) contains more detailed reasoning compared to that of the first-instance court. In particular, the Court of Appeal referred to the suspicions against R., including under Article 152-3 § 3 of the Criminal Code (Violation of the rules for purchase, export, re-export or trading of metals). It was noted that according to the police decision of 9 April 2001 concerning the discontinuance of the criminal proceedings in respect of R., the precious metals and substances containing precious metals had been obtained through crime, and their legal owner had not been identified. The Court of Appeal also referred to the confiscation request of 25 July 2002 by the police to the court, in which evidence had been set out demonstrating that the property had been obtained through crime; according to the Court of Appeal this evidence had included witness statements by K. and the applicant. The Court of Appeal noted that the applicant had been interviewed as a witness in the criminal proceedings and she had stated that she did not know the origin of the items and that they had been obtained by R. The Court of Appeal further noted that the applicant had not claimed title to the property or claimed that it had been her and her husband's joint property. On that basis, the Court of Appeal concluded that the property had been obtained through crime and had been lawfully confiscated.

85. Thus, the Court observes that Court of Appeal, in upholding the first-instance court's confiscation decision, mainly referred to two documents drawn up by the police, the first of which set out suspicions against R., and the second of which requested confiscation of the property, and to the statements of two witnesses, including the applicant. The Court notes that the Court of Appeal merely referred to the documents drawn up by the police, without making any attempt to assess the suspicions raised or conclusions drawn in these documents. As concerns the witness statements, K.'s statements were merely referred to, with no mention of their content. The applicant's statements were summarised briefly, and from this concluded that the property had been obtained through crime or

that its legal owner could not be identified. The Court observes, however, that according to the applicant's statements this property was obtained by her husband, who had placed his money in precious metals (see paragraph 23 above). In these circumstances, the Court is unable to conclude that the lack of reasoning in the first-instance court's decision was remedied by the Court of Appeal.

86. The foregoing considerations are sufficient to enable the Court to conclude that the requirements of a fair trial were not complied with in the present case. Having reached this conclusion, the Court considers it unnecessary to further examine the question whether Article 6 § 1 was also breached on account of the lack of oral hearing.

There has accordingly been a violation of Article 6 § 1 of the Convention.

II. Alleged Violation of Article 1 of Protocol No. 1 to the Convention

[...]

(a) General principles

101. The Court reiterates that Article 1 of Protocol No. 1 to the Convention, which guarantees in substance the right to property, comprises three distinct rules. The first, which is expressed in the first sentence of the first paragraph and is of a general nature, lays down the principle of peaceful enjoyment of property. The second rule, in the second sentence of the same paragraph, covers deprivation of possessions and makes it subject to certain conditions. The third, contained in the second paragraph, recognises that the Contracting States are entitled, among other things, to control the use of property in accordance with the general interest. The second and third rules, which are concerned with particular instances of interference with the right to peaceful enjoyment of property, must be construed in the light of the general principle laid down in the first rule (see, among many authorities, *Immobiliare Saffi v. Italy* [GC], no. 22774/93, § 44, ECHR 1999-V, and *Broniowski v. Poland* [GC], no. 31443/96, § 134, ECHR 2004V).

102. The Court's constant approach has been that confiscation, even though it does involve deprivation of possessions, nevertheless constitutes control of the use of property within the meaning of the second paragraph of Article 1 of Protocol No. 1 (see *Sun v. Russia*, no. 31004/02, § 25, 5 February 2009; *Riela and Others v. Italy* (dec.), no. 52439/99, 4 September 2001; *Arcuri and Others v. Italy* (dec.), no. 52024/99, 5 July 2001; *C.M. v. France* (dec.), no. 28078/95, 26 June 2001; *Air Canada v. the United Kingdom*, 5 May 1995, § 34, Series A no. 316A; and *AGOSI v. the United Kingdom*, 24 October 1986, § 51, Series A no. 108). Accordingly, it considers that the same approach must be followed in the present case.

103. The Court considers that confiscation in criminal proceedings is in line with the general interest of the community, because the forfeiture of money or assets obtained through illegal activities or paid for with the proceeds of crime is a necessary and effective means of combating criminal activities (see *Raimondo v. Italy*, 22 February 1994, § 30, Series A no. 281A). Confiscation in this context is therefore in keeping with the goals of the Council of Europe Convention on Laundering, Search, Seizure and Confiscation of the Proceeds from Crime, which requires State Parties to introduce confiscation of instrumentalities and the proceeds of crime in respect of serious offences. Thus, a confiscation order in respect of criminally acquired property operates in the general interest as a deterrent to those considering engaging in criminal activities, and also guarantees that crime does not pay (see *Denisova and Moiseyeva v. Russia*, no. 16903/03, § 58, 1 April 2010, with further references to *Phillips v. the United Kingdom*, no. 41087/98, § 52, ECHR 2001VII, and *Dassa Foundation and Others v. Liechtenstein* (dec.), no. 696/05, 10 July 2007).

104. The Court further reiterates that, although the second paragraph of Article 1 of Protocol No. 1 contains no explicit procedural requirements, it has been its constant requirement that domestic proceedings afford the aggrieved individual a reasonable opportunity of putting his or her case to the responsible authorities for the purpose of effectively challenging measures interfering with the rights guaranteed by this provision. In ascertaining whether this condition has been satisfied, a comprehensive view must be taken of the applicable procedures (see *Denisova and Moiseyeva*, cited

above, § 59; *Jokela v. Finland*, no. 28856/95, § 45, ECHR 2002-IV; and *AGOSI*, cited above, § 55).

(b) Application of the principles to the present case

105. Turning to the present case, the Court notes at the outset that pursuant to the Property Act the possessor of movable property is deemed its owner until the contrary is proved. Possession, in turn, is deemed lawful until the contrary is proved (see paragraph 42 above). The Court further notes that the disputed property was in R.'s possession when it was seized and that the applicant has presented the Court with an intestate succession certificate according to which she inherited one third of R.'s property (see paragraph 20 above). Thus, pursuant to the domestic law, the applicant is to be considered as having inherited the seized property unless the presumptions mentioned above were rebutted.

106. The Court further notes that the Viru County Court, when ordering the confiscation of the property, relied on Article 63 (3) of the Code of Criminal Procedure. Thus, the confiscation in question had, in principle, a legal basis. Furthermore, the Court is satisfied that confiscation of property obtained through crime is in line with the general interest of the community (see paragraph 103 above). The Court therefore proceeds to examine whether a fair balance was struck between the legitimate aim and the applicant's fundamental rights, and whether sufficient procedural guarantees were in place.

107. The Court observes that under Article 63 (3) of the Code of Criminal Procedure, relied on by the County Court, property obtained through crime could be confiscated. Having regard also to the presumption of innocence enshrined in Article 6 § 2 of the Convention, the Court notes that in the present case neither R. nor any other accused in the criminal proceedings were convicted of any offence. While in respect of the attempted smuggling of prohibited goods M. and J. were prosecuted, although the criminal proceedings were later discontinued due to lack of public interest, the Court notes that this episode concerned waste containing precious metals, and had no direct link to other items and substances also seized from R., such as gold, silver and diamonds. Although it can

be understood that R. was also suspected of a crime related to these items and substances under Article 152-3 § 3 of the Criminal Code (see paragraph 14 above), there is no information in the case file allowing the Court to conclude that any substantial investigation or judicial determination in this respect – that is, in respect of the suspected offence of purchase of items made of precious metals from the population – was carried out. Indeed, the suspicion in question appears to have been based merely on the fact that the items and substances in question were found at R.'s home and workplace. Thus, as the commission of any crimes was not established by the domestic authorities, the Court is unable to see how the property could be confiscated as obtained through crime under Article 63 (3) of the Code of Criminal Procedure. The Court also notes in this connection that it has not been shown that possession of such items and substances was unlawful in itself.

108. As regards the question whether the confiscation of this part of the property might have been based on the consideration that the property had been obtained as proceeds of crime, the Court is not convinced by the investigating authorities' reliance on R.'s tax return for 2000, according to which he admittedly could not have obtained such an amount of precious metals by lawful means (see paragraph 14 above), subsequently complemented by K.'s statements that R. had been living beyond his means (see paragraph 22 above). In this connection, the Court firstly notes that Article 63 (3) of the Code of Criminal Procedure, on which the confiscation decision was based, concerned property received as a result of a criminal offence and not property acquired as proceeds of crime. Moreover, it has not been demonstrated, as regards either of these grounds, that domestic law provided for confiscation of the property of a suspect who died during the criminal proceedings and in whose respect the proceedings were discontinued for that reason without him having been convicted. Secondly, and in any event, the domestic authorities appear to have carried out no assessment as to the sums R. might have obtained through crime and invested in precious metals. In these circumstances, the Court is bound to conclude that the confiscation of the gold and silver items and diamonds was an arbitrary measure, its scope being determined by the somewhat incidental seizure of evidence at the outset of the proceedings. The Court notes that no individual assessment of which

pieces of property to confiscate appears to have been carried out (see, by contrast, *Silickienė*, cited above, § 68; see also *Phillips*, cited above, § 53, where the Court was satisfied that the procedure followed in the making of the confiscation order had been fair and respected the rights of the defence). The Court reiterates in this connection that the original County Court confiscation order did not contain a list of the items to be confiscated. Although this deficiency was remedied by the same court, the fact remains that the first-instance court gave no reasons for the confiscation. The Court of Appeal referred to the material in the case file, but provided no analysis of evidence for its own part. These deficiencies, coupled with the procedural shortcomings already dealt with under Article 6 § 1 (see paragraphs 80 to 86 above) are sufficient to enable the Court to conclude that the fair balance which should be struck between the protection of the right of property and the requirements of general interest was upset in the present case.

109. Accordingly, there has been a violation of Article 1 of Protocol No. 1 to the Convention.

III. Alleged Violation of Article 6 § 1 of the Convention in respect of the Complaint Concerning Length of the Proceedings

[...]

118. The Court reiterates that the reasonableness of the length of proceedings must be assessed in the light of the circumstances of the case and with reference to the following criteria: the complexity of the case; the conduct of the applicant and the relevant authorities; and what was at stake for the applicant in the dispute (see, among many other authorities, *Frydlender v. France* [GC], no. 30979/96, § 43, ECHR 2000-VII).

119. The Court considers that the proceedings at issue in the present case were not complicated. As regards the conduct of the applicant, it does not appear that any delays could be attributed to her. At the same time, there were remarkable delays in the conduct of the proceedings by the authorities, notably there was a period of almost five years between the quashing of the first judgment by an appeal court and the re-hearing of the case at the first level of jurisdiction.

As regards the question of what was at stake for the applicant, the Court notes that the pecuniary claim in question was not in itself such as to require special diligence in the conduct of the proceedings.

120. Having examined all the materials submitted to it and having regard to its case-law on the subject, the Court considers that in the instant case the length of the proceedings was excessive and failed to meet the "reasonable time" requirement.

121. There has accordingly been a breach of Article 6 § 1 of the Convention on account of the length of the proceedings.

IV. Alleged Violation of Article 13 of the Convention

[...]

127. The Court reiterates that Article 13 guarantees an effective remedy before a national authority for an alleged breach of the requirement under Article 6 § 1 to hear a case within a reasonable time (see *Kudła v. Poland* [GC], no. 30210/96, § 156, ECHR 2000-XI).

128. In the present case, the Court has already found that there was no effective remedy available to the applicant that she would have been required to use (see paragraph 116 above). This conclusion also applies in respect of Article 13 of the Convention.

129. Accordingly, the Court considers that in the present case there has been a violation of Article 13 of the Convention on account of the lack of a remedy under domestic law whereby, at the time when she lodged her application, the applicant could have obtained a ruling upholding her right to have her case heard within a reasonable time, as set forth in Article 6 § 1 of the Convention.

(*Rummi v. Estonia*, app. no. 63362/09, 15 January 2015, Judgment of the Chamber)

6/4

On 15 January, the European Court of Human Rights gave a judgment in the case of *Veits v. Estonia*, where the applicant complained that she had not been invited to take part in the court proceedings involving the determination of her civil rights and obligations (Article 6 § 1), that she had been deprived of her apartment, of which she had been the *bona fide* owner (Article 1 of Protocol No. 1), and that she had had at her disposal no effective domestic remedy for her complaint about the peaceful enjoyment of possessions (Article 13). The Chamber found the following:

I. Alleged Violation of Article 6 § 1 of the Convention

[...]

57. As the Court framed in the *Silickienė* judgment (cited above, § 47), in a case like the present one it is called to determine whether the way in which the confiscation was applied in respect of the applicant offended the basic principles of a fair procedure inherent in Article 6 § 1 (see, *mutatis mutandis, Salabiaku v. France,* 7 October 1988, § 30, Series A no. 141-A). It must be ascertained whether the procedure in the domestic legal system afforded the applicant, in the light of the severity of the measure to which she was liable, an adequate opportunity to put her case to the courts, pleading, as the case might be, illegality or arbitrariness of that measure and that the courts had acted unreasonably (see *AGOSI v. the United Kingdom,* 24 October 1986, § 55, Series A no. 108; also see, *mutatis mutandis, Arcuri and Others v. Italy* (dec.), no. 52024/99, 5 July 2001, and *Riela and Others v. Italy* (dec.), no. 52439/99, 4 September 2001). It is not, however, within the province of the Court to substitute its own assessment of the facts for that of the domestic courts and, as a general rule, it is for these courts to assess the evidence before them (see *Edwards v. the United Kingdom,* 16 December 1992, § 34, Series A no. 247-B).

58. The Court notes that the domestic courts in the present case determined the applicant's civil rights without inviting her to take part in the proceedings, despite the opportunity provided under Article 40-1 of the Code of Criminal Procedure to involve her in the proceedings as a third party. It would appear that the judicial authorities could have done so of their own motion. At the same time, the applicant has not argued that she took any action herself to seek to be involved in the proceedings. The Court further notes that it has not been disputed that the applicant was aware of the criminal

proceedings in general and – at least through her mother V., who was her legal representative until she reached the age of majority – of the attachment of the apartment in particular. Nor has it been argued that the applicant's mother was excluded from representing her because of a conflict of interests. While it is true that the attachment order itself was of a temporary nature and the failure to challenge it did not amount to a failure to exhaust domestic remedies, the fact that it was possible to contest it nevertheless constituted a procedural guarantee allowing the arguments against the attachment to be presented to the court, and thus the applicant's title to the property to be supported (see *Silickienė*, cited above, § 48). Furthermore, and more importantly, the applicant's mother V. and grandmother N. presented arguments to the court against the confiscation of the apartment, and also appealed on that issue. In this connection, the Court considers it to be of importance that there is no dispute that the applicant acquired the apartment as a gift from her mother when she was thirteen years old, and that she did not know the circumstances of the acquisition of the apartment. At the same time, the details concerning the acquisition of the apartment were well known to the applicant's mother and grandmother who, as mentioned above, countered the confiscation and presented the arguments they were in a position to present, having been directly involved in the transactions related to the acquisition of the apartment. However, the courts were not persuaded by these arguments, found, on evidence, that the apartment had been obtained through crime, and held that its bona fide acquisition by the applicant could not have occurred (see paragraph 19 above). Thus, the arguments in favour of the applicant were presented to the courts by her mother and grandmother, and the courts dealt with those arguments but rejected them on their merits. The applicant has not pointed to any further arguments or evidence that could have been adduced on her behalf in the domestic proceedings, had she been party to those proceedings.

59. The Court reiterates that, as a general principle, persons whose property is confiscated should be formally granted the status of parties to the proceedings in which the confiscation is ordered (see *Silickienė*, cited above, § 50). However, in the specific circumstances of the present case it accepts that the applicant's interests were *de facto* protected by her mother V. and grandmother N., and that it

cannot be said that her interests remained unrepresented in the proceedings where her civil rights were determined.

60. Therefore, the Court concludes that the applicant's right to a fair trial was not breached in the present case.

There has accordingly been no violation of Article 6 § 1 of the Convention.

II. Alleged Violation of Article 1 of Protocol No. 1 to the Convention

[...]

(a) General principles

69. The Court reiterates that Article 1 of Protocol No. 1 to the Convention, which guarantees in substance the right to property, comprises three distinct rules. The first, which is expressed in the first sentence of the first paragraph and is of a general nature, lays down the principle of peaceful enjoyment of property. The second rule, in the second sentence of the same paragraph, covers deprivation of possessions and makes it subject to certain conditions. The third, contained in the second paragraph, recognises that the Contracting States are entitled, among other things, to control the use of property in accordance with the general interest. The second and third rules, which are concerned with particular instances of interference with the right to peaceful enjoyment of property, must be construed in the light of the general principle laid down in the first rule (see, among many authorities, *Immobiliare Saffi v. Italy* [GC], no. 22774/93, § 44, ECHR 1999-V, and *Broniowski v. Poland* [GC], no. 31443/96, § 134, ECHR 2004V).

70. The Court's constant approach has been that confiscation, while it involves deprivation of possessions, also constitutes control of the use of property within the meaning of the second paragraph of Article 1 of Protocol No. 1 (see *Sun v. Russia*, no. 31004/02, § 25, 5 February 2009; *Riela and Others*, cited above; *Arcuri and Others*, cited above; *C.M. v. France* (dec.), no. 28078/95, 26 June 2001; *Air Canada v. the United Kingdom*, 5 May 1995, § 34, Series A no. 316A; and *AGOSI*,

cited above, § 51). Accordingly, it considers that the same approach must be followed in the present case.

71. The Court considers that confiscation in criminal proceedings is in line with the general interest of the community, because the forfeiture of money or assets obtained through illegal activities or paid for with the proceeds of crime is a necessary and effective means of combating criminal activities (see *Raimondo v. Italy*, 22 February 1994, § 30, Series A no. 281A). Confiscation in this context is therefore in keeping with the goals of the Council of Europe Convention on Laundering, Search, Seizure and Confiscation of the Proceeds from Crime, which requires State Parties to introduce confiscation of instrumentalities and the proceeds of crime in respect of serious offences. Thus, a confiscation order in respect of criminally acquired property operates in the general interest as a deterrent to those considering engaging in criminal activities, and also guarantees that crime does not pay (see *Denisova and Moiseyeva v. Russia*, no. 16903/03, § 58, 1 April 2010, with further references to *Phillips v. the United Kingdom*, no. 41087/98, § 52, ECHR 2001VII, and *Dassa Foundation and Others v. Liechtenstein* (dec.), no. 696/05, 10 July 2007).

72. The Court further reiterates that, although the second paragraph of Article 1 of Protocol No. 1 contains no explicit procedural requirements, it has been its constant requirement that the domestic proceedings afford the aggrieved individual a reasonable opportunity of putting his or her case to the responsible authorities for the purpose of effectively challenging the measures interfering with the rights guaranteed by this provision. In ascertaining whether this condition has been satisfied, a comprehensive view must be taken of the applicable procedures (see *Denisova and Moiseyeva*, cited above, § 59; *Jokela v. Finland*, no. 28856/95, § 45, ECHR 2002-IV; and *AGOSI*, cited above, § 55).

(b) Application of the principles to the present case

73. Turning to the present case, the Court notes that the Harju County Court, when ordering the confiscation of the apartment in question, relied on Article 83 § 3 (2) of the Penal Code. Under that provision, a court may confiscate the object of an intentional of-

fence if it belongs to a third person at the time of the making of the judgment and the person had acquired it on account of the actions of the offender, for example as a gift. Thus, the Court is satisfied that the confiscation had a legal basis. Furthermore, the Court considers that the confiscation of property obtained through crime is in line with the general interest of the community (see paragraph 71 above). It therefore needs to examine whether a fair balance was struck between the legitimate aim and the applicant's fundamental rights, and whether there were sufficient procedural guarantees in place.

74. In this connection, the Court reiterates that the applicant was not charged with or convicted of any offence related to the confiscated property. Indeed, she was a minor at the time of the commission of the offences. However, as established by the domestic courts, the apartment in question – in which the applicant did not live – had been acquired by the applicant's mother and grandmother through crime and had been transferred to the applicant free of charge. The Court considers that the domestic rules according to which in such circumstances the property could be confiscated and its acquirer could not rely on bona fide ownership did not amount to a disproportionate interference with the applicant's property rights. The Court reiterates that the domestic courts dealt with, and rejected with sufficient reasoning, the arguments by the applicant's mother V. and grandmother N. to the effect that the apartment in question had not been obtained through crime, and that the applicant's apartment at 9 Mahtra Street had been sold in order to pay back a loan taken for buying the apartment in dispute. The Court considers that its findings in respect of Article 6 § 1 (see paragraphs 57 to 60 above) are also relevant in the context of Article 1 of Protocol No. 1 as regards the question whether the domestic proceedings afforded the applicant a reasonable opportunity of putting her case to the authorities in order to effectively challenge the confiscation measure. Thus, without repeating the above conclusions in further detail, the Court notes that it is satisfied that the applicant's interests were *de facto* represented in the domestic proceedings by her mother and grandmother, and the fact that she was not personally involved in the proceedings did not, in the particular circumstances of the present case, upset the fair balance between the protection of the right to property and the requirements of the general interest.

Accordingly, there has been no violation of Article 1 of Protocol No. 1 to the Convention.

III. Alleged Violation of Article 13 of the Convention

[...]

81. Having regard to its findings as regards Article 6 § 1 of the Convention (see paragraphs 57 to 60 above) and in respect of the procedural guarantees under Article 1 of Protocol No. 1 to the Convention (see paragraphs 73 and 74 above), the Court considers it unnecessary also to examine these issues under Article 13 of the Convention.

(*Veits* v. *Estonia*, app. no. 12951/11, 15 January 2015, Judgment of the Chamber)

6/5

On 16 June, the European Court of Human Rights gave a judgment in the case of *Delfi AS* v. *Estonia*, where the applicant company complained that holding it liable for the comments posted by the readers of its Internet news portal infringed its freedom of expression (Article 10). It is considered a landmark decision regarding the scope and limitations of online freedom of expression. The Grand Chamber found the following:

I. Alleged Violation of Article 10 of the Convention

[...]

1. Preliminary remarks and the scope of the Court's assessment

110. The Court notes at the outset that user-generated expressive activity on the Internet provides an unprecedented platform for the exercise of freedom of expression. That is undisputed and has been recognised by the Court on previous occasions (see *Ahmet Yıldırım v. Turkey*, no. 3111/10, § 48, ECHR 2012, and *Times Newspapers Ltd (nos. 1 and 2) v. the United Kingdom*, nos. 3002/03 and 23676/03, § 27, ECHR 2009). However, alongside these benefits, certain dangers may also arise. Defamatory and other types of clearly unlawful speech, including hate speech and speech inciting violence, can be disseminated like never before, worldwide, in a matter of seconds,

and sometimes remain persistently available online. These two conflicting realities lie at the heart of this case. Bearing in mind the need to protect the values underlying the Convention, and considering that the rights under Article 10 and 8 of the Convention deserve equal respect, a balance must be struck that retains the essence of both rights. Thus, while the Court acknowledges that important benefits can be derived from the Internet in the exercise of freedom of expression, it is also mindful that liability for defamatory or other types of unlawful speech must, in principle, be retained and constitute an effective remedy for violations of personality rights.

111. On this basis, and in particular considering that this is the first case in which the Court has been called upon to examine a complaint of this type in an evolving field of technological innovation, the Court considers it necessary to delineate the scope of its inquiry in the light of the facts of the present case.

112. Firstly, the Court observes that the Supreme Court recognised (see § 14 of its judgment of 10 June 2009 as set out in paragraph 31 above) that "[p]ublishing of news and comments on an Internet portal is also a journalistic activity. At the same time, because of the nature of Internet media, it cannot reasonably be required of a portal operator to edit comments before publishing them in the same manner as applies for a printed media publication. While the publisher [of a printed media publication] is, through editing, the initiator of the publication of a comment, on the Internet portal the initiator of publication is the writer of the comment, who makes it accessible to the general public through the portal. Therefore, the portal operator is not the person to whom information is disclosed. Because of [their] economic interest in the publication of comments, both a publisher of printed media and an Internet portal operator are publishers/disclosers as entrepreneurs".

113. The Court sees no reason to call into question the above distinction made by the Supreme Court. On the contrary, the starting-point of the Supreme Court's reflections, that is, the recognition of differences between a portal operator and a traditional publisher, is in line with the international instruments in this field, which manifest a certain development in favour of distinguishing between the legal principles regulating the activities of the traditional print and

audiovisual media on the one hand and Internet-based media operations on the other. In the recent Recommendation of the Committee of Ministers to the member States of the Council of Europe on a new notion of media, this is termed a "differentiated and graduated approach [that] requires that each actor whose services are identified as media or as an intermediary or auxiliary activity benefit from both the appropriate form (differentiated) and the appropriate level (graduated) of protection and that responsibility also be delimited in conformity with Article 10 of the European Convention on Human Rights and other relevant standards developed by the Council of Europe" (see § 7 of the Appendix to Recommendation CM/Rec(2011)7, quoted in paragraph 46 above). Therefore, the Court considers that because of the particular nature of the Internet, the "duties and responsibilities" that are to be conferred on an Internet news portal for the purposes of Article 10 may differ to some degree from those of a traditional publisher, as regards third-party content.

114. Secondly, the Court observes that the Supreme Court of Estonia found that the "legal assessment by the courts of the twenty comments of a derogatory nature [was] substantiated. The courts [had] correctly found that those comments [were] defamatory since they [were] of a vulgar nature, degrade[d] human dignity and contain[ed] threats" (see § 15 of the judgment as set out in paragraph 31 above). Further, in § 16 of its judgment, the Supreme Court reiterated that the comments degraded "human dignity" and were "clearly unlawful". The Court notes that this characterisation and analysis of the unlawful nature of the comments in question (see paragraph 18 above) is obviously based on the fact that the majority of the comments are, viewed on their face, tantamount to an incitement to hatred or to violence against L.

115. Consequently, the Court considers that the case concerns the "duties and responsibilities" of Internet news portals, under Article 10 § 2 of the Convention, when they provide for economic purposes a platform for user-generated comments on previously published content and some users – whether identified or anonymous – engage in clearly unlawful speech, which infringes the personality rights of others and amounts to hate speech and incitement to violence against them. The Court emphasises that the present case relates to a large professionally managed Internet news portal run on

a commercial basis which published news articles of its own and invited its readers to comment on them.

116. Accordingly, the case does not concern other fora on the Internet where third-party comments can be disseminated, for example an Internet discussion forum or a bulletin board where users can freely set out their ideas on any topics without the discussion being channelled by any input from the forum's manager; or a social media platform where the platform provider does not offer any content and where the content provider may be a private person running the website or a blog as a hobby.

117. Furthermore, the Court notes that the applicant company's news portal was one of the biggest Internet media publications in the country; it had a wide readership and there was a known public concern about the controversial nature of the comments it attracted (see paragraph 15 above). Moreover, as outlined above, the impugned comments in the present case, as assessed by the Supreme Court, mainly constituted hate speech and speech that directly advocated acts of violence. Thus, the establishment of their unlawful nature did not require any linguistic or legal analysis since the remarks were on their face manifestly unlawful. It is against this background that the Court will proceed to examine the applicant company's complaint.

2. Existence of an interference

118. The Court notes that it was not in dispute between the parties that the applicant company's freedom of expression guaranteed under Article 10 of the Convention had been interfered with by the domestic courts' decisions. The Court sees no reason to hold otherwise.

119. Such an interference with the applicant company's right to freedom of expression must be "prescribed by law", have one or more legitimate aims in the light of paragraph 2 of Article 10, and be "necessary in a democratic society".

3. Lawfulness

120. The Court reiterates that the expression "prescribed by law" in the second paragraph of Article 10 not only requires that the impugned measure should have a legal basis in domestic law, but also refers to the quality of the law in question, which should be accessible to the person concerned and foreseeable as to its effects (see, among other authorities, *VgT Verein gegen Tierfabriken v. Switzerland*, no. 24699/94, § 52, ECHR 2001VI; *Rotaru v. Romania* [GC], no. 28341/95, § 52, ECHR 2000-V; *Gawęda v. Poland*, no. 26229/95, § 39, ECHR 2002-II; and *Maestri v. Italy* [GC], no. 39748/98, § 30, ECHR 2004-I). However, it is primarily for the national authorities, notably the courts, to interpret and apply domestic law (see *Centro Europa 7 S.r.l. and Di Stefano v. Italy* [GC], no. 38433/09, § 140, ECHR 2012; *Kruslin v. France*, 24 April 1990, § 29, Series A no. 176-A; and *Kopp v. Switzerland*, 25 March 1998, § 59, *Reports of Judgments and Decisions* 1998-II).

121. One of the requirements flowing from the expression "prescribed by law" is foreseeability. Thus, a norm cannot be regarded as a "law" within the meaning of Article 10 § 2 unless it is formulated with sufficient precision to enable the citizen to regulate his conduct; he must be able – if need be with appropriate advice – to foresee, to a degree that is reasonable in the circumstances, the consequences which a given action may entail. Those consequences need not be foreseeable with absolute certainty. Whilst certainty is desirable, it may bring in its train excessive rigidity, and the law must be able to keep pace with changing circumstances. Accordingly, many laws are inevitably couched in terms which, to a greater or lesser extent, are vague, and whose interpretation and application are questions of practice (see, for example, *Lindon, Otchakovsky-Laurens and July v. France* [GC], nos. 21279/02 and 36448/02, § 41, ECHR 2007IV, and *Centro Europa 7 S.r.l. and Di Stefano*, cited above, § 141).

122. The level of precision required of domestic legislation – which cannot provide for every eventuality – depends to a considerable degree on the content of the law in question, the field it is designed to cover and the number and status of those to whom it is addressed (see *Centro Europa 7 S.r.l. and Di Stefano*, cited above, § 142). The Court has found that persons carrying on a professional activity,

who are used to having to proceed with a high degree of caution when pursuing their occupation, can on this account be expected to take special care in assessing the risks that such activity entails (see *Lindon, Otchakovsky-Laurens and July*, cited above, § 41, with further references to *Cantoni v. France*, 15 November 1996, § 35, *Reports* 1996V, and *Chauvy and Others v. France*, no. 64915/01, §§ 43-45, ECHR 2004VI).

123. In the present case the parties' opinions differed as to whether the interference with the applicant company's freedom of expression was "prescribed by law". The applicant company argued that there was no domestic law according to which an intermediary was to be taken as a professional publisher of comments posted on its website by third parties regardless of whether it was aware of their specific content. On the contrary, the applicant company relied on the domestic and European legislation on Internet service providers and argued that it expressly prohibited the imposition of liability on service providers for third-party content.

124. The Government referred to the relevant provisions of the civil law and domestic case-law to the effect that media publishers were liable for their publications along with the authors. They added that there was no case-law on the basis of which the applicant company could have presumed that the owner of an Internet news portal as a new media publication was not liable for the comments posted on its articles. In their view the Court should proceed from the facts as established and the law as applied and interpreted by the domestic courts and not take account of the applicant company's references to EU law. In any event, the EU law referred to by the applicant company actually supported the domestic courts' interpretations and conclusions.

125. The Court observes that the difference in the parties' opinions as regards the law to be applied stems from their diverging views on the issue of how the applicant company is to be classified. According to the applicant company, it should be classified as an intermediary as regards the third-party comments, whereas the Government argued that the applicant company was to be seen as a media publisher, including with regard to such comments.

126. The Court observes (see paragraphs 112 and 113 above) that the Supreme Court recognised the differences between the roles of a publisher of printed media, on the one hand, and an Internet portal operator engaged in media publications for an economic purpose, on the other. However, the Supreme Court found that because of their "economic interest in the publication of comments, both a publisher of printed media and an Internet portal operator [were] publishers/disclosers" for the purposes of section 1047 of the Obligations Act (see § 14 of the judgment as set out in paragraph 31 above).

127. The Court considers that, in substance, the applicant argues that the domestic courts erred in applying the general provisions of the Obligations Act to the facts of the case as they should have relied upon the domestic and European legislation on Internet service providers. Like the Chamber, the Grand Chamber reiterates in this context that it is not its task to take the place of the domestic courts. It is primarily for the national authorities, notably the courts, to interpret and apply domestic law (see, among others, *Centro Europa 7 S.r.l. and Di Stefano*, cited above, § 140, and *Rekvényi v. Hungary* [GC], no. 25390/94, § 35, ECHR 1999III). The Court also reiterates that it is not for it to express a view on the appropriateness of methods chosen by the legislature of a respondent State to regulate a given field. Its task is confined to determining whether the methods adopted and the effects they entail are in conformity with the Convention (see *Gorzelik and Others v. Poland* [GC], no. 44158/98, § 67, ECHR 2004I). Thus, the Court confines itself to examining whether the Supreme Court's application of the general provisions of the Obligations Act to the applicant's situation was foreseeable for the purposes of Article 10 § 2 of the Convention.

128. Pursuant to the relevant provisions of the Constitution, the Civil Code (General Principles) Act and the Obligations Act (see paragraphs 33 to 38 above), as interpreted and applied by the domestic courts, the applicant company was considered a publisher and deemed liable for the publication of the clearly unlawful comments. The domestic courts chose to apply these norms, having found that the special regulation contained in the Information Society Services Act transposing the Directive on Electronic Commerce into Estonian law did not apply to the present case since

the latter related to activities of a merely technical, automatic and passive nature, unlike the applicant company's activities, and that the objective pursued by the applicant company was not merely the provision of an intermediary service (see § 13 of the Supreme Court's judgment as set out in paragraph 31 above). In this particular context the Court takes into account the fact that some countries have recognised that the importance and the complexity of the subject matter, involving the need to ensure proper balancing of different interests and fundamental rights, call for the enactment of specific regulations for situations such as that pertaining in the present case (see paragraph 58 above). Such action is in line with the "differentiated and graduated approach" to the regulation of new media recommended by the Council of Europe (see paragraph 46 above) and has found support in the Court's case-law (see, *mutatis mutandis, Editorial Board of* Pravoye Delo *and Shtekel v. Ukraine*, no. 33014/05, §§ 63-64, ECHR 2011). However, although various approaches are possible in legislation to take account of the nature of new media, the Court is satisfied on the facts of this case that the provisions of the Constitution, the Civil Code (General Principles) Act and the Obligations Act, along with the relevant case-law, made it foreseeable that a media publisher running an Internet news portal for an economic purpose could, in principle, be held liable under domestic law for the uploading of clearly unlawful comments, of the type at issue in the present case, on its news portal.

129. The Court accordingly finds that, as a professional publisher, the applicant company should have been familiar with the legislation and case-law, and could also have sought legal advice. The Court observes in this context that the Delfi news portal is one of the largest in Estonia. Public concern had already been expressed before the publication of the comments in the present case and the Minister of Justice had noted that victims of insults could bring a suit against Delfi and claim damages (see paragraph 15 above). Thus, the Court considers that the applicant company was in a position to assess the risks related to its activities and that it must have been able to foresee, to a reasonable degree, the consequences which these could entail. It therefore concludes that the interference in issue was "prescribed by law" within the meaning of the second paragraph of Article 10 of the Convention.

4. Legitimate aim

130. The parties before the Grand Chamber did not dispute that the restriction of the applicant company's freedom of expression had pursued the legitimate aim of protecting the reputation and rights of others. The Court sees no reason to hold otherwise.

5. Necessary in a democratic society

(a) General principles

131. The fundamental principles concerning the question whether an interference with freedom of expression is "necessary in a democratic society" are well established in the Court's case-law and have been summarised as follows (see, among other authorities, *Hertel v. Switzerland*, 25 August 1998, § 46, *Reports* 1998VI; *Steel and Morris v. the United Kingdom*, no. 68416/01, § 87, ECHR 2005II; *Mouvement raëlien suisse v. Switzerland* [GC], no. 16354/06, § 48, ECHR 2012; and *Animal Defenders International v. the United Kingdom* [GC], no. 48876/08, § 100, ECHR 2013):

"(i) Freedom of expression constitutes one of the essential foundations of a democratic society and one of the basic conditions for its progress and for each individual's self-fulfilment. Subject to paragraph 2 of Article 10, it is applicable not only to 'information' or 'ideas' that are favourably received or regarded as inoffensive or as a matter of indifference, but also to those that offend, shock or disturb. Such are the demands of pluralism, tolerance and broadmindedness without which there is no 'democratic society'. As set forth in Article 10, this freedom is subject to exceptions, which ... must, however, be construed strictly, and the need for any restrictions must be established convincingly ...

(ii) The adjective 'necessary', within the meaning of Article 10 § 2, implies the existence of a 'pressing social need'. The Contracting States have a certain margin of appreciation in assessing whether such a need exists, but it goes hand in hand with European supervision, embracing both the legislation and the decisions applying it, even those given by an independent court. The Court is therefore empowered to give the final ruling on whether a 'restriction' is reconcilable with freedom of expression as protected by Article 10.

(iii) The Court's task, in exercising its supervisory jurisdiction, is not to take the place of the competent national authorities but rather to review under Article 10 the decisions they delivered pursuant to their power of appreciation. This does not mean that the supervision is limited to ascertaining whether the respondent State exercised its discretion reasonably, carefully and in good faith; what the Court has to do is to look at the interference complained of in the light of the case as a whole and determine whether it was 'proportionate to the legitimate aim pursued' and whether the reasons adduced by the national authorities to justify it are 'relevant and sufficient'... In doing so, the Court has to satisfy itself that the national authorities applied standards which were in conformity with the principles embodied in Article 10 and, moreover, that they relied on an acceptable assessment of the relevant facts ..."

132. Furthermore, the Court has emphasised the essential function the press fulfils in a democratic society. Although the press must not overstep certain bounds, particularly as regards the reputation and rights of others and the need to prevent the disclosure of confidential information, its duty is nevertheless to impart – in a manner consistent with its obligations and responsibilities – information and ideas on all matters of public interest (see *Jersild v. Denmark*, 23 September 1994, § 31, Series A no. 298; *De Haes and Gijsels v. Belgium*, 24 February 1997, § 37, *Reports* 1997I; and *Bladet Tromsø and Stensaas v. Norway* [GC], no. 21980/93, § 58, ECHR 1999III). Journalistic freedom also covers possible recourse to a degree of exaggeration, or even provocation (see *Prager and Oberschlick v. Austria*, 26 April 1995, § 38, Series A no. 313, and *Bladet Tromsø and Stensaas*, cited above, § 59). The limits of permissible criticism are narrower in relation to a private citizen than in relation to politicians or governments (see, for example, *Castells v. Spain*, 23 April 1992, § 46, Series A no. 236; *Incal v. Turkey*, 9 June 1998, § 54, *Reports* 1998IV; and *Tammer v. Estonia*, no. 41205/98, § 62, ECHR 2001I).

133. Moreover, the Court has previously held that in the light of its accessibility and its capacity to store and communicate vast amounts of information, the Internet plays an important role in enhancing

the public's access to news and facilitating the dissemination of information in general (see *Ahmet Yıldırım*, cited above, § 48, and *Times Newspapers Ltd*, cited above, § 27). At the same time, the risk of harm posed by content and communications on the Internet to the exercise and enjoyment of human rights and freedoms, particularly the right to respect for private life, is certainly higher than that posed by the press (see *Editorial Board of* Pravoye Delo *and Shtekel*, cited above, § 63).

134. In considering the "duties and responsibilities" of a journalist, the potential impact of the medium concerned is an important factor and it is commonly acknowledged that the audiovisual media often have a much more immediate and powerful effect than the print media (see *Purcell and Others v. Ireland*, no. 15404/89, Commission decision of 16 April 1991, Decisions and Reports 70, p. 262). The methods of objective and balanced reporting may vary considerably, depending among other things on the media in question (see *Jersild*, cited above, § 31).

135. The Court has held that "punishment of a journalist for assisting in the dissemination of statements made by another person in an interview would seriously hamper the contribution of the press to discussion of matters of public interest and should not be envisaged unless there are particularly strong reasons for doing so" (see *Jersild*, cited above, § 35; *Thoma v. Luxembourg*, no. 38432/97, § 62, ECHR 2001III; and, *mutatis mutandis*, *Verlagsgruppe News GmbH v. Austria*, no. 76918/01, § 31, 14 December 2006, and *Print Zeitungsverlag GmbH v. Austria*, no. 26547/07, § 39, 10 October 2013).

136. Moreover, the Court has held that speech that is incompatible with the values proclaimed and guaranteed by the Convention is not protected by Article 10 by virtue of Article 17 of the Convention. The examples of such speech examined by the Court have included statements denying the Holocaust, justifying a pro-Nazi policy, linking all Muslims with a grave act of terrorism, or portraying the Jews as the source of evil in Russia (see *Lehideux and Isorni v. France*, 23 September 1998, §§ 47 and 53, *Reports* 1998VII; *Garaudy v. France* (dec.), no. 65831/01, ECHR 2003IX; *Norwood v. the United Kingdom* (dec.), no. 23131/03, ECHR 2004XI; *Witzsch v. Germany*

(dec.), no. 7485/03, 13 December 2005; and *Pavel Ivanov v. Russia* (dec.), no. 35222/04, 20 February 2007).

137. The Court further reiterates that the right to protection of reputation is a right which is protected by Article 8 of the Convention as part of the right to respect for private life (see *Chauvy and Others*, cited above, § 70; *Pfeifer v. Austria*, no. 12556/03, § 35, 15 November 2007; and *Polanco Torres and Movilla Polanco v. Spain*, no. 34147/06, § 40, 21 September 2010). In order for Article 8 to come into play, however, an attack on a person's reputation must attain a certain level of seriousness and be made in a manner causing prejudice to personal enjoyment of the right to respect for private life (see *A. v. Norway*, no. 28070/06, § 64, 9 April 2009, and *Axel Springer AG v. Germany* [GC], no. 39954/08, § 83, 7 February 2012).

138. When examining whether there is a need for an interference with freedom of expression in a democratic society in the interests of the "protection of the reputation or rights of others", the Court may be required to ascertain whether the domestic authorities have struck a fair balance when protecting two values guaranteed by the Convention which may come into conflict with each other in certain cases, namely on the one hand freedom of expression protected by Article 10, and on the other the right to respect for private life enshrined in Article 8 (see *Hachette Filipacchi Associés v. France*, no. 71111/01, § 43, 14 June 2007; *MGN Limited v. the United Kingdom*, no. 39401/04, § 142, 18 January 2011; and *Axel Springer AG*, cited above, § 84).

139. The Court has found that, as a matter of principle, the rights guaranteed under Articles 8 and 10 deserve equal respect, and the outcome of an application should not, in principle, vary according to whether it has been lodged with the Court under Article 10 of the Convention by the publisher of an offending article or under Article 8 of the Convention by the person who has been the subject of that article. Accordingly, the margin of appreciation should in principle be the same in both cases (see *Axel Springer AG*, cited above, § 87, and *Von Hannover v. Germany (no. 2)* [GC], nos. 40660/08 and 60641/08, § 106, ECHR 2012, with further references to the cases of *Hachette Filipacchi Associés*, cited above, § 41; *Timciuc v. Romania* (dec.), no. 28999/03, § 144, 12 October 2010; and *Mosley v. the United*

Kingdom, no. 48009/08, § 111, 10 May 2011). Where the balancing exercise between those two rights has been undertaken by the national authorities in conformity with the criteria laid down in the Court's case-law, the Court would require strong reasons to substitute its view for that of the domestic courts (see *Axel Springer AG*, cited above, § 88, and *Von Hannover (no. 2)*, cited above, § 107, with further references to *MGN Limited*, cited above, §§ 150 and 155, and *Palomo Sánchez and Others v. Spain* [GC], nos. 28955/06, 28957/06, 28959/06 and 28964/06, § 57, 12 September 2011). In other words, there will usually be a wide margin afforded by the Court if the State is required to strike a balance between competing private interests or competing Convention rights (see *Evans v. the United Kingdom* [GC], no. 6339/05, § 77, ECHR 2007I; *Chassagnou and Others v. France* [GC], nos. 25088/94, 28331/95 and 28443/95, § 113, ECHR 1999III; and *Ashby Donald and Others v. France*, no. 36769/08, § 40, 10 January 2013).

(b) Application of the above principles to the present case

(i) Elements in the assessment of proportionality

140. The Court notes that it is not disputed that the comments posted by readers in reaction to the news article published on the applicant company's Internet news portal, as presented in the portal's commenting area, were of a clearly unlawful nature. Indeed, the applicant company removed the comments once it was notified by the injured party, and described them as "infringing" and "illicit" before the Chamber (see paragraph 84 of the Chamber judgment). Moreover, the Court is of the view that the majority of the impugned comments amounted to hate speech or incitements to violence and as such did not enjoy the protection of Article 10 (see paragraph 136 above). Thus, the freedom of expression of the authors of the comments is not at issue in the present case. Rather, the question before the Court is whether the domestic courts' decisions, holding the applicant company liable for these comments posted by third parties, were in breach of its freedom to impart information as guaranteed by Article 10 of the Convention.

141. The Court observes that although the applicant company immediately removed the comments in question from its website

upon notification by L.'s lawyers (see paragraphs 18 and 19 above), the Supreme Court held the applicant company liable on the basis of the Obligations Act as it should have prevented the publication of comments with clearly unlawful contents. It then referred to section 1047(3) of the Obligations Act, according to which disclosure of information or other matters is not deemed to be unlawful if the person who discloses the information or other matters or the person to whom such matters are disclosed has a legitimate interest in the disclosure, and if the person who discloses the information has verified the information or other matters with a thoroughness which corresponds to the "gravity of the potential violation". The Supreme Court thus held that, after the disclosure, the applicant company had failed to remove the comments – the unlawful content of which it should have been aware of – from the portal on its own initiative. The inactivity of the applicant company was thus deemed unlawful as it had not "proved the absence of culpability" under section 1050(1) of the Obligations Act (see § 16 of the Supreme Court judgment as set out in paragraph 31 above).

142. In the light of the Supreme Court's reasoning, the Court must, according to its consistent case-law, examine whether the domestic courts' finding of liability on the part of the applicant company was based on relevant and sufficient grounds in the particular circumstances of the case (see paragraph 131 above). The Court observes that in order to resolve the question whether the domestic courts' decisions holding the applicant company liable for the comments posted by third parties were in breach of its freedom of expression, the Chamber identified the following aspects as relevant for its analysis: the context of the comments, the measures applied by the applicant company in order to prevent or remove defamatory comments, the liability of the actual authors of the comments as an alternative to the applicant company's liability, and the consequences of the domestic proceedings for the applicant company (see paragraphs 85 et seq. of the Chamber judgment).

143. The Court agrees that these aspects are relevant for the concrete assessment of the proportionality of the interference in issue within the scope of the Court's examination of the present case (see paragraphs 112 to 117 above).

(ii) Context of the comments

144. As regards the context of the comments, the Court accepts that the news article about the ferry company, published on the Delfi news portal, was a balanced one, contained no offensive language and gave rise to no arguments about unlawful statements in the domestic proceedings. The Court is aware that even such a balanced article on a seemingly neutral topic may provoke fierce discussions on the Internet. Furthermore, it attaches particular weight, in this context, to the nature of the Delfi news portal. It reiterates that Delfi was a professionally managed Internet news portal run on a commercial basis which sought to attract a large number of comments on news articles published by it. The Court observes that the Supreme Court explicitly referred to the fact that the applicant company had integrated the comment environment into its news portal, inviting visitors to the website to complement the news with their own judgments and opinions (comments). According to the findings of the Supreme Court, in the comment environment, the applicant company actively called for comments on the news items appearing on the portal. The number of visits to the applicant company's portal depended on the number of comments; the revenue earned from advertisements published on the portal, in turn, depended on the number of visits. Thus, the Supreme Court concluded that the applicant company had an economic interest in the posting of comments. In the view of the Supreme Court, the fact that the applicant company was not the writer of the comments did not mean that it had no control over the comment environment (see § 13 of the judgment as set out in paragraph 31 above).

145. The Court also notes in this regard that the "Rules of comment" on the Delfi website stated that the applicant company prohibited the posting of comments that were without substance and/or off-topic, were contrary to good practice, contained threats, insults, obscene expressions or vulgarities, or incited hostility, violence or illegal activities. Such comments could be removed and their authors' ability to post comments could be restricted. Furthermore, the actual authors of the comments could not modify or delete their comments once they were posted on the applicant company's news portal – only the applicant company had the technical means to do this. In the light of the above and the Supreme Court's reason-

ing, the Court agrees with the Chamber's finding that the applicant company must be considered to have exercised a substantial degree of control over the comments published on its portal.

146. In sum, the Court considers that it was sufficiently established by the Supreme Court that the applicant company's involvement in making public the comments on its news articles on the Delfi news portal went beyond that of a passive, purely technical service provider. The Court therefore finds that the Supreme Court based its reasoning on this issue on grounds that were relevant for the purposes of Article 10 of the Convention.

(iii) Liability of the authors of the comments

147. In connection with the question whether the liability of the actual authors of the comments could serve as a sensible alternative to the liability of the Internet news portal in a case like the present one, the Court is mindful of the interest of Internet users in not disclosing their identity. Anonymity has long been a means of avoiding reprisals or unwanted attention. As such, it is capable of promoting the free flow of ideas and information in an important manner, including, notably, on the Internet. At the same time, the Court does not lose sight of the ease, scope and speed of the dissemination of information on the Internet, and the persistence of the information once disclosed, which may considerably aggravate the effects of unlawful speech on the Internet compared to traditional media. It also refers in this connection to a recent judgment of the Court of Justice of the European Union in the case of *Google Spain and Google*, in which that court, albeit in a different context, dealt with the problem of the availability on the Internet of information seriously interfering with a person's private life over an extended period of time, and found that the individual's fundamental rights, as a rule, overrode the economic interests of the search engine operator and the interests of other Internet users (see paragraph 56 above).

148. The Court observes that different degrees of anonymity are possible on the Internet. An Internet user may be anonymous to the wider public while being identifiable by a service provider through an account or contact data that may be either unverified or subject to some kind of verification – ranging from limited verification

(for example, through activation of an account via an e-mail address or a social network account) to secure authentication, be it by the use of national electronic identity cards or online banking authentication data allowing rather more secure identification of the user. A service provider may also allow an extensive degree of anonymity for its users, in which case the users are not required to identify themselves at all and they may only be traceable – to a limited extent – through the information retained by Internet access providers. The release of such information would usually require an injunction by the investigative or judicial authorities and would be subject to restrictive conditions. It may nevertheless be required in some cases in order to identify and prosecute perpetrators.

149. Thus, in the case of *K.U. v. Finland*, concerning an offence of "malicious misrepresentation" of a sexual nature against a minor, the Court found that "[a]lthough freedom of expression and confidentiality of communications are primary considerations and users of telecommunications and Internet services must have a guarantee that their own privacy and freedom of expression will be respected, such guarantee cannot be absolute and must yield on occasion to other legitimate imperatives, such as the prevention of disorder or crime or the protection of the rights and freedoms of others" (see *K.U. v. Finland*, no. 2872/02, § 49, ECHR 2008). The Court in that case rejected the Government's argument that the applicant had had the possibility of obtaining damages from the service provider, finding that this was not sufficient in the circumstances of the case. It held that there had to be a remedy enabling the actual offender to be identified and brought to justice, whereas at the relevant time the regulatory framework of the respondent State had not provided for the possibility of ordering the Internet service provider to divulge the information required for that purpose (ibid., §§ 47 and 49). Although the case of *K.U. v. Finland* concerned a breach classified as a criminal offence under the domestic law and involved a more sweeping intrusion into the victim's private life than the present case, it is evident from the Court's reasoning that anonymity on the Internet, although an important value, must be balanced against other rights and interests.

150. As regards the establishment of the identity of the authors of the comments in civil proceedings, the Court notes that the parties'

positions differed as to its feasibility. On the basis of the information provided by the parties, the Court observes that the Estonian courts, in the "pre-trial taking of evidence" procedure under Article 244 of the Code of Civil Procedure (see paragraph 40 above), have granted requests by defamed persons for the disclosure by online newspapers or news portals of the IP addresses of authors who had posted allegedly defamatory comments and for the disclosure by Internet access providers of the names and addresses of the subscribers to whom the IP addresses in question had been assigned. The examples provided by the Government show mixed results: in some cases it has proved possible to establish the computer from which the comments had been made, while in other cases, for various technical reasons, this has proved impossible.

151. According to the Supreme Court's judgment in the present case, the injured person had the choice of bringing a claim against the applicant company or the authors of the comments. The Court considers that the uncertain effectiveness of measures allowing the identity of the authors of the comments to be established, coupled with the lack of instruments put in place by the applicant company for the same purpose with a view to making it possible for a victim of hate speech to effectively bring a claim against the authors of the comments, are factors that support a finding that the Supreme Court based its judgment on relevant and sufficient grounds. The Court also refers, in this context, to the *Krone Verlag (no. 4)* judgment, where it found that shifting the risk of the defamed person obtaining redress in defamation proceedings to the media company, which was usually in a better financial position than the defamer, was not as such a disproportionate interference with the media company's right to freedom of expression (see *Krone Verlags GmbH & Co. KG v. Austria (no. 4)*, no. 72331/01, § 32, 9 November 2006).

(iv) Measures taken by the applicant company

152. The Court notes that the applicant company highlighted the number of comments on each article on its website, and therefore the places of the most lively exchanges must have been easily identifiable for the editors of the news portal. The article in issue in the present case attracted 185 comments, apparently well above

average. The comments in question were removed by the applicant company some six weeks after they were uploaded on the website, upon notification by the injured person's lawyers to the applicant company (see paragraphs 17 to 19 above).

153. The Court observes that the Supreme Court stated in its judgment that "[o]n account of the obligation arising from law to avoid causing harm, the [applicant company] should have prevented the publication of comments with clearly unlawful contents". However, it also held that "[a]fter the disclosure, the [applicant company had] failed to remove the comments – the unlawful content of which it should have been aware of – from the portal on its own initiative" (see § 16 of the judgment as set out in paragraph 31 above). Therefore, the Supreme Court did not explicitly determine whether the applicant company was under an obligation to prevent the uploading of the comments on the website or whether it would have sufficed under domestic law for the applicant company to have removed the offending comments without delay after publication, to escape liability under the Obligations Act. The Court considers that when assessing the grounds upon which the Supreme Court relied in its judgment entailing an interference with the applicant's Convention rights, there is nothing to suggest that the national court intended to restrict the applicant's rights to a greater extent than that required to achieve the aim pursued. On this basis, and having regard to the freedom to impart information as enshrined in Article 10, the Court will thus proceed on the assumption that the Supreme Court's judgment must be understood to mean that the subsequent removal of the comments by the applicant company, without delay after publication, would have sufficed for it to escape liability under domestic law. Consequently, and taking account of the above findings (see paragraph 145) to the effect that the applicant company must be considered to have exercised a substantial degree of control over the comments published on its portal, the Court does not consider that the imposition on the applicant company of an obligation to remove from its website, without delay after publication, comments that amounted to hate speech and incitements to violence, and were thus clearly unlawful on their face, amounted, in principle, to a disproportionate interference with its freedom of expression.

154. The pertinent issue in the present case is whether the national court's findings that liability was justified, as the applicant company had not removed the comments without delay after publication, were based on relevant and sufficient grounds. With this in mind, account must, firstly, be taken of whether the applicant company had instituted mechanisms that were capable of filtering comments amounting to hate speech or speech entailing an incitement to violence.

155. The Court notes that the applicant company took certain measures in this regard. There was a disclaimer on the Delfi news portal stating that the writers of the comments – and not the applicant company – were accountable for them, and that the posting of comments that were contrary to good practice or contained threats, insults, obscene expressions or vulgarities, or incited hostility, violence or illegal activities, was prohibited. Furthermore, the portal had an automatic system of deletion of comments based on stems of certain vulgar words and it had a notice-and-take-down system in place, whereby anyone could notify it of an inappropriate comment by simply clicking on a button designated for that purpose, to bring it to the attention of the portal administrators. In addition, on some occasions the administrators removed inappropriate comments on their own initiative.

156. Thus, the Court notes that the applicant company cannot be said to have wholly neglected its duty to avoid causing harm to third parties. Nevertheless, and more importantly, the automatic word-based filter used by the applicant company failed to filter out odious hate speech and speech inciting violence posted by readers and thus limited its ability to expeditiously remove the offending comments. The Court reiterates that the majority of the words and expressions in question did not include sophisticated metaphors or contain hidden meanings or subtle threats. They were manifest expressions of hatred and blatant threats to the physical integrity of L. Thus, even if the automatic word-based filter may have been useful in some instances, the facts of the present case demonstrate that it was insufficient for detecting comments whose content did not constitute protected speech under Article 10 of the Convention (see paragraph 136 above). The Court notes that as a consequence of this

failure of the filtering mechanism, such clearly unlawful comments remained online for six weeks (see paragraph 18 above).

157. The Court observes in this connection that on some occasions the portal administrators did remove inappropriate comments on their own initiative and that, apparently some time after the events of the present case, the applicant company set up a dedicated team of moderators. Having regard to the fact that there are ample possibilities for anyone to make his or her voice heard on the Internet, the Court considers that a large news portal's obligation to take effective measures to limit the dissemination of hate speech and speech inciting violence – the issue in the present case – can by no means be equated to "private censorship". While acknowledging the "important role" played by the Internet "in enhancing the public's access to news and facilitating the dissemination of information in general" (see *Ahmet Yıldırım*, cited above, § 48, and *Times Newspapers Ltd*, cited above, § 27), the Court reiterates that it is also mindful of the risk of harm posed by content and communications on the Internet (see *Editorial Board of* Pravoye Delo *and Shtekel*, cited above, § 63; see also *Mosley*, cited above, § 130).

158. Moreover, depending on the circumstances, there may be no identifiable individual victim, for example in some cases of hate speech directed against a group of persons or speech directly inciting violence of the type manifested in several of the comments in the present case. In cases where an individual victim exists, he or she may be prevented from notifying an Internet service provider of the alleged violation of his or her rights. The Court attaches weight to the consideration that the ability of a potential victim of hate speech to continuously monitor the Internet is more limited than the ability of a large commercial Internet news portal to prevent or rapidly remove such comments.

159. Lastly, the Court observes that the applicant company has argued (see paragraph 78 above) that the Court should have due regard to the notice-and-take-down system that it had introduced. If accompanied by effective procedures allowing for rapid response, this system can in the Court's view function in many cases as an appropriate tool for balancing the rights and interests of all those involved. However, in cases such as the present one, where third-party

user comments are in the form of hate speech and direct threats to the physical integrity of individuals, as understood in the Court's case-law (see paragraph 136 above), the Court considers, as stated above (see paragraph 153), that the rights and interests of others and of society as a whole may entitle Contracting States to impose liability on Internet news portals, without contravening Article 10 of the Convention, if they fail to take measures to remove clearly unlawful comments without delay, even without notice from the alleged victim or from third parties.

(v) Consequences for the applicant company

160. Finally, turning to the question of what consequences resulted from the domestic proceedings for the applicant company, the Court notes that the company was obliged to pay the injured person the equivalent of EUR 320 in compensation for non-pecuniary damage. It agrees with the finding of the Chamber that this sum, also taking into account the fact that the applicant company was a professional operator of one of the largest Internet news portals in Estonia, can by no means be considered disproportionate to the breach established by the domestic courts (see paragraph 93 of the Chamber judgment). The Court notes in this connection that it has also had regard to the domestic post-*Delfi* case-law on the liability of the operators of Internet news portals (see paragraph 43 above). It observes that in these cases the lower courts have followed the Supreme Court's judgment in *Delfi* but no awards have been made for non-pecuniary damage. In other words, the tangible result for the operators in post-*Delfi* cases has been that they have taken down the offending comments but have not been ordered to pay compensation for non-pecuniary damage.

161. The Court also observes that it does not appear that the applicant company had to change its business model as a result of the domestic proceedings. According to the information available, the Delfi news portal has continued to be one of Estonia's largest Internet publications and by far the most popular for posting comments, the number of which has continued to increase. Anonymous comments – now existing alongside the possibility of posting registered comments, which are displayed to readers first – are still predominant and the applicant company has set up a team of moderators

carrying out follow-up moderation of comments posted on the portal (see paragraphs 32 and 83 above). In these circumstances, the Court cannot conclude that the interference with the applicant company's freedom of expression was disproportionate on that account either.

(vi) Conclusion

162. Based on the concrete assessment of the above aspects, taking into account the reasoning of the Supreme Court in the present case, in particular the extreme nature of the comments in question, the fact that the comments were posted in reaction to an article published by the applicant company on its professionally managed news portal run on a commercial basis, the insufficiency of the measures taken by the applicant company to remove without delay after publication comments amounting to hate speech and speech inciting violence and to ensure a realistic prospect of the authors of such comments being held liable, and the moderate sanction imposed on the applicant company, the Court finds that the domestic courts' imposition of liability on the applicant company was based on relevant and sufficient grounds, having regard to the margin of appreciation afforded to the respondent State. Therefore, the measure did not constitute a disproportionate restriction on the applicant company's right to freedom of expression.

Accordingly, there has been no violation of Article 10 of the Convention.

(*Delfi AS* v. *Estonia*, app. no. 64569/09, 16 June 2015, Judgment of the Grand Chamber)

6/6

On 9 July, the European Court of Human Rights gave a judgment in the case of *Tolmachev* v. *Estonia*, where the applicant complained that his complaint was not examined by the court because of his absence and that his right to defend himself though counsel was breached (Article 6 §§ 1 and 3 (c) as well as Article 13). The Chamber found the following:

I. Alleged violation of Article 6 §§ 1 and 3 (c) of the Convention

[...]

42. The Court notes at the outset that in the present case the applicant was fined by the police who dealt with the misdemeanour matter in extra-judicial proceedings. Had the applicant not complained to the County Court about the decision made by the police, this decision – and the applicant's conviction – would have become final and the sentence enforceable. It is against that background that the Court proceeds to the examination of the case.

43. In this connection, the Court reiterates that while entrusting the prosecution and punishment of minor offences to administrative authorities is not inconsistent with the Convention, it is to be stressed that the person concerned must have an opportunity to challenge any decision made against him before a tribunal that offers the guarantees of Article 6 (see *Kadubec v. Slovakia*, 2 September 1998, § 57, *Reports of Judgments and Decisions* 1998VI; *Malige v. France*, 23 September 1998, § 45, *Reports of Judgments and Decisions* 1998VII; and *Öztürk v. Germany*, 21 February 1984, § 56, Series A no. 73).

44. In the present case the applicant had an opportunity to file a complaint with the County Court against the decision made by the police, and he made use of this opportunity. It has not been put in question that the County Court was a "judicial body that [had] full jurisdiction" (see, for example, *Gradinger v. Austria*, 23 October 1995, §§ 42 and 44, Series A no. 328C, with further references), and the Court sees no reason to hold otherwise. The Court observes that under domestic law the County Court had to examine the matter in its entirety, regardless of the limits of the complaint filed, and as regards both points of fact and law (see paragraphs 13 and 25 above).

45. The Court has had regard to the applicant's arguments related to the service of the summons and scheduling of the hearing for the day following the County Court's pertinent ruling. It notes, however, that these issues were not raised before the Court of Appeal. In any event, the Court observes that the summons for the hearing of 21 March 2013 were sent out in the beginning of February (see

paragraphs 8 and 9 above). Against that background, the County Court's ruling of 20 March 2013, by which the hearing was (again) scheduled for 21 March 2013 (see paragraph 10 above), has no relevance to the question whether the applicant was informed of the date of the hearing well in advance. As regards the applicant's argument that the summons was not served on anyone, the Court, having had regard to the pertinent provisions of the domestic law (see paragraph 22 above), has no reason to conclude that the summons that the County Court's security official attempted to serve on the applicant's mother, living at the address indicated by the applicant as his residence (see paragraph 9 above), were not properly served. Furthermore, there is no dispute that the applicant's counsel received summons. Thus, the Court sees no reason to doubt that the applicant was summoned to the court hearing in accordance with domestic law. Furthermore, it notes that the applicant did not deny that he was aware of the date of the hearing. Accordingly, the Court considers that there is no call to further deal with this issue and it proceeds on the presumption that the applicant was or had to be aware of the County Court hearing in due time.

46. The Court further observes that the applicant did not appear at the hearing but instructed his counsel to pursue the case. However, the County Court found that the applicant's presence was required for the resolution of the matter. As he failed to appear and the County Court did not consider it possible to resolve the case in his absence, the County Court refused to examine the applicant's complaint and the decision made by the police became final. Thus, the Court has to determine whether the County Court's decision, in such circumstances, was in accordance with Article 6 of the Convention.

47. The Court reiterates that it is of capital importance that a defendant should appear, both because of his right to a hearing and because of the need to verify the accuracy of his statements and compare them with those of the victim – whose interests need to be protected – and of the witnesses. The legislature must accordingly be able to discourage unjustified absences (see, *inter alia*, *Poitrimol v. France*, 23 November 1993, § 35, Series A no. 277A; *Van Geyseghem v. Belgium* [GC], no. 26103/95, § 33, ECHR 1999I; *Van Pelt v. France*, no. 31070/96, § 66, 23 May 2000; and *Neziraj v. Germany*,

no. 30804/07, § 47, 8 November 2012). However, it is also of crucial importance for the fairness of the criminal justice system that the accused be adequately defended, both at first instance and on appeal. The Court has consistently found that the latter interest prevailed and that, consequently, the fact that a defendant, in spite of having been properly summoned, did not appear, could not – even in the absence of an excuse – justify depriving him of his right under Article 6 § 3 of the Convention to be defended by counsel (see *Lala v. the Netherlands*, 22 September 1994, § 33, Series A no. 297A; *Pelladoah v. the Netherlands*, 22 September 1994, § 40, Series A no. 297B; *Van Geyseghem*, loc. cit.; *Van Pelt*, loc. cit.; *Harizi v. France*, no. 59480/00, § 49, 29 March 2005; *Kari-Pekka Pietiläinen v. Finland*, no. 13566/06, § 31, 22 September 2009; and *Neziraj*, cited above, §§ 48-49). It is for the courts to ensure that a trial is fair and, accordingly, that counsel who attends trial for the apparent purpose of defending the accused in his absence is given the opportunity to do so (see *Lala*, cited above, § 34; *Pelladoah*, cited above, § 41; and *Kari-Pekka Pietiläinen*, loc. cit.)

48. Thus, the right of everyone charged with a criminal offence to be defended effectively by a lawyer is one of the basic features of a fair trial. An accused does not lose this right merely on account of not attending a court hearing. Even if the legislature must be able to discourage unjustified absences, it cannot penalise them by creating exceptions to the right to legal assistance. The legitimate requirement that defendants must attend court hearings can be satisfied by means other than deprivation of the right to be defended (see *Van Geyseghem*, cited above, § 34; *Van Pelt*, cited above, § 67; *Kari-Pekka Pietiläinen*, cited above, § 32; and *Neziraj*, cited above, § 51).

49. The Court considers that the right to be defended by a lawyer is intertwined, in the present case, with the right of effective access to the court and the right to a hearing in one's presence. Indeed, the Court has emphasised in a number of cases that the duty to guarantee the right of a criminal defendant to be present in the courtroom ranks as one of the essential requirements of Article 6 (see, among others, *Hermi v. Italy* [GC], no. 18114/02, §§ 58-59, ECHR 2006XII).

50. At the same time, the Court reiterates that neither the letter nor the spirit of Article 6 of the Convention prevents a person from

waiving of his own free will, either expressly or tacitly, the entitlement to the guarantees of a fair trial (see *Kwiatkowska v. Italy* (dec.), no. 52868/99, 30 November 2000). However, if it is to be effective for Convention purposes, a waiver of the right to take part in the trial must be established in an unequivocal manner and be attended by minimum safeguards commensurate to its importance (see *Poitrimol*, cited above, § 31). Furthermore, it must not run counter to any important public interest (see *Sejdovic v. Italy* [GC], no. 56581/00, § 86, ECHR 2006II, and *Håkansson and Sturesson v. Sweden*, 21 February 1990, § 66, Series A no. 171-A).

51. The Court observes that in the present case the County Court dealt with the misdemeanour matter in complaints proceedings – it formally examined the applicant's complaint against a decision taken by the police. The Court has held that the personal attendance of the defendant does not take on the same crucial significance for an appeal hearing as it does for the trial hearing (see *Hermi*, cited above, § 60, and *Kamasinski v. Austria*, 19 December 1989, § 106, Series A no. 168). However, having regard to the special features of the proceedings involved and taking account of the entirety of the proceedings in the domestic legal order (see *Hermi*, loc. cit.; *Ekbatani v. Sweden*, 26 May 1988, § 27, Series A no. 134; and *Monnell and Morris v. the United Kingdom*, 2 March 1987, § 56, Series A no. 115), the Court considers that the County Court's role in the present case was not the same as that of a traditional court of appeal. Although the proceedings were set in motion by the applicant's complaint against a decision by the police by which he had been sanctioned, and this decision would have become final and enforceable if not challenged or if the County Court declined to examine the complaint – as it happened in the instant case –, the County Court's role, nevertheless, was similar to that of an ordinary first-instance court. It had to examine the matter in its entirety without being bound by the limits of the complaint filed or facts established by a lower instance. In these circumstances, the Court is of the view that the applicant's presence at the County Court's hearing was important in order to secure him a fair trial.

52. The Court observes that the County Court found, on the basis of the case-file and issues raised in the applicant's complaint, that it could not decide the case without the applicant's presence. It is

not for this Court to overrule such an assessment which was reasoned, had regard to the County Court's role in the examination of the complaints in the misdemeanour proceedings and lacked any signs of arbitrariness. The Court considers that the trial court, in such circumstances, was better placed to assess whether it could proceed with the case merely with the participation of the applicant's counsel or whether it was imperative for the applicant to be present. The Court also emphasises in this connection that the proceedings conducted by the police in respect of the applicant, taken separately, did not offer the fair trial guarantees enshrined in Article 6 of the Convention. The Convention requirements could only be complied with on the condition that the applicant had an opportunity to challenge the decision of the police before a tribunal in proceedings that did offer the fair trial guarantees of Article 6. The Court has no reason to doubt that the County Court's finding that it could not resolve the case in the applicant's absence proceeded from and was in line with the fair trial requirements including the principle of immediacy (see, for example, *P.K. v. Finland* (dec.), no. 37442/97, 9 July 2002).

53. However, the Court notes that the County Court's refusal to proceed with the examination of the applicant's complaint resulted in the discontinuation of the court proceedings and entering into force of the sanction imposed on the applicant by the police. In the light of the case-law summarised above (see paragraphs 47 and 48), the Court considers that such an outcome was not compatible with the Convention. Assuming that the applicant waived his right to take part in the hearing – an issue which the Court does not need to determine in the present case –, there is nothing to indicate that the applicant waived his right to be defended through legal assistance of his own choosing, a distinct right protected under Article 6 § 3 (c) of the Convention.

54. The Court observes, in this connection, that the applicant's counsel was present and ready to defend the applicant at the County Court's hearing of 21 March 2013. He submitted that the applicant was abroad and could therefore not take part in the hearing, and asked the court to examine the matter without the applicant's participation. Nevertheless, as mentioned above, the County Court decided to refuse to examine the complaint because of the ap-

plicant's absence. The Court has taken note of the Government's argument that the applicant's complaint mainly related to factual circumstances where counsel could not have substituted the applicant. However, it is not for the Court to speculate whether the applicant's counsel would have also put forward any legal issues to be dealt with, had the hearing on the merits of the case taken place, or to what extent the factual circumstances could have been examined in the applicant's absence. It merely notes that it does not appear that the County Court asked the applicant's counsel how in his view, having regard to the arguments raised in the complaint, the case could have been resolved without the applicant being present. The Court considers that it would have been precisely in the course of the examination of the case at a court hearing when the applicant's counsel could have provided such explanations – an opportunity he was not given.

55. As regards the Government's argument that the applicant's counsel had not requested the adjournment of the hearing, the Court considers that such a request would not have been pertinent, having regard to the applicant's position that the case should have been examined in his absence. If the domestic courts came to the conclusion that the applicant's presence was imperative – as they did in the present case –, there was nothing to prevent them from adjourning the hearing and ascertaining whether the applicant's attendance could be secured regardless of his alleged residence abroad. The Court notes in this connection that pursuant to the Code of Misdemeanour Procedure a defendant who failed to appear at a hearing regardless of being ordered to do so could be subject to a fine or compelled attendance (Article 43 of the Code of Misdemeanour Procedure, see paragraph 24 above).

56. In these circumstances, the Court considers that the discontinuation of the applicant's case cannot be considered justifiable, having regard to the rights of the defence and the requirements of the fair trial.

57. There has accordingly been a violation of Article 6 §§ 1 and 3 (c) of the Convention.

(*Tolmachev* v. *Estonia*, app. no. 73748/13, 9 July 2015, Judgment of the Chamber)

6/7
On 3 September, the European Court of Human Rights gave a judgment in the case of *Sõro* v. *Estonia*, where the applicant complained that his right to respect for his private and family life had been breached owing to the publication of the information that he had worked as a driver of the KGB (Article 8). The Chamber found the following:

I. Alleged violation of Article 8 of the Convention

[...]

56. The Court considers that the publication of the information about the applicant's service in the KGB concerned facts about his personal past that were made available to the public and also affected his reputation. It therefore constituted an interference with his right to respect for his private life (compare *Sidabras and Džiautas v. Lithuania*, nos. 55480/00 and 59330/00, §§ 42-50, ECHR 2004VIII).

57. The Court further notes that the lawfulness of the interference was not in dispute between the parties. It observes that the interference in question was based on the Diclosure Act that had been adopted by the Riigikogu and published according to the rules in force. Nor has it been disputed that the text of the law was sufficiently clear to enable those affected to foresee the consequences it entailed. The law's accessibility and public awareness of it is also confirmed by the information provided by the Government according to which 1,153 persons submitted a confession to the Estonian Internal Security Service within one year of the entry into force of the Disclosure Act in order not to have information about their service in or collaboration with the security and intelligence organisations published. Thus, the Court is satisfied that the impugned interference was lawful for the purposes of the second paragraph of Article 8 of the Convention.

58. As regards the purpose of the interference, the Court notes that the registration and disclosure of the former employees and collaborators of the security and intelligence organisations of the regimes

that had operated in Estonia were part of the measures taken to ensure the transparency, clarity and internal peace in the society, as well as to avoid security threats. The Court has also taken note of the cases referred to by the Government where former employees or collaborators of the KGB had provided a foreign country with state secrets leading to their conviction of treason (see paragraph 54 above). The Court concludes that the interference in question pursued legitimate aims within the meaning of paragraph 2 of Article 8, namely the protection of national security and public safety, the prevention of disorder as well as well as the protection of the rights and freedoms of others (compare, *mutatis mutandis, Sidabras and Džiautas*, cited above, §§ 54-55).

59. Accordingly, the Court proceeds to the examination of whether the measure was "necessary in a democratic society". The Court observes in this connection that there is no uniform approach among High Contracting Parties as to the measures to dismantle the heritage of former communist totalitarian systems (see *Matyjek v. Poland* (dec.), no. 38184/03, § 36, ECHR 2006VII). Different measures have been applied and their application has given rise to a number of cases before the Court concerning a variety of issues such as restrictions on the persons' eligibility to stand for elections (see *Ždanoka v. Latvia* [GC], no. 58278/00, ECHR 2006IV, and *Ādamsons v. Latvia*, no. 3669/03, 24 June 2008) or to their employment (see *Vogt v. Germany*, 26 September 1995, Series A no. 323; *Volkmer v. Germany* (dec.), no. 39799/98, 22 November 2001; *Sidabras and Džiautas*, cited above; *Rainys and Gasparavičius v. Lithuania*, nos. 70665/01 and 74345/01, 7 April 2005; and *Žičkus v. Lithuania*, no. 26652/02, 7 April 2009) as well as lack of access to the information on the basis of which the persons' collaboration with former secret services was established (see *Matyjek v. Poland*, no. 38184/03, 24 April 2007) or reduction of pensions of the persons concerned (see *Cichopek and Others v. Poland* (dec.) no. 15189/10 and other applications, 14 May 2013). Against this background, the Court turns to the proportionality analysis of the impugned measures in the present case.

60. The Court reiterates that in a number of previous cases it has criticised the lack of individualisation of the impugned measures. Thus, in *Ādamsons* it considered that the group of persons – former KGB agents – to which the restrictions to stand for elections applied,

had been designed in a too broad manner without having regard to the period of service of the persons concerned, specific tasks assigned to them or their individual behaviour (see *Ādamsons*, cited above, § 125). Similarly, in *Žičkus* the lack of differentiation in domestic law between different levels of former involvement with the KGB was pointed out by the Court (see *Žičkus*, cited above, § 33). In addition to the lack of differentiation in domestic law as regards the premises for the application of the restrictions, the Court has also addressed the issue of broadly fashioned restrictions applied to the individuals concerned. Thus, in *Sidabras and Džiautas*, it noted that with the exception of references to "lawyers" and "notaries", domestic law contained no definition of the specific private sector jobs, functions or tasks which the applicants were barred from holding (see *Sidabras and Džiautas*, cited above, § 59).

61. The Court is of the view that the above considerations also apply to the present case. It notes that the Disclosure Act made no distinction between different levels of former involvement with the KGB. It is true that under the applicable procedure the applicant was informed beforehand of the text of the announcement to be published, and given a possibility to contest the factual information contained in it. However, there was no procedure put in place to assess the specific tasks performed by individual employees of the former security services in order to differentiate the danger they could possibly pose several years after the termination of their career in these institutions. The Court is not convinced that there existed a reasonable link between the legitimate aims sought by the enactment of the Disclosure Act and the publication of information about all former employees of the former security services including drivers, as in the applicant's case, regardless of the specific function they performed in these services.

62. The Court also notes that although the Disclosure Act came into force three and a half years after Estonia had declared its independence on 20 August 1991, the publication of the information about the former employees of the security services was stretched over several years. Thus, in the applicant's case the information in question was only published in 2004 – almost thirteen years after the restoration of the Estonian independence. The Court is of the opinion that any threat the former servicemen of the KGB could ini-

tially pose to the newly created democracy must have considerably decreased with the passage of time. It notes that it does not appear from the file that any assessment of the possible threat posed by the applicant at the time of the publication of the information was carried out (compare *Žičkus*, loc. cit.).

63. Lastly, the Court observes that the Disclosure Act in itself did not impose any restrictions on the applicant's employment. Nevertheless, according to the applicant he was derided by his colleagues and forced to quit his job. The Court considers that even if such a result was not sought by the Disclosure Act, it is nevertheless indicative of the seriousness of the interference with the applicant's right to respect for his private life.

64. The foregoing considerations are sufficient to enable the Court to conclude that the applicant's right to respect for his private life was subject to a disproportionate interference in the present case.

There has accordingly been a violation of Article 8 of the Convention.

(*Sõro* v. *Estonia*, app. no. 22588/08, 3 September 2015, Judgment of the Chamber)

Part Six: VIII. D. The Position of the Individual (including the Corporation) in International Law – Human rights and fundamental freedoms – Other aspects of human rights and fundamental freedoms

6/8

On 4 March, Foreign Minister Keit Pentus-Rosimannus spoke at the 28th Human Rights Council. Among other issues, she addressed the situation in occupied territories as well as online freedom of opinion and expression. In connection with occupied Ukrainian and Georgian territories, she said that:

> The latest UNHCR data speak of 1,801,700 persons of concern in Ukraine. A year ago there were almost none. Let us be clear. This is not an internal conflict. The calamity Ukraine is suffering has been

inflicted from outside. Behind each person there is a huge tragedy and violation of their human rights. That is why we consider the role of HRM(M)U vital, to which Estonia has contributed and will also, in order to document and deter serious violations of human rights, in particular the systemic intimidation and persecution of Crimean Tatars by the occupying power. Their freedom of expression and peaceful assembly continues to be curtailed and limitations have been imposed on the freedom of religion and belief in Crimea. International human rights monitors must be provided with unrestricted access to the whole territory of Ukraine, including Crimea.

We reiterate our strong support for the sovereignty and territorial integrity of Ukraine, also confirmed by the General Assembly in its resolution 68/262. And we should not be fooled by the attempts to distort the principle of self-determination – we are not talking of a nation called Crimeans wanting to establish their own state.

Regarding Georgia, we see worrying developments in the occupied territories. The *de facto* authorities are fortifying the [Administrative Boundary Line] and cutting parts of Georgia off from the rest of the country. We do not recognize the so called "Treaty on Alliance and Strategic Partnership" signed by Russia and de facto authorities in Abkhazia, a region that is an integral part of Georgia. Such steps are not in any way conducive to stabilizing the situation. Instead, all efforts should be made in the Geneva international discussions to achieve progress on security and humanitarian issues that continue to affect communities in Georgia. As previous [High Commissionaire] Navi Pillay mentioned about Tskhinvali region "one of the most inaccessible places on earth, with no access permitted for international agencies". Including herself."

Regarding online freedom of opinion and expression she stated that:

"The right to freedom of opinion and expression is the cornerstone of every democracy. Estonia has been a confident supporter of the internet resolutions adopted by the Human Rights Council over the last years and continues holding one of the top ranks of online freedom in the world. At the same time, we are deeply concerned about increasing restrictions to the right to freedom of opinion and expression in many countries. As one of the founding members of the Freedom Online Coalition in 2011, we call on the states restricting freedom of expression, including on the Internet, to lift such restrictions and to join the voice of those who are promoting and protecting human rights and fundamental freedoms."

(Available at the website of the Ministry of Foreign Affairs, <www.vm.ee/en/news/statement-estonia-un-human-rights-council-28th-session-4-march-2015>, visited on 30 November 2016)

6/9
On 19 May, the Estonian Permanent Representative to the Council of Europe, Gea Rennel, delivered a statement at 125th Session of the Committee of Ministers of the Council of Europe. She emphasised again free access to the Internet and online freedom opinion and expression, which have become a priority for Estonia.

> We welcome the particular focus in the Secretary General's report on the freedom of expression. This right is an enabler of many other rights and should be at the very core of the Council of Europe activities. Effective protection of the freedom of expression on the Internet requires the protection of the Internet eco-system which is open, free and secure. It is vital to base this on the broader platform of Internet governance which offers a basis for defending human rights online, including concepts such as cybercrime or protection of privacy. The Council of Europe has various instruments in this regard and we should make best out of them.

> Today we have to look beyond current challenges to be better prepared for the future. In this context, while keeping our eyes on the horizon, let me highlight the importance of the digital society. There are many angles to approach the topic, but I am certain that most of us agree that over time digital technology and the Internet will become ever more prominent players in shaping the world of tomorrow.

> The World Bank governance indicators have shown that there is a clear correlation between economic growth and different freedoms. The Internet allows for effective access to information, knowledge

and skills, contributes to innovation and enables wider political participation. The latter has been underlined also in the report. Developing new restrictions on the Internet basically means limiting these perspectives dramatically. It is the free, open and democratic nature of the Internet that has made it a driving force of progress towards development in its various forms. Therefore it is absolutely crucial to protect and strengthen the freedoms both offline and online. Roughly half of the world's Internet users have encountered restrictive measures being imposed on their net activities by various authorities. Manipulations with information flow and restrictions have also been prominent features of the Ukrainian-Russian conflict.

(Available at the website of the Ministry of Foreign Affairs, <www.vm.ee/en/news/statement-ambassador-permanent-representative-estonia-council-europe-gea-rennel-125th-session>, visited on 30 November 2016)

6/10

On 1 July, the Supreme Court of Estonia rendered a judgment in the case 3-4-1-2-15, where it dismissed two requests by appeals court to declare unconstitutional Sections 4(3) and 22(3) of the *Riigikogu* (Parliament) Election Act which respectively stipulate that "A person who has been convicted of a criminal offence by a court and is imprisoned is not allowed to participate in voting" and "A person is not entered in the list of voters if he or she has been convicted of a criminal offence by a court pursuant to information kept in the criminal records database and if, as of the thirtieth day before election day, he or she is serving a prison sentence until the election day". The issue was about blanket exclusion from voting for everybody who were convicted of a criminal offence and imprisoned. The requests were dismissed because the individuals in questions had committed serious crimes and their exclusion was seen as a proportional measure. While reasoning, the Court referred also to the Protocol 1 of the European Convention of Human Rights and international law.

> 51. In the opinion of the Supreme Court *en banc*, the desire to temporarily remove persons who have seriously harmed the legal values that serve as the basis for communal life, including those that are considered worthy of protection under the Penal Code, from exercising public authority via the elections of the *Riigikogu* must be considered as the first reason for the restriction of the right to

vote of persons convicted by a court and serving a prison sentence in a penal institution. Such removal serves, above all, the purpose of the legitimacy of the public authority, allowing only persons who have not called the aforementioned values into doubt by their acts to participate in the legitimisation of authority via elections. Also, such restriction protects the rights of the persons who have not expressed such disrespect towards the values serving as the basis for communal life by their acts and fosters the rule of law, which is also a legal value of a constitutional rank.

52. Thus, these purposes are legitimate for restricting the right to vote. This does not mean that the right to vote, which is of utmost importance in a democratic society, could be restricted lightly.

[...]

54. The Court *en banc* has no doubts about the appropriateness or necessity of the restriction for attainment of the aforementioned legitimate purposes. Next, the Court *en banc* will examine whether the restriction is proportional in the narrow sense for attainment of the purposes.

[...]

56. The right to vote in parliamentary elections ensures the functioning of the democratic organisation of the state. It is an important fundamental right, but the exclusion of certain persons or strictly limited small groups of persons from voting does not undermine the democratic formation of the will on the whole. In § 58 of the [Penal Code], the constitutional legislature has explicitly allowed for restricting the right to vote of persons serving a prison sentence.

57. In its case law, the European Court of Human Rights has held that an automatic voting ban on all persons who are serving a prison sentence is disproportionate (see, for instance, *Hirst vs United Kingdom* (no. 2), no. 74025/01, 6 October 2005, para. 82). The Court *en banc* finds that an absolute ban on the right to vote, which is imposed on a group of persons limited based on certain features and does not allow for any weighing of the ban, may render a dispropor-

tionate result. In the present case, this is so in the case of the given applicants, too. The Court *en banc* explains its opinion as follows.

58. Applicant 1 has been convicted of: a murder in an exceptionally torturous and cruel manner; secret theft, if committed by a group, for at least a second time and by removing an obstacle or lock; hooliganism; theft of a motor vehicle, if committed at least for a second time and by a group of persons; and of fraud, if committed by a person who has been convicted of a similar criminal offence before and by an official and to a large degree [...]. Applicant 1 was released from prison in 2008 before serving the full sentence but committed a new crime during the probation period. He is currently serving a prison sentence of over six years for these criminal offences, taking into account the non-served portion of the previous sentence.

59. Thus, applicant 1 has been convicted of multiple especially severe criminal offences, including of a murder in an exceptionally torturous and cruel manner. Murder is one of the most serious types of criminal offences under the Penal Code. Applicant 1 committed a new crime after being released from prison on probation. Given the dangerousness of the criminal offences, a long-term prison sentence has been imposed on him. Given that the Constitution *expressis verbis* allows for restricting the right to vote of persons serving a prison sentence and the criminal offences committed by applicant 1, notably murder under aggravating circumstances, as well as that the person continued committing criminal offences after partially serving the prison sentence and was released on probation before the prescribed time and the length of the sentence based on the severity of his crimes, the restriction of the right to vote of applicant 1 is, according to the Supreme Court *en banc*, proportionate.

60. Applicant 2 has been convicted of the following: a secret theft to a large degree; theft or robbery of a firearm, ammunition or explosives if committed by a group of persons; murder; twice of robbery, if committed by a group of persons and using a weapon or another object used as a weapon, by a person who has committed a similar criminal offence before, and if it was related to the removal of an obstacle or lock preventing access to the location of property; twice of theft of a document proving a person's identity and citizenship or of another official personal document; using the official personal

document of another person; twice of escaping from custody; twice of illegal making, acquisition, possession, use, transportation, sale or forwarding of a firearm or ammunition as well as illegal carrying or delivery of ammunition; illegal carrying or delivery of a firearm; secret theft, if committed by a group, for at least a second time and by removing an obstacle or lock preventing access to the location of property; murder under aggravating circumstances if committed in connection with the victim's performance of a service or public duty (i.e. murder of the police officer who tried to apprehend him) and by a person who has committed a murder before; secret theft to a large degree; public theft or robbery of a firearm, ammunition or explosives; secret theft, if committed by a group of persons and involving the removal of an obstacle or lock preventing access to the location of property; instigation to murder committed in an exceptionally torturous and cruel manner and at least for a second time, and torture [...]. In one court case, the court of the first instance sentenced applicant 2 to death by firing squad, but the circuit court transformed the sentence to life in prison.

61. Thus, applicant 2 has been convicted of many severe criminal offences committed at different times, incl. for two murders, on one occasion for killing a police officer who was performing his service duties, for an attempted murder and instigation to murder, and he has twice escaped from custody and also continued committing severe crimes in prison. Based on the dangerousness of these especially severe criminal offences, applicant 2 has been sentenced to life in prison, which, according to the sanction system of the Penal Code, is an exceptional and the severest type of penalty. Given that the Constitution *expressis verbis* allows for restricting the right to vote of persons serving a prison sentence and the criminal offences committed by applicant 2, above all, the killing of a police officer who was performing his service duties, the number of many serious criminal offences, the commitment of offences during imprisonment and the life sentence imposed on him based on the severity of the criminal offences, the restriction of the right to vote of applicant 2 is proportionate.

62. Based on the findings in paragraphs 59 and 61 [...], the requests [...] must be dismissed.

III

63. The Supreme Court *en banc* also notes that it interprets § 57 of the Constitution similarly to the interpretation of Article 3 of Protocol no. 1 of the ECHR by the European Court of Human Rights. The ECtHR has held that a general, an automatic and non-selective voting ban of prisoners in parliamentary elections is against the Convention (*Hirst vs United Kingdom (no. 2)*, no 74025/01, 6 October 2005, para. 82). In *Frodl vs. Austria*, the ECtHR held that the right to vote may only be limited in the case of a narrowly defined group of persons who serve a long prison sentence (no. 20201/04, 8 April 2010, para. 28). In *Söyler vs Turkey*, the ECtHR took the view that deprivation of all persons serving a prison sentence of the right to vote is not in accordance with the Convention (no. 29441/07, 17 September 2013, para. 42). According to the Court *en banc*, a ban according to which no person who is serving a prison sentence can vote in parliamentary elections is in accordance with § 57 of the Constitution.

64. The Court *en banc* emphasises that the state must implement international agreements and can do so via its various bodies. Various bodies contribute to the implementation of international agreements within the limits of their competence. The Supreme Court reviews the constitutionality of rules based on a specific request and type of procedure. Both the *Riigikogu* and the Chancellor of Justice submitted in their opinions presented to the Supreme Court that depriving all persons who are serving a prison sentence from the right to vote in parliamentary elections is against the Constitution. The *Riigikogu* can, on its own initiative, replace the unconstitutional rules with constitutional ones. The Chancellor of Justice is competent to initiate abstract constitutional review proceedings regarding rules that, in the estimate of the Chancellor of Justice, are unconstitutional.

(Available at the website of the Supreme Court, <www.riigikohus.ee/?id=1601>, visited 30 November 2016)

6/11

On 2 October, the Supreme Court of Estonia rendered a judgment in the case 3-4-1-31-15, where it declared that the Code of Administrative Court

Procedure (CACP) is not unconstitutional to the extent it obliges potential applicants to files complaints against the decisions of the Social Insurance Board (SIB) in the jurisdictional district where the SEB has its headquarters, not in the jurisdictional district where they reside. The applicant in question found that it is cumbersome to file a complaint in another jurisdictional district and such a demand is unconstitutional. He claimed that the CACP regulation violated several rights guaranteed under the Constitution, i.e. the prohibition of discrimination, the right of recourse to the courts and the right to attend any hearing held by a court in his case. The Court weighed different arguments and made a brief reference also to international law.

> 59. International law does not require either that the state should ensure the hearing of a case in a court as close to a person's home as possible. Also, no such recommendation has been made by international organisations. The European Commission for the Efficiency of Justice in its optional guidance (*Guidelines on the Creation of Judicial Maps to Support Access to Justice within a Quality Judicial System*, CEPEJ(2013)7) has noted that the state should evaluate different factors when deciding on the optimum allocation of resources (p. 4). It is found that the geographical distribution of courts is often a remnant from earlier times and fails to take account of society's current needs, development of transportation, or opportunities offered by modern means of communication. There is no given optimum number of people to be served by a court (ibid., pp. 5–6). The highest productivity at European level is attained in courts with the number of judges between 40 and 80 (ibid., p. 8). The greater the use of information technology solutions the more remote the location of the court could be, and remote participation in hearings also reduces procedural costs (ibid., p. 10). Availability of legal advice in a region, and whether it is possible to recruit judges meeting high professional standards in a particular region, including in the future, are also factors to be considered (ibid., p. 11).

> 60. The European Network of the Councils of Justice in its report Judicial reform in Europe Report 2011–2012 also notes that the distance of courts from people is growing as a result of reorganisation of judicial systems, but due to new technological solutions this is not seen as an obstacle (p. 6). Concentration of courts should be motivated, inter alia, by the need to more effectively use available

resources (ibid., p. 8). In the Chamber's opinion, information technology solutions in Estonia are legally ensured and also widespread in practice.

61. In view of the low intensity of the interference with fundamental rights, the soundness of the legitimate aim, and the legislator's broad discretion in assigning jurisdiction, the Chamber is of the opinion that the contested regulation is constitutional."

(Available at the website of the Supreme Court, <www.riigikohus.ee/?id=1640>, visited 30 November 2016)

Part Six: IX. The Position of the Individual (including the Corporation) in International Law – Crimes under international law

6/12

On 4 March, Foreign Minister Keit Pentus-Rosimannus spoke at the 28th Human Rights Council. Among other issues, she spoke about crimes committed by governments against their people.

> Systematic, widespread and gross human rights violations have been and are being committed by the Democratic People's Republic of Korea, its institutions and officials. The United Nations Human Rights Council's Commission of Inquiry on Human Rights in the Democratic People's Republic of Korea (DPRK) revealed in its report last year that in many instances, the violations of human rights found by the Commission and documented in its report, meet the high threshold required for proof of crimes against humanity in international law. The perpetrators enjoy impunity. The United Nations must ensure that those most responsible for the crimes against humanity committed in the DPRK will be held accountable.

(Available at the website of the Ministry of Foreign Affairs, <www.vm.ee/en/news/statement-estonia-un-human-rights-council-28th-session-4-march-2015>, visited on 30 November 2016)

Part Eight: II. B. Jurisdiction of the State – Types of jurisdiction – Jurisdiction to adjudicate

8/1

On 26 August, Foreign Minister Marina Kaljurand stated that Estonia condemns the unlawful conviction of Ukrainian citizens Oleg Sentsov and Olexander Kolchenko by the military court of Russia. She added that the unlawful arrest of Ukrainian citizens in illegally annexed Crimea as well as making them stand to trial is a violation of international law and human rights.

> Russia must adhere to international commitments and immediately release all unlawfully detained Ukrainian citizens."

Oleg Sentsov and Olexander Kolchenko were pro-Ukrainian activists who were detained in Crime in May 2014. According to the Federal Security Service (FSB) of the Russian Federation, they were members of the sabotage and terrorist cell Right Sector and they planned terrorist and sabotage attacks in a number of Crimean towns. Their detention and trial was controversial and was seen by supporters as a punishment for pro-Ukrainian activities in the illegally annexed Crimea.

(Available at the website of the Ministry of Foreign Affairs, <www.vm.ee/en/news/estonia-condemns-unlawful-conviction-ukrainian-citizens-russia>, visited on 30 November 2016)

Part Eight: III. A. Jurisdiction of the State – Extra-territorial exercise of jurisdiction – General

8/2

On 2 June 2015, Foreign Minister Keit Pentus-Rosimannus stated that Russia has been violating international law for nearly nine months by having abducted and by illegally detaining a security police officer, Eston Kohver.

> The illegal detention and holding of apparent court proceedings of Eston Kohver, who was abducted from Estonian territory by the FSB (Federal Security Service of the Russian Federation), have not had any connection to a fair court proceeding from the very start. Esto-

nian authorities are doing everything in their power to have Eston Kohver released so that he can return home.

(Available at the website of the Ministry of Foreign Affairs, <www.vm.ee/en/news/foreign-minister-russia-has-violated-international-law-9-months-illegally-detaining-eston>, visited on 30 November 2016)

8/3

On 5 September 2014, a security police officer, Eston Kohver, while on duty to prevent cross-border crime, was abducted by the Russian Security Services on Estonian territory near the Estonian-Russian border. He was taken by force to Russia and was held in custody in Moscow. On 19 August 2015, he was sentenced to 15 years in prison for espionage, illegal crossing of the border, and illegal possession and smuggling of a weapon. He did not admit any guilt for these acts. On the same day, the Prime Minister released a statement:

> The abduction of Eston Kohver on the territory of the Republic of Estonia by FSB on 5 September 2014, and the illegal detention that followed in the Russian Federation, has been illegitimate since the beginning. It has been a clear and grave violation of international law by the Russian Federation.
>
> The staged court case that formed a verdict suitable for the Russian authorities has nothing to do with a fair trial.
>
> Considering the circumstances of his illegal detention and how the court evidence has been gathered, we know that Eston Kohver has not been free in his decisions.
>
> The authorities of Estonia continue to fully support Eston Kohver and are doing everything possible to free him from Russia.

(Available at the website of the Government, <www.valitsus.ee/en/news/statement-prime-minister-roivas-eston-kohvers-verdict>, visited on 30 November 2016)

8/4

On 26 September, Eston Kohver (see items 8/2 and 8/3) was released by Russia as a result of prisoners exchanged. In return, Estonia released

Aleksei Dressen who had spied for Russia and had been convicted for treason. On the same day, the Prime Minister commented the event:

> One year and three weeks ago Estonian security officer Eston Kohver was abducted by Russian Security Services from Estonian territory. His illegal detention – a clear and grave violation of international law – is finally over. Eston Kohver is safe and sound at home, in Estonia, with his family and loved ones.

(Available at the website of the Government, <www.valitsus.ee/en/news/statement-prime-minister-taavi-roivas-eston-kohvers-release>, visited on 30 November 2016)

Part Nine: II. A. State Territory – Boundaries and frontiers – Delimitation

9/1

On 27 October, the Foreign Affairs Committee of the *Riigikogu* (Parliament) started the legislative proceedings of the bill on the ratification of the State Border Treaty and the Maritime Border Treaty between the Republic of Estonia and the Russian Federation. The treaties were signed on 18 February 2014 by then Foreign Minister Urmas Paet and Russian Foreign Minister Sergei Lavrov.

For years, there have been debates whether and how new border treaties affect the Peace Treaty of Tartu (1920) where Russia "unreservedly recognises" the independence of Estonia and renounced in perpetuity all rights to the territory of Estonia. The treaty is regarded as the "birth certificate" of Estonia. While Estonia holds that the treaty is still valid, Russia claims that the treaty lost its validity in 1940, when Estonia was incorporated to the Soviet Union. Also, Russia does not recognise that Estonia restored its independence in 1991 (i.e. state continuity), but considers Estonia a new state that was created in 1991. As a result, according to Russia, the Peace Treaty of Tartu is not applicable because the other party of that bilateral treaty does not exist anymore. Some fear that if Estonia ratifies new peace treaties, Estonia would also abandon the Peace Treaty of Tartu. It should be noted that the delimitation of borders was merely one issue address in the latter treaty (Article III).

The Chairman of the Foreign Affairs Committee Sven Mikser said that:

> [W]e once again acknowledged that the border treaties establish only where the border line between the two states runs, and their ratification will not attempt to solve any other disagreements, including those concerning history.

Foreign Minister Marina Kaljurand emphasised that the treaties are technical agreements that establish the state border on the land and the border between territorial waters. She added that the treaties will make the state border clearer and easier to guard:

> I am convinced that a legally drawn up and correctly marked state border will strengthen the security of the Republic of Estonia even more.

The treaties determine the state border between Estonia and Russia, and delimit the areas of Narva River and the maritime areas of the Gulf of Finland between the two countries. The state border that is agreed upon mostly coincides with the existing guarded temporary control line. In comparison to the present control line, certain lands will be transferred by both sides. According to the treaties, the changes on both sides of the control line will be equal on the lakes and on the mainland. On the Estonian side, most of the plots of land that are to be transferred are already owned by the state, but some still belong to private persons and the state has to acquire them.

(Available at the website of the *Riigikogu*, <www.riigikogu.ee/en/press-releases/the-riigikogu-is-conducting-the-legislative-proceedings-on-the-bill-on-the-ratification-of-the-estonian-russian-border-treaties>, visited on 30 November 2016)

Part Sixteen: I. Use of Force – Prohibition of the use of force

16/1

On 12 February, Foreign Minister Keit Pentus-Rosimannus gave an annual speech on Estonia's foreign policy in the *Riigikogu* (parliament). Among other issues, she addressed the conflict in Ukraine and its wider consequences to the European security architecture.

Today we are faced with Russian aggression in Ukraine. This has affected and will continue to affect the future of our bilateral and multilateral relations and activities, both in our region and beyond, in the most direct way. The most recent developments have put in doubt the viability of the European co-operative security architecture, which is based on the OSCE Helsinki Final Act. [...]

I will start with what has likely scraped peoples' souls all over Estonia. There is a war two thousand kilometres away from us. Our position about the Russian aggression against Ukraine is clear – it is a serious violation of the fundamental principles of international relations and international law, a violation which has now resulted more than 5,000 casualties. Borders have been redrawn by force. A million and a half people have been forced to leave their homes. One and a half million people. There should be consequences for those responsible.

Did the conflict in Ukraine come as a complete surprise? Not at all. Just to recall Estonian National Security Concept adopted by the Parliament in 2010, stating that Russia is prepared to use military force to achieve its goals. We came to such a conclusion after the Russia-Georgia war in 2008. But the year 2002 was also very telling, when Russia essentially stopped the withdrawal of its military forces from Moldova and Georgia, thereby violating its commitments taken within the OSCE, as well as one of the basic principles of European security, namely the principle of host nation consent to the stationing of foreign forces. Unfortunately, we see that such a violation of the principles, a failure to respect the sovereignty of neighbouring countries, has been characteristic of the behaviour of Russia throughout this new 21st century. The mistake that was made by the international community following the war in Georgia, as they hurried to resume partnership relations with Putin's Russia, must not be repeated. A regime which sponsors the killing of civilians and annexes territories cannot be a partner. Not long as the behaviour does not change. In real terms. Not just on paper.

(Available at the website of the Ministry of Foreign Affairs, <www.vm.ee/en/news/address-foreign-minister-keit-pentus-rosimannus-riigikogu-behalf-government-estonia>, visited on 30 November 2016)

16/2

On 19 May, the Estonian Permanent Representative to the Council of Europe, Gea Rennel, delivered a statement at 125th Session of the Committee of Ministers of the Council of Europe. She addressed the situation in Ukraine and the consequences of the use of force.

> I would like to focus today on our common values enshrined in the Statute of Council of Europe. Let us remind that the Council of Europe was formed to achieve greater unity between its member states for the purpose of safeguarding and realizing the common ideals and principles. Using direct military force or hidden means of warfare for the purpose of aggression are not part of the values and principles dear to us. Vice versa – occupation or acquisition of a sovereign territory by another state must be condemned in the strictest terms. This is also clearly pointed out in Secretary General's recent report.
>
> The report also aptly reminds us that the current crisis is actually a crisis of values, which could have been avoided if each and every member state would have honored their commitments and obligations undertaken upon joining the Council of Europe. It is more than regretful that one of the member states has redrawn international borders unilaterally and through force. This act of violence has caused a lot of pain and suffering. The aggression has resulted in a tragic war. Thousands of people have lost their lives and many more have been forced to leave their homes. But, the annexation of Crimea in 2014 and subsequent military activities in South East Ukraine are unfortunately part of a longer chain of events.
>
> Since 2008 when Georgia became under a military attack by the Russian Federation, the use of force leading to occupation of neighboring sovereign states has become an unfortunate practice in the area of Council of Europe. This has led to the creation of black holes beyond the reach of international human rights monitoring mechanisms where grave violations of human rights and minority rights occur on a regular basis.
>
> Unfortunately the situation in Georgia has deteriorated within last few months. The so called treaties signed by the Russian Federation with occupied regions of Georgia only undermine the efforts

to return to the stable path of development. These treaties envisage policies and standards that suggest further possible breach of international law and order.

Now turning to Ukraine, we have to admit that the situation there is alarming, to say the least. It is clear that weapons and violence will not bring peace and stability. Sustainable political solution can only be based on the principles of the peaceful settlement, the full respect of Ukraine's independence, sovereignty and territorial integrity within its internationally recognized borders and the protection of human rights. We call upon all parties concerned to strictly respect Minsk Agreements and to take the necessary further steps for their swift imlementation.

(Available at the website of the Ministry of Foreign Affairs, <www.vm.ee/en/news/statement-ambassador-permanent-representative-estonia-council-europe-gea-rennel-125th-session>, visited on 30 November 2016)

ANNEX I. A. *Agreements signed by Estonia before 2015 but entered into force in regard to Estonia in 2015 – Bi- and multilateral agreements*

Title	Conclusion	Entry into Force
Amendments to the Agreement between the Kingdom of the Netherlands and the Republic of Estonia on mutual administrative assistance for the proper application of customs law and for the prevention, investigation and combating of customs offences	17.06.2014	01.02.2015
Cooperation Agreement between the Government of the Republic of Estonia and the Government of the Italian Republic on the Fight against Organized Crime, Terrorism and Illicit Drug Trafficking	08.09.2009	09.03.2015

Title	Conclusion	Entry into Force
Agreement between the Government of the Republic of Estonia and the Government of the Republic of Finland on the Prevention of, Preparation for and Resolution of Emergency Situation	29.01.2014	10.05.2015
Agreement between the Government of the Republic of Estonia and the Government of the Republic of Lithuania on Mutual Protection of Classified Information	28.05.2013	23.05.2015
Agreement between the Government of the Republic of Estonia and the Government of the Republic of Armenia in the fields of Education and Research	22.09.2014	27.05.2015
Agreement between the Government of the Republic of Estonia and the Cabinet of Ministers of Ukraine on the conditions of placement of Diplomatic Mission of the Republic of Estonia to Ukraine and Diplomatic Mission of Ukraine to the Republic of Estonia	11.04.2013	04.09.2015
Protocol Between the Government of the Republic of Estonia and the Swiss Federal Council Amending the Convention of 11 June 2002 between the Government of the Republic of Estonia and the Swiss Federal Council for the Avoidance of Double Taxation with Respect to Taxes on Income and on Capital	25.08.2014	16.10.2015

Title	Conclusion	Entry into Force
Headquarters Agreement between the Government of the Republic of Estonia and the European Agency for the Operational Management of Large-Scale IT Systems in the Area of Freedom, Security and Justice	19.12.2014	12.11.2015
Convention between the Republic of Estonia and the Grand Duchy of Luxembourg for the Avoidance of Double Taxation and the Prevention of Fiscal Evasion with Respect to Taxes on Income and on Capital	07.07.2014	11.12.2015
Protocol amending the Agreement between the Government of the Republic of Estonia and the Government of the People's Republic of China for the Avoidance of Double Taxation and the Prevention of Fiscal Evasion with Respect to Taxes on Income	09.12.2014	18.12.2015

ANNEX I. B. *Agreements signed by Estonia before 2015 but entered into force in regard to Estonia in 2015 – Conventions*

Title	Conclusion	Entry into Force
Amendments to the Annex of the Protocol of 1978 relating to the International Convention for the Prevention of Pollution from Ships, 1973 (Amendments to Annexes I and II)	17.05.2013	01.01.2015
Amendments to Annex B to the Protocol of 1988 Relating to the International Convention on Load Lines, 1966, as amended	21.06.2013	01.01.2015
Council of Europe Convention on Action against Trafficking in Human Beings	16.05.2005	01.06.2015

Title	Conclusion	Entry into Force
Amendments to the Annex of the Protocol of 1997 to Amend the International Convention for the Prevention of Pollution from Ships, 1973, as modified by the Protocol of 1978 relating thereto (Amendments to Annex VI and the NOx Technical Code 2008)	04.04.2014	01.09.2015
Convention for the Establishment of a European Space Agency	30.05.1975	01.09.2015

ANNEX II. A. *Agreements signed by Estonia in 2015 – Bi- and multilateral agreements*

Title	Conclusion	Entry into Force
Agreement between the Government of the Republic of Estonia and the Government of Georgia on International Road Transport of Passengers and Goods	13.01.2015	01.05.2015
Agreement between the Government of the Republic of Estonia and the Government of the Republic of Latvia on Co-operation in the Combating of the Effects of Marine Pollution	16.01.2015	16.01.2015
Implementing Protocol between the Government of the Republic of Estonia and the Cabinet of Ministers of Ukraine on the Implementation of the Agreement between the European Community and Ukraine on Readmission of Persons	14.01.2015	13.04.2016

Title	Conclusion	Entry into Force
Agreement between the Government of the Republic of Estonia and the European Space Agency Concerning the Accession of Estonia to the Convention for the Establishment of a European Space Agency and Related Terms and Conditions	04.02.2015	01.09.2015
Agreement between the Government of the United States of America and the Government of the Republic of Estonia	09.06.2015	09.06.2015
Arrangement between the Republic of Estonia and the Republic of Finland on Visa Representation	02.07.2015	03.07.2015
Agreement between the Government of the Republic of Estonia and the Government of the State of Kuwait on Visa Exemption for Holders of Diplomatic Passports	25.09.2015	11.05.2016
Protocol between the Republic of Estonia and Georgia to amend the Agreement between the Republic of Estonia and Georgia on the Promotion and Reciprocal Protection of Investments	02.11.2015	21.11.2016
Agreement between the Government of the Republic of Estonia and the Government of the Republic of Uzbekistan on Visa Exemption for Holders of Diplomatic Passports	03.12.2015	05.08.2016
Arrangement between the Republic of Estonia and the Republic of Italy on Visa Representation	11.12.2015	01.01.2016

Title	Conclusion	Entry into Force
Agreement between the Government of the Republic of Estonia and the Government of Turkmenistan on Visa Exemption for Holders of Diplomatic Passports	12.12.2015	01.04.2016

ANNEX II. B. *Agreements signed by Estonia in 2015 – Conventions*

Title	Conclusion	Entry into Force
Amendments to the Annex of the Protocol of 1978 relating to the International Convention for the Prevention of Pollution from Ships, 1973 (Amendments to Annexes I, II, IV and V)	15.05.2015	
Amendments to the Annex of the International Convention for the Prevention of Pollution from Ships, 1973, as modified by the Protocol of 1978 relating thereto (Amendments to Annex I)	15.05.2015	
Amendments to Part A of the Seafarers' Training, Certification and Watchkeeping (STCW) Code	11.06.2015	
Amendments to the International Convention on Standards of Training, Certification and Watchkeeping for Seafarers (STCW), 1978, as amended	11.06.2015	
Amendments to the Protocol of 1988 Relating to the International Convention for the Safety of Life at Sea, 1974	11.06.2015	
Paris Agreement	12.12.2015	04.12.2016

Republic of Latvia Materials on International Law 2015

Edited by Kristaps Tamužs*

[*Editorial Notes:*

1. Republic of Latvia Materials on International Law 2015 (RLMIL 2015) have been classified according to the Recommendation (97)11 of 12 June 1997 of the Committee of Ministers of Council of Europe, as applied by the British Yearbook of International Law from the year 1997, with certain minor amendments.

2. The RLMIL mostly concern the opinions made by the institutions and officials of Latvia. Often, different officials expressed views on same issues. In order to prevent unnecessary repetition, the editor has selected materials from the highest possible level. The statements of the officials and in particular the decisions of the courts have been occasionally edited in order to ensure brevity, focus and consistency.

3. There were several recurring topics in the speeches given and statements made by officials, for example, the conflict in Ukraine and the Latvian officials' strong endorsement of the Minsk agreement. A concern was raised on several occasions about the ongoing humanitarian crisis in Syria. The President as well as the Minister of Foreign Affairs also continued to express Latvia's continued support for a reform of the United Nations Security Council.

The work of the Latvian Ministry of Foreign Affairs as well as other state institutions primarily focused on the Latvian presidency of the European Union during the first half of 2015. Within this framework Latvia also hosted the summit meeting of the Eastern Partnership on 21 and 22 May

---

* LL.M.; Legal Advisor, the Constitutional Court of the Republic of Latvia; Visiting Lecturer, Riga Graduate School of Law and Riga Stradiņš University. The case-law of the Supreme Court of Latvia cited in the Republic of Latvia Materials on International Law 2015 have been kindly selected and edited by Ms. Anita Zikmane, head of the Division of Case-law and Research of the Supreme Court.

2015. Latvia's presidency focused on a united, active and principled implementation of the Common Foreign and Security Policy of the European Union.

4. On 21 October 2014 Latvia was elected as a member of the UN Human Rights Council and its two-year mandate commenced in 2015.

5. In 2015 the European Court of Human Rights communicated 18 cases to the Latvian Government, handed down seven judgments and declared eight cases inadmissible by a decision of a seven-judge Chamber. Further 11 cases were declared inadmissible by decisions of three-judge committees and 387 cases were declared inadmissible by unpublished decisions of either a single-judge formation or a three-judge committee.]

Part One: I. B. International Law in general – Nature, basis, purpose – History

1/1

On 23 July, in commemoration of the 75th anniversary of the Sumner Welles Declaration, Professor Paulis Lazda presented a lecture at the Ministry of Foreign Affairs entitled "Latvia's Uninterrupted de iure Independence: Sumner Welles' Policy of Denying the Legitimacy of the Soviet Russian Occupation".

During the event the State Secretary of the Foreign Ministry, Mr. Andrejs Pildegovičs, highlighted that

> already on 23 July 1940 the Acting Secretary of State of the United States of America, Sumner Welles, denounced the USSR's use of military force against the Baltic States and put forward an important foreign policy doctrine on the non-recognition of the legitimacy and legality of their occupation – neither *de iure* nor *de facto*.
>
> The occupation by the Soviet Union was condemned as illegitimate, predatory and "contrary to the rule of reason, of justice and of law, which are the basis of modern civilisation itself".
>
> This Declaration became the foundation for a long-term policy of democratic nations that to a great extent determined and influenced relations with the USSR for five decades. The Truman Doc-

trine of 1947 did not recognize changes in the world that were made through the use of force. As the result, the "empire of evil" (the USSR) collapsed and the Baltic States regained their freedom.

...

The policy of *de iure* non-recognition of occupation is quite relevant also in the current circumstances. Considering how the occupation of the Baltic States took place and the ensuing policy of non-recognition of this action by democracies across the world, confidence is inspired that it will be pursued also in other cases, such as, for instance, the illegal and illegitimate annexation of Crimea by the Russian Federation. We are convinced that Crimea will one day be able to make its own free choices, and its people will eventually again be given true freedom of choice.

The conceptual basis for the policy adopted by democratic, civilised countries to oppose any attempt to set a precedent through annexation of territory is rooted in the policy of non-recognition of Baltic occupation."

In his report, Professor Paulis Lazda underscored the significance of the document and the strong character of Sumner Welles.

"It was the Welles doctrine that as early as in July 1940 denounced Soviet occupation as unacceptable for both legal and humanitarian reasons, thereby perpetuating the existence Latvia and the other Baltic States in a political sense. The Welles Declaration in fact 'delegitimised' the USSR, challenging the legal base of its actions and exhibited its imperial ambition. 'Soviet' Latvia did not become a recognised and legitimate part of the USSR, instead it came to be regarded as a territory occupied by force. ...

Sumner Welles rejected compromises and called for foreign policy to be built on a foundation of modern principles. His firm position protected Latvia and the other Baltic States, such that their existence de iure was uninterrupted until the restoration of independence in 1991.

(Available at the website of the Ministry of Foreign Affairs, <http://www.mfa.gov.lv/en/news/latest-news/47468-the-75th-anniversary-of-the-sumner-welles-declaration-commemorated-in-latvia>, visited on 18 July 2017)

1/2

The Sumner Welles Declaration was also invoked by the President of Latvia, Mr. Raimonds Vējonis, during his speech at the 70th session of the United Nations General Assembly:

> In July, we marked the 75th anniversary since the Sumner Welles Declaration on the non-recognition policy of the illegal Soviet annexation of the Baltic States. This policy reflected the international law-based principle that change of borders by force is not acceptable. The firm stance of the international community in support of this principle has been of great importance to us.

(Available at the website of the Chancery of the President, <http://www.president.lv/pk/content/?cat_id=603&art_id=23483>, visited on 24 July 2017)

Part Four: II. Relationship between International Law and Internal Law – Application and implementation of international law in internal law

The Constitutional Court of the Republic of Latvia continued to demonstrate its commitment to the doctrine of the Latvian legal system's openness to international law by extensively invoking the provisions of various instruments of international law, including in particular the European Convention on Human Rights.

4/1

In its judgment of 5 February 2015 in the case no. 2014-03-01 the Constitutional Court dealt with a challenge to the constitutionality of a legal provision that disqualified non-party entities from participation in local elections in larger municipalities.

> 20.1. It follows from the explanations provided at the court hearing by the Saeima's representative that the legitimate aim of the dif-

ferential treatment is the strengthening of the system of political parties ...

Political parties are an important element of a democratic state. As the Constitutional Court has already recognised in its case-law, a political party is an association of persons that has a certain ideology and the main aim of which is gaining political power to implement this ideology ... in accordance with the aims and principles put into the party's programme ... Political parties form the link between the society and the state power, ensuring an organised participation of the society in political processes. The European Court of Human Rights ... has recognised that political parties differ from other organisations involved in politics by making a proposal to electors regarding a comprehensive model of society and are able to implement this proposal if they come to the power (see the ECHR Grand Chamber judgement of 13 February 2003 in the case "*Refah Partısı [the Welfare Party] v. Turkey*", applications no. 41340/98, 41342/98, 41343/98 and 41344/98, para. 87). ...

Thus, strengthening the system of political parties is aimed at the protection of a democratic state order and may be recognised as being a legitimate aim for establishing a differential treatment.

...

20.2. ... It is possible to establish any representative body – a parliament or a local government council – if the electors have the possibility to choose for which of the submitted lists of candidates to vote. Also the ECHR, in underscoring the necessity of the possibility to choose, in its case-law with regard to Article 3 of Protocol no. 1 to the European Convention ... in connection with election of legislator has noted that free manifestation of the people's opinion is unimaginable where a system of political parties that would represent opinions that are widespread among the population of the state is non-existent (see the ECHR Judgement of 15 April 2014 in the case "*Oran v. Turkey*", applications no. 28881/07 and 37920/07, para. 57). These insights are applicable also to the election of a local government council as a representative body.

(Available at the website of the Constitutional Court, <http://www.satv.tiesa.gov.lv/wp-content/uploads/2014/01/2014-03-01_Spriedums_ENG.pdf>, visited on 24 July 2017)

4/2

The Constitutional Court's judgment of 25 March 2015 in the case no. 2014-11-0103 addressed the issue of calculation of tax payable by the producers of electrical energy by small hydro-electrical power plants.

> 19. Any restriction upon the fundamental rights must be based upon circumstances and arguments regarding its necessity, i.e., the restriction must be established for the sake of important interests – a legitimate aim ... The Constitutional Court has recognised that in the legal proceedings before the Constitutional Court the duty to identify the legitimate aim falls upon the institution, which has adopted the contested act ...
>
> The Saeima states that the restriction upon the fundamental rights has been established to balance the public interest to live in a benevolent environment with economic development. I.e., the legitimate aim of the restriction upon the fundamental rights is said to be ensuring other persons' rights and public welfare. ...
>
> A number of the European Union and international documents have emphasised the importance of water as resource. The Constitutional Court has recognised that the regulatory enactments of the European Union, insofar as the fundamental principles of the Satversme are not affected, must be taken into consideration in the interpretation of the national regulatory enactments ... The 1st recital in the Preamble to the Water Framework Directive notes that water should be treated as heritage and should be protected. Moreover, a requirement to the member states of the European Union to provide incentives to use water resources efficiently follows from Article 9 of the Water Framework Directive.
>
> [P]ara. 19 in the final report the United Nations 2012 Conference on Sustainable Development recognizes the critical importance of water as resource in ensuring sustainable development (see: Report of the United Nations Conference on Sustainable Development. Rio de Janeiro, Brazil, 20 – 22 June 2012. United Nations: New York, 2012,

p. 23 ...). Even though th[is] document ... is not legally binding, nevertheless the findings that it comprises should be recognised as being sufficiently authoritative ... It follows from the above that a tax to be paid for using such an important resource as water can serve the purpose of protecting public welfare.

...

Thus, the restriction upon the fundamental rights has a legitimate aim – the protection of public welfare.

20. Upon establishing the legitimate aim of the restriction of fundamental rights, its compliance with the principle of proportionality must be examined. Since in the case under review the constitutionality of a restriction upon the right to own property which follows from the obligation to pay a tax is being examined, the Constitutional Court must establish whether the specificity of the tax law influences the scope of constitutional review.

The Constitutional Court has recognised that in the field of tax law the legislator cannot be required to meet the same standards as, for example, in the field of ensuring and protecting civil or political rights ... The State enjoys broad discretion in establishing and implementing its taxation policy... It comprises the right to choose tax rates and the categories of persons that the taxes apply to, as well as the right to provide details of the respective regulation. In examining the limits of the legislator's discretion with regard to establishing a tax for a specific object, it must be taken into consideration that the Satversme *expressis verbis* authorizes the legislator to adopt the State budget, i.e., to determine the revenue and expenditure of the State. The Satversme authorises the legislator to implement such fiscal policy that would ensure the revenue necessary for the State ...

Thus, the State must provide for its sustainable development, *inter alia*, also in a way to ensure that the State budget would always have the resources necessary for performing the functions of the State. Moreover, the Constitutional Court has already noted that a person's right to own property cannot be examined in insolation from a person's constitutional duty to pay taxes established in due procedure ...

The finding that the rights that follow from Article 105 of the Satversme should be interpreted in interconnection with Article 1 of Protocol no. 1 to the European Convention ... has become embedded in the case-law of the Constitutional Court. It follows from the case-law of the European Court of Human Rights ... that the cases related to the establishment of the obligation to pay taxes are predominantly examined in the context of control of the use of property ... It has also been recognised in the case-law of the ECHR that a tax, as to its nature, must not be confiscatory (see, for example, the ECHR judgement of 25 July 2013 in the case *"Khodorkovskiy and Lebedev v. Russia"*, applications no. 11082/06 and 13772/05, para. 870). Whereas the Constitutional Court has recognised that in reviewing the legality of restricting fundamental rights it could chiefly examine whether the payment of the tax has not placed an excessive burden on the addressee and whether the legal regulation on taxes complies with the general principles of law ... Thus, in assessing whether the payment of a tax is not an excessive burden for the addressee, it must be considered, *inter alia*, whether the applied tax as to its nature is not confiscatory.

Thus, the specificity of the tax law influences the scope of the constitutional review.

...

25.2. The Constitutional Court underscores that in assessing whether the legitimate aim can be reached by other means, it must be taken into consideration that a more lenient measure is not just any other measure, but such that would allow reaching the legitimate aim in at least the same quality ... Moreover, in particular in assessing whether more lenient measures for reaching the legitimate aim exist, the Constitutional Court must abide by the limits of review that follow from the nature of the tax ...

As noted above, the natural resources tax should be considered an environmental tax. The Constitutional Court has recognised that tax laws perform also a regulatory function, i.e., balance the interests of the State and those of taxpayers, as well as influence the taxpayers' behaviour ... Thus, the legislator, in exercising its discretion in establishing taxation policy, has the right to support or restrict, through the natural resources tax, the use of a particular economic activity, technology or natural resource, thus providing for sustainable development of the State. I.e., the legislator has the right to select such measures for reaching the defined legitimate aim that can influence a person's interest to take up particular types of commercial activities or employ particular technologies in his or her commercial activities. *Inter alia*, the legislator can, by using the tax, also increase the costs of the respective commercial activity and, thus, decrease the amount of income that the person had planned to gain from the respective activity.

Thus, if the legislator, by exercising its discretion, has decided to introduce a tax with a regulatory function, the absence of such a tax cannot be recognised as being a more lenient measure. In such a case, similarly to the case under review, the legislator wishes to reach two purposes by the restriction upon the fundamental rights – to leave a particular impact upon a person's behaviour and to ensure revenue for the State budget. This means that the absence of an obligation to pay the natural resources tax would not allow reaching the legitimate aim of the restriction upon the fundamental rights in at least the same quality.

If the Constitutional Court has established that the principle for calculating the tax which the legislator has chosen has a reasonable explanation, based upon unbiased and rational considerations, then the Constitutional Court has no right to provide that the legislator should select another tax rate, another principle for calculating the tax or should include other elements in the formula for calculating the tax. Likewise, the ECHR, in examining case with regard to restrictions upon human rights in connection with the obligation to pay tax, does not assess the choices made by states in the field of taxation, unless such choice lacks reasonable grounds (see, for example, the ECHR judgement of 4 July 2013 in the case "*R.Sz. v. Hungary*", application no. 41838/11, para. 48). It has been established in the case under review that the legislator considered alternatives to the contested norms, and certainty has been gained that the principle for calculating the tax has a reasonable explanation, which is based upon unbiased and rational considerations.

Thus, there are no more lenient means that would allow reaching the legitimate aim of the restriction upon the fundamental rights in at least the same quality

(Available at the website of the Constitutional Court, <http://www.satv.tiesa.gov.lv/wp-content/uploads/2014/04/2014-11-0103_Spriedums_ENG.pdf>, visited on 24 July 2017)

4/3

Case no. 2014-13-01, in which the Constitutional Court adopted a judgment on 16 April 2015, concerned the constitutionality of a provision of the Law of Civil Procedure, which made it impossible to obtain a reversal of the execution of a court judgment in labour disputes, save for some narrowly defined circumstances.

> 11. ... The ECHR has indicated that the concept of fair trial contains the right to demand that the State ensure an effective enforcement of a judgment of a court (see, for example, the 22 June 2004 judgment of the ECHR in the case *"Pini and Others v. Romania"*, applications no. 78028/01 and 78030/01, paras. 174-189, and the 24 July 2003 judgment in the case *"Ryabykh v. Russia"*, application no. 52854/99, paras. 54-56). The ECHR has also emphasised that the rights guaranteed by Article 6 of the Convention would be illusory if a final, binding judicial decision would not be enforceable to the detriment of one party to the proceedings (see the 7 May 2002 judgment in the case *"Burdov v. Russia"*, application no. 59498/00, para. 34, and the 4 November 2014 decision in the case *"Popov and Others v. Russia"*, application no. 20347/09, para. 17). Taking this into account, Article 92 of the Satversme is to be interpreted in such a way that it includes the guarantees of an effective enforcement of a judicial decision, since without such guarantees the remaining principles of a fair trial would become meaningless.

(Available, only in Latvian, at the website of the Constitutional Court, <http://www.satv.tiesa.gov.lv/wp-content/uploads/2016/02/2014-13-01_Spriedums.pdf>, visited on 24 July 2017)

4/4

The Constitutional Court's judgment of 2 July 2015 in case no. 2015-01-01 extensively referred to the practice of the ECHR and also to UN documents in order to resolve the potential conflict between an obligation of private individuals to display the national flag on certain specified days and the negative freedom of expression.

> 11.1. ... In establishing the content of fundamental rights defined in the Satversme, Latvia's international commitments in the field of human rights must be taken into consideration ... The international human rights provisions on the constitutional level are a means for determining the content and the scope of fundamental rights and at the same time are directly applicable in Latvia, insofar these are legally binding upon the state. The State's obligation to abide by the international commitments in the field of human rights that it has assumed follows from Article 89 of the Satversme, laws and international treaties binding upon Latvia. The Constitutional Court underscores the aim of reaching harmony between the norms of human rights included in the Satversme and the international human rights provisions ...
>
> The Constitutional Court has recognised that the content of Article 100 of the Satversme can be revealed in full by taking into account Article 19 of the ... International Covenant on Civil and Political Rights ..., as well as Article 10 of the Convention ... Legal literature emphasizes the substantive link between the inclusion of Chapter VIII "Fundamental Human Rights", thus, also Article 100, into the Satversme with the Convention and the Covenant ...
>
> 11.2. The initial historical objective of human rights – to protect a person against unfounded interference by the State in the sphere of his liberty – can be discerned also in the content of the right to freedom of speech.
>
> The United Nations Commission on Human Rights has recognised the negative aspect of the freedom of speech, underscoring that any form of effort to coerce a person to express one's opinion is to be considered as a violation of "the freedom not to express one's opinion (General Comment no. 34: Freedom of opinion and expression (Art. 19): 10/09/2011. CCPR/C/GC/34, para. 10). This has been recog-

nised also within the European system of human rights protection (see the report by the European Commission on Human Rights of 1 March 1994 in the case "*Goodwin v. the United Kingdom*", para. 48).

The case-law of the ECHR includes references to the possible infringement of the negative aspect in the freedom of speech (see, for example, the judgement of 3 April 2012 by the Grand Chamber in the case "*Gillberg v. Sweden*", application no. 41723/06, para. 84), it has also been recognised that an individual may express one's opinion by showing one's attitude and by behaviour (see, for example, the judgement of 23 September 1998 in the case "*Steel and Others v. the United Kingdom*", application no. 24838/94, paras. 90 and 92). Thus, the showing of attitude may manifest itself as not expressing one's opinion. An individual may choose to be "free from" expressing one's opinion and thus exercise his or her rights to the freedom of speech in its negative aspect.

...

11.4. The Constitutional Court has recognised in its case-law that everyone has the right to freely receive information and express their opinion in any form – orally, in writing, visually, using artistic means of expression, etc. ....

The freedom of speech, alongside its traditional manifestations, for example, speeches, diversity of opinion in mass media, participation in demonstrations and other events, comprises also various forms of artistic expression, for example, fiction, painting, music, as well as other combined forms of expression, *inter alia*, use of symbols (see, for example, ECHR judgement of 21 March 2002 in the case "*Nikula v. Finland*", application no. 31611/96, para. 46, and judgement of 21 October 2014 in the case "*Murat Vural v. Turkey*", application no. 9540/07, paras. 44 and 46).

It is recognised in para. 52 of the ECHR judgement of 24 July 2012 in the case "*Fáber v. Hungary*", application no. 40721/08, that the use of a flag with a symbolic meaning is to be recognised as an expression of the freedom of speech. It is also emphasized in legal literature that the freedom of speech may manifest itself as "symbolic expression" ... Thus, placing of the Latvian national flag on a residential building owned by a natural person is also one of the expressions of the freedom of speech.

The petitioner also recognises the symbolic meaning of the Latvian national flag; however, on that particular day she had chosen not to express her opinion by placing the Latvian national flag on the residential building. Thus, the petitioner exercised her right to the freedom of speech in its negative aspect.

Thus the scope of the first sentence in Article 100 of the Satversme comprises also placing of the Latvian national flag on a residential building owned by a natural person and the choice not to place it.

...

16.1. The Constitutional Court must establish whether the restriction upon the freedom of speech that the contested norms comprise is an appropriate measure for reaching the legitimate aim in a democratic society.

The Saeima notes that the established rights restriction is appropriate for reaching its legitimate aim, since placing of the Latvian national flag on residential building ensures not only that all the residents of the particular building participate in a common commemoration of the respective historical events, but also that "a noteworthy part of the rest of society is reached" by this. ...

The Saeima ..., in providing grounds for the obligation to place the Latvian national flag on residential buildings, underscore[s] that the history of development of Latvia as a democratic state and the political situation, requiring that common historic memory is maintained and consolidated, must be taken into consideration. The historical and constitutional peculiarities of each state may determine the choice of special measures for reaching the legitimate aim that has been set. In Latvia the obligation to place, on the dates specified by the Saeima, the Latvian national flag on residential buildings should be considered as being such special choice. The grounds for introducing such special measures have also been recognised in the ECHR case-law (see, for example, the judgement of

16 March 2006 by the Grand Chamber of ECHR in the case "*Ždanoka v. Latvia*", application no. 58278/00, paras. 95 and 121).

In reviewing the appropriateness of the selected measure in the case under review, it must be taken into consideration that the expression of beliefs showing loyalty to the state should be separated from expressing opinions showing loyalty to a particular ideology or political force (see the judgement of 27 April 2010 by the Grand Chamber of ECHR in the case "*Tănase v. Moldova*", application no. 7/08, paras. 166 and 167). The necessity to separate the views has been recognised also by the Saeima ..., emphasizing that the imposed obligation does not demand expressing opinion that would be loyal to any political force. ...

Thus, it can be concluded that the obligation to place, on the dates specified by the contested norms of the Law on the National Flag, the Latvian national flag on residential buildings owned by private persons is an appropriate measure for reaching the legitimate aim.

...

16.5. The Constitutional Court notes: the fact that a penalty is envisaged for failing to place the Latvian national flag on residential buildings owned by natural persons on the dates specified by the Saeima changes the legal nature of the restriction upon an individual's fundamental rights. I.e., it could be possible that the Latvian national flag is placed on the residential building only because of the potential penalty and not in commemoration of the historical events important for the Latvian state. ...

I. Ijabs expresses the opinion that no "pressing social need" can be discerned in connection with the imperative obligation to place the Latvian national flag on residential buildings owned by natural persons, which has been indicated in the ECHR case-law as a necessary precondition for recognising a restriction upon an individual's right as being proportional (see, for example, the judgement of 8 July 2008 in the case "*Vajnai v. Hungary*", application no. 33629/06, para. 43, and the judgement of 6 May 2003 in the case "*Perna v. Italy*", application no. 48898/99, para. 39(b)).

The Constitutional Court notes: if it is possible that an individual will be punished for not expressing one's opinion, then this aspect influences not only the incentives for the individual's actions in a particular situation, but also for other expressions of an individual's freedom of speech.

...

16.7. In the case under review, the penalty envisaged in the contested ... norm for failure to place the Latvian national flag on residential buildings owned by natural persons not only leaves an impact upon the actual actions taken by an individual; i.e., forces him to perform the obligation –to place the Latvian national flag on his residential building on the dates specified in law (primary impact), but also causes a negative impact upon the manifestations of the freedom of speech in society in general (secondary impact). The ECHR case-law underscores that the possible penalty that has been envisaged for an individual in the field of the freedom of speech leaves a negative impact upon the freedom of speech in society as a whole (see, for example, the judgement of 10 December 2007 by the Grand Chamber of the ECHR in the case "*Stoll v. Switzerland*", application no. 69698/01, paras. 153 and 154). In relation to this it has been recognised that the introduction of even minor penalties in the field of freedom of speech leaves a negative impact (chilling effect) upon society in general and therefore is admissible only in exceptional cases (see, for example, the ECHR judgement of 21 March 2002 in the case "*Nikula v. Finland*", application no. 31611/96, paras. 54 and 55, and the judgement of 14 March 2013 in the case "*Eon v. France*", application no. 26118/10, para. 61).

If a legislator establishes an administrative penalty linked to a restriction upon the negative aspect of the freedom of speech, then it should provide sufficient substantiation for it. It has been recognised in the ECHR case-law that the decisive condition for establishing the disproportionality of the penalty linked to a restriction upon the freedom of speech is not the severity of the penalty but the fact that the legislator has not provided a sufficient substantiation for the necessity of the penalty (see, for example, the judgement of 26 September 1995 by the Grand Chamber of ECHR in the case "*Vogt v. Germany*", application no. 17851/91, paras. 52(ii), 52(iii) and

53, the ECHR judgement of 27 May 2003 in the case *"Skałka v. Poland"*, application no. 43425/98, paras. 35 and 38, and the judgement of 14 March 2013 in the case *"Eon v. France"*, application no. 26118/10, para. 52). The case materials do not lead to assurance that with regard to the contested ... norm the Saeima has provided a sufficient substantiation regarding the existence of an exceptional situation.

The restriction upon an individual's freedom of speech by establishing a penalty cannot be justified by general assumptions regarding special social need (see, for example, the ECHR judgement of 8 July 2008 in the case *"Vajnai v. Hungary"*, application no. 33629/06, para. 55). The Saeima has pointed to the circumstances that were relevant at the time when the contested norms were adopted; however, it has not substantiated the current necessity for an administrative penalty as an element of the restriction upon the freedom of speech in a democratic society. The freedom of speech in its negative aspect manifests itself as refraining from actions. If an individual by his actions had endangered democratic society or other persons' interests, then there would be grounds to apply, for example, Section 93 of the Criminal Law, which provides for criminal liability for desecration of state symbols, *inter alia*, the Latvian national flag. An individual's freedom of speech in its negative aspect does not manifest itself as such a potentially endangering action but as refraining from actions.

(Available at the website of the Constitutional Court, <http://www.satv.tiesa.gov.lv/wp-content/uploads/2015/01/2015-01-01_Spriedums_ENG.pdf>, visited on 24 July 2017)

4/5

The Constitutional Court adopted a judgment in the case no. 2015-03-01 on 21 December 2015. The case concerned the constitutionality of accountability mechanisms that had been introduced with the purpose of controlling the activities of insolvency administrators. The particular dispute concerned the legal status of insolvency administrators who are also sworn attorneys.

21.2.2. ... The European Court of Human Rights ... has noted that the mutual exchange of information between an advocate and his client, irrespectively of its purpose, deserves a special protection. An advocate cannot perform his duties of office if he cannot guarantee confidentiality in the client's matters. Confidentiality of advocates is one of the principles of legal proceedings that are recognised in states governed by the rule of law. However, the confidentiality principle is not absolute. ECHR has examined the obligation of sworn attorneys to report on suspicious transactions and has recognised that it is not an incommensurate restriction upon the principle of advocates' confidentiality (see the ECHR judgement of 6 December 2012 in the case *"Michaud v. France"*, application no. 12323/11, paras. 117, 118 and 123–131).

The protection of the mutual exchange of information between an advocate and his client as a professional secret follows from the rights of the client not to assist in incriminating himself (see the ECHR judgement of 24 July 2008 in the case *"André and Another v. France"*, application no. 18603/03, para. 41). In view of the fact that the information indicated in an advocate's bank account statements is protected by professional secrecy, ECHR has recognised that law enforcement institutions when scrutinising an advocate's bank account statements had to invite representatives of an independent institution – the bar association – to participate (see the ECHR judgement of 1 December 2015 in the case *"Brito Ferrinho Bexiga Villa-Nova v. Portugal"*, application no. 69436/10, para. 57).

Legal assistance provided by an advocate is effective and ensures protection of a person's rights and lawful interests in a fair trial only if confidentiality regarding the client's matters is guaranteed. There may be situations when the confidentiality principle prohibits requesting information not only about the content of legal assistance provided by an advocate but also about the concrete persons it has been provided to. This prohibition applies also to state institutions, which must respect an advocate's independence.

(Available at the website of the Constitutional Court, <http://www.satv.tiesa.gov.lv/wp-content/uploads/2015/01/2015-03-01_Spriedums_ENG.pdf>, visited on 24 July 2017)

4/6

On 12 November 2015 the Constitutional Court adopted a judgment in the case no. 2015-06-01, in which it was asked to examine the constitutionality of a legal provision that limited the disclosure of information about disciplinary cases against judges. In its judgment the Court had to arrive at a balance between the right to receive information and the guarantees of judicial independence and impartiality.

> 11.1. The Constitutional Court has recognised that the content of Article 100 of the Satversme can be revealed in full by taking into account Article 19 of the ... International Covenant on Civil and Political Rights ..., as well as Article 10 of the Convention ...
>
> The UN Human Rights Committee has indicated that Article 19(2) of the ICCPR protects the right of access to information that is possessed by state institutions, including judicial institutions, regardless of the way the information is stored, its sources or the time of its creation. States ought to provide for the necessary procedure enabling the individuals' access to information by adopting a certain legal framework with regards to open information (see General Comment no. 34: Freedom of opinion and expression (Art. 19): 10/09/2011. CCPR/C/GC/34, paras. 7 and 18).
>
> On the other hand, the case-law of the European Court of Human Rights ... indicates that Article 10(1) of the Convention cannot be interpreted in such a way that it guarantees a comprehensive right to access the information possessed by state institutions ...
>
> The impugned norm pertains to information that is related to one of the branches of state power, namely, the judicial power. The information in question is possessed by a state institution.
>
> The task of ... the judicial power is to ensure adjudication that guarantees the implementation of the constitution, the laws and other normative acts, the adherence to the principle of rule of law and the protection of human rights and freedoms ... The judicial powers protects fairness as one of the basic values of a state governed by the rule of law and it acts in accordance with the public interest.
>
> Information concerning the functioning of the justice system falls within the public interest. This has also been recognised by the case-law of the ECHR (see, for example, the ECHR Grand Chamber

judgment of 23 April 2015 in the case *"Morice v. France"*, application no. 29369/10, para. 128). ...

13.2. It follows from international documents and the normative acts of other states that the right to obtain information about disciplinary cases against judges may be restricted.

For instance, para. 17 of the United Nations Basic Principles on the Independence of the Judiciary requires that the examination of disciplinary cases against judges be kept confidential at the initial stage, unless otherwise requested by the judge (see Basic Principles on the Independence of the Judiciary. Adopted by the Seventh United Nations Congress on the Prevention of Crime and the Treatment of Offenders held at 18 Milan from 26 August to 6 September 1985 and endorsed by General Assembly resolutions 40/32 of 29 November 1985 and 40/146 of 13 December 1985) ...

16.2. The case-law of the Constitutional Court and the ECHR as well as international documents and legal literature point out the particular role of the judges within the society and also the need to protect the independence and maintain the authority of the judicial power.

The Constitutional Court has recognized that the protection of judges against all unfounded interference with the adjudication and their exercise of their tasks is significant in order to protect the rule of law for the benefit of the society and the state. The protection of the judicial independence serves the interests of anyone who is concerned by judicial proceedings. The need to protect the independence of judges is closely linked to the independence of the judicial power and therefore also to the implementation of the principle of separation of powers ... The ECHR has emphasised the importance, in a democratic society, of maintaining the authority of the judiciary (see the ECHR Grand Chamber judgment of 23 April 2015 in the case *"Morice v. France"*, application no. 29369/10, para. 170). In order for the judicial power to be able to successfully carry out its tasks, it ought to be trusted by the public. That is why it is necessary to protect the public trust in the judicial power against essentially groundless accusations, in particular taking into account the fact that the criticised judges and the judges in general

> are bound by the duty of confidentiality which prevents them from responding to such accusations (see, for example, the ECHR judgment of 26 April 1995 in the case *"Prager and Oberschlick v. Austria"*, application no, 15974/90, para. 34, and the judgment of 24 February 1997 in the case *"De Haes and Gijsels v. Belgium"*, application no. 19983/92, para. 37).

> ... the preamble of the Bangalore Principles of Judicial Conduct indicates that a competent, independent and impartial judiciary is essential if the courts are to fulfil their role in upholding constitutionalism and the rule of law (see the Bangalore Principles of Judicial Conduct, 29 April, 2003, United Nations Commission on Human Rights resolution 2003/43). The Universal Charter of the Judge, adopted by the International Association of Judges in 1999, in its Article 11 provides that the administration of disciplinary action towards judges must be organized in such a way that it does not compromise the judges' genuine independence (see the Universal Charter of the Judge. Adopted by the Central Council of the International Association of Judges, 1999). Albeit the above-mentioned documents have not been confirmed in accordance with the order how international treaties are confirmed, the Constitutional Court finds that they disclose significant general principles of functioning of the judicial power.

(Available, only in Latvian, at the website of the Constitutional Court, <http://www.satv.tiesa.gov.lv/wp-content/uploads/2016/02/2015-06-01_Spriedums.pdf>, visited on 25 July 2017)

4/7

On 23 November 2015 the Constitutional Court pronounced its judgment in the case no. 2015-10-01, which dealt with the prohibition for judges to receive benefits for taking care of their disabled children.

> 13. Article 110 of the Satversme provides: "The State shall protect and support marriage – a union between a man and a woman, the family, the rights of parents and rights of the child. The State shall provide special support to disabled children, children left without parental care or who have suffered from violence."

Among the rights guaranteed by Article 110 of the Satversme there is the right of children with a disability to special support and protection by the state ... Article 110 places an obligation on the state to guarantee to families with children at least the minimum of internationally recognised rights, including social rights ...

The right of children with disabilities to special protection is set down in the Convention on the Rights of People with Disabilities, to which Latvia is a state party. Article 7 of this Convention provides that states parties shall take all necessary measures to ensure the full enjoyment by children with disabilities of all human rights and fundamental freedoms on an equal basis with other children and also that in all actions concerning children with disabilities, the best interests of the child shall be a primary consideration.

The right of children with disabilities to special care is also guaranteed by the Convention on the Rights of a Child, to which Latvia is a state party. In accordance with Article 23(1) of this Convention states parties recognize that a mentally or physically disabled child should enjoy a full and decent life, in conditions which ensure dignity, promote self-reliance and facilitate the child's active participation in the community. Paragraph 2 of the same Article provides that states parties recognize the right of the disabled child to special care and shall encourage and ensure the extension, subject to available resources, to the eligible child and those responsible for his or her care, of assistance for which application is made and which is appropriate to the child's condition and to the circumstances of the parents or others caring for the child ... The United Nations Committee on the Rights of the Child indicates that the support to be provided to the family is meant to reduce the stress of the child's parents and to ensure the maintenance of a healthy family environment (see Committee on the Rights of the Child, General Comment No. 9, The Rights of Children with Disabilities, U.N.Doc. CRC/C/GC/9, 27 February 2007, p. 41).

17.2. The nature of the impugned norm is relevant for the resolution of the case ...

The purpose of the [law On Prevention of Conflict of Interest in Activities of Public Officials] is to ensure that the actions of public officials are in the public interest, prevent the influence of a personal or financial interest of any public official, his or her relatives or counterparties upon the actions of the public official, to promote openness regarding the actions of the public officials and their liability to the public, as well as public confidence regarding the actions of public officials ... The Constitutional Court accepts as justified the finding in the case-law of the ECHR that the status of a state official is characterised by a special bond of trust and loyalty with the state (see, for example, the ECHR decision of 18 November 2014 in the case *"Spūlis and Vaškevičs v. Latvia"*, applications no. 2631/10 and 12253/10, para. 41). The condition of particular reliability and loyalty to the state forms the basis of the limitations linked to the status of state officials; such limitations are not to be considered *per se* disproportional from the perspective of the principle of equality.

In order to achieve the purpose of the law ..., the impugned norm lists those state officials who are only allowed to carry out [additional activities], which [are] listed in that norm. The impugned norm is equally applicable to all the officials listed therein, including judges, without recognising any differences between them. Hence the impugned norm *per se* is neutral towards all judges. However, it places a judge in a different situation if the judge needs to provide assistant services to her child with a disability. Hence, the impugned norm, albeit neutral, nevertheless creates a different treatment of a judge who is prevented from providing assistant services to her child with a disability.

17.3. In order to establish whether the different treatment deriving from the impugned norm has an objective and reasonable basis, it needs to be determined whether the different treatment has a legitimate aim.

The Constitutional Court has established that in the proceedings before the Constitutional Court it is the institution which has issued the impugned legal act which has an obligation to indicate and substantiate the legitimate aim of the different treatment ... The Parliament ... indicates that the legitimate aim ... is to ensure the independence of the judicial power, to protect the right and legitimate interests of others and the democratic order of the state ...

On the other hand, the petitioner considers that the different treatment has no legitimate aim.

Article 83 of the Satversme provides that "judges shall be independent and subject only to the law". The independence of judges and courts guaranteed by this constitutional norm is one of the basic principles of a democratic state based on the rule of law ... The principle of judicial independence that is included in Article 83 of the Satversme requires the judicial system to ensure both the judicial independence globally and the independence of the judge in each individual case ...

The requirement of judicial independence that derives from international law documents falls within the scope of the right to a fair trial. Article 6 of the European Convention ... provides that everyone is entitled to a fair and public hearing within a reasonable time by an independent and impartial tribunal established by law. The wording of Article 14 of the [ICCPR] is similar. The Consultative Council of European Judges has emphasised that the independence of the court ought to be guaranteed with respect to both parties to a particular case but also with respect to the society at large (see Opinion No 1 (2001) of the Consultative Council of European Judges on Standards Concerning the Independence of the Judiciary and the Irremovability of Judges, Strasbourg, 23 November 2001, para. 11). Even though this document is not legally binding on the states, it nevertheless provides an authoritative opinion on the meaning of the principle of judicial independence. Hence the judicial independence guarantees the safeguarding of the rule of law, which serves the interests of the society and the state ...

In order to ensure a fair trial and judges' independence in each court proceedings, an appropriate legal regulation has been developed. In order to ensure judges' independence and impartiality in each specific case, the state in every law that governs the conduct of court proceedings has developed procedures for recusal and self-recusal of judges, has introduced a prohibition of hearing the same case more than once and has provided for other guarantees. On the other hand, at the institutional level the independence of the judicial power and the judges is ensured by means of a number of legal acts, including the Satversme and the [law On Prevention of Conflict of Interest in Activities of Public Officials].

Hence the impugned norm forms a part of the legal regime that ensures the openness and responsibility before the society of a judge as a public official and also ensures the independence of the judicial power in a democratic state.

18.2. In the case before the Court the interference with the petitioner's right to an [equal treatment] is caused exactly by the fact that the impugned norm is a neutral one or, in other words, it does not provide for a different treatment of persons in different situations. In certain situations an insufficient differentiation between groups of persons in different situations may lead to a violation of the principle of equal treatment (see the judgment of the Grand Chamber of the ECHR of 12 April 2006 in the case "*Stec and Others v. the United Kingdom*", applications no. 65731/01 and 65900/01, para. 51).

The Constitutional Court points out that the legislator is entitled to develop a system of normative acts that treats a particular group [of persons] differently, as long as such a system is [compatible] with the principle of equal treatment. One of the ways to ensure a different treatment of a group [of persons] which because of some significant characteristic is placed in different circumstances from other groups is to provide for the existence of appropriately differentiated categories [of persons] in the normative acts (see, for example, the judgment of the ECHR of 6 April 2000 in the case "*Thlimmenos v. Greece*", application no. 34369/97, para. 48) ...

The Constitutional Court recognises that it is impossible to govern each person's specific situation by law; nevertheless, it points out that the law ought to provide for a sufficiently differentiated treatment in order for a norm not to breach the principle of equality ... in different legal and factual circumstances. The ECHR in its case-law has postulated that the state enjoys a margin of appreciation in assessing whether and to what extent differences in otherwise similar situations justify a different treatment (see the judgment of the Grand Chamber of the ECHR of 12 April 2006 in the case "*Stec and Others v. the United Kingdom*", applications no. 65731/01 and 65900/01, para. 51). The state enjoys a margin of appreciation in assessing whether and to what extent a different treatment is admissible and justifiable; however, the scope of this margin will vary according to the circumstances, the subject-matter and the background. In order to take into account the needs of specific persons, it may be necessary to use broad categorisations to cover various factual circumstances (see, for example, the judgment of the Grand Chamber of the ECHR of 16 March 2010 in the case *"Carson and Others v. the United Kingdom"*, application no. 42184/05, paras. 61 and 62).

(Available, only in Latvian, at the website of the Constitutional Court, <http://www.satv.tiesa.gov.lv/wp-content/uploads/2016/02/2015-10-01_Spriedums.pdf>, visited on 31 July 2017)

4/8

In its judgment of 27 November 2015 in the case No. SKA-1142/205 the Administrative Cases Department of the Supreme Court of the Republic of Latvia dealt with questions concerning the obligations deriving from the European Convention on Human Rights and the Hague Convention on the Civil Aspects of International Child Abduction.

> 12. ... As it has also been correctly pointed out in the appeal on points of law, the case-law of the ECHR, which has also been analysed by the Supreme Court, clearly indicates that state institutions including courts are obliged to ensure a fair balance between the competing interests of the child, of the two parents, and of public order; however, it must be taken into account that the best interests of the child must be of primary consideration; namely, in all decisions relating to children their interests are the most important ones (see, for example, the judgment of the Grand Chamber of the ECHR of 26 November 2013 in the case *"X. v. Latvia"*, application no. 27853/09, para. 95). It also follows from the case-law of the ECHR that the relationship between parents and children comes within the sphere of "family life" under Article 8 of the Convention and that it is exactly the right to a mutual contact that forms an important element of the right to an enjoyment of a family life (see, for example, the judgment of the ECHR of 27 July 2006 in the case *"Iosub Caras v. Romania"*, application no. 7198/04, paras. 28 and 29).

On the other hand, in order to take into account the interests of the child, it is important to take into account the specific circumstances of the particular case. ... The Regional Court, after examining the evidence in the case-file has determined that no harm has been done to the children as a result of the actions of the *bāriņtiesa* [a guardianship and curatorship institution] and therefore the interests of the children have not been violated.

13. In this type of cases the ensuring of the interests of children is directly related to the promptness of the proceedings. Namely, the case-law of the ECHR in cases pertaining to potential violations deriving from a refusal to return a child, from insufficiently adequate and effective enforcement of a decision to return a child as well as situations when the return of children may lead to a disproportionate interference with their rights indicates that the national authorities ought to be guided by the principle that, if a decision ordering a child's return is in force, the specific concept of "best interests of the child" within the meaning of the Hague Convention is best served by an immediate return of the child (the judgment of the ECHR of 15 January 2015 in the case "*M.A. v. Austria*", application no. 4097/13, para. 136, as well as the judgment of the Grand Chamber of the ECHR of 26 November 2013 in the case "*X. v. Latvia*", application no. 27853/09, para. 101 and the case-law cited therein). Accordingly, pursuant to Article 11 of the Hague Convention, the courts or administrative institutions ought to operate promptly in ensuring the return of the child.

Accordingly, within the context of the actual return of the child the interests of the child are served if a [court] decision on the children's return is enforced as quickly as possible. ...

14. The arguments included in the appeal on points of law concerning the obligatory character of the wishes expressed by the children are contrary to the conclusion supported by the case-law of the ECHR that, in applying the Hague Convention, the opinion of the child ought to be taken into account, but his disagreement with (objections to) the return are not an obstacle to the return (the judgment of the ECHR of 9 September 2014 in the case "*Gajtani v. Switzerland*", application no. 43730/07, para. 107).

> In the 21 July 2015 judgment of the ECHR in the case "*G.S. v. Georgia*" (application no. 2361/13) it was indicated that even if the child during the proceedings for return has expressed a wish to stay with the parent who has unlawfully abducted the child, a refusal to return would be unfounded, since it would give an unjustified advantage to the parent who had wrongfully removed or retained the child. It has also been found that a refusal to order a return on the basis that a separation from a parent would violate the child's rights would be unfounded because, albeit a separation from the abducting parent might be difficult for the child, it would not automatically meet the "grave risk" test, namely, it would not be a situation which goes beyond what a child might reasonably bear (see para. 56 of the "*G.S.*" judgment).

(Available, only in Latvian, at the website of the Supreme Court, <http://at.gov.lv/files/files/1142-ska-2015.doc>, visited on 31 July 2017)

4/9

In its decision of 7 August 2015 in the case no. SKK-303/2015 the Criminal Cases Department of the Supreme Court dealt with the distinction between impermissible police entrapment and lawful investigative actions.

> The ECHR in its judgments has repeatedly emphasised ... the fact that when a criminal case is examined by a court the state institutions are obliged to respond to the arguments of the defence about a possible entrapment (unless such arguments are completely unconvincing) and for that reason to examine evidence about the behaviour of the accused prior to the commencement of special investigative actions against him. In verifying whether the accused has been entrapped to commit a crime, it is essential to verify: a) the reasons why the operation had been mounted; b) the extent of the police's involvement in the offence; and c) the nature of any incitement or pressure to which the applicant had been subjected (see the judgment of the ECHR of 22 July 2003 in the case "*Edwards and Lewis v. the United Kingdom*", applications no. 39647/98 and 40461/98, and the judgment of 5 February 2008 in the case "*Ramanauskas v. Lithuania*", application no. 74420/01). If it is concluded that there has been an entrapment, all evidence obtained in such a manner are to be declared inadmissible. The fact that the accused has confessed does not alter the fact that there has been an entrap-

ment, since in such a situation a confession is not evidence which might be used to prove the guilt of the accused (see the judgment of the ECHR of 9 June 1998 in the case *"Teixeira de Castro v. Portugal"*, application no. 25829/94, the judgment of 26 October 2006 in the case *"Khudobin v. Russia"*, application no. 59696/00, the judgment of 5 February 2008 in the case *"Ramanauskas v. Lithuania"*, application no. 74420/01, and the judgment of 21 February 2008 in the case *"Pyrgiotakis v. Greece"*, application no. 15100/06).

In case the reliability of evidence has been disputed, it is essential to ensure that the reliability of evidence is tested. The domestic court is obliged to verify the reasons for the investigative actions, the extent of police's involvement in the offence and the nature of the actions to which the applicant has been subjected in order to come to a conclusion whether the right to a fair trial guaranteed by Article 6 of the Convention has been violated (see the judgment of the ECHR of 9 June 1998 in the case *"Teixeira de Castro v. Portugal"*, application no. 25829/94, the judgment of 5 February 2008 in the case *"Ramanauskas v. Lithuania"*, application no. 74420/01, the judgment of 24 June 2008 in the case *"Miliniene v. Lithuania"*, application no. 74355/01, the judgment of 10 March 2009 in the case *"Bykov v. Russia"*, application no. 4378/02, and the judgment of 8 January 2013 in the case *"Baltiņš v. Latvia"*, application no. 25282[/07]). Furthermore, the evidence submitted by the prosecution has to meet a very high standard in order for the allegations of entrapment to be convincingly refuted; in other words, the standard of proof is clear and convincing evidence, not reasonable doubt (see the judgment of the ECHR of 5 February 2008 in the case *"Ramanauskas v. Lithuania"*, application no. 74420/01).

(Available, only in Latvian, at the website of the Supreme Court, <http://at.gov.lv/files/files/skk-303-2015.doc>, visited on 31 July 2017)

Part Four: III. Relationship between International Law and Internal Law – Remedies under internal law for violations of international law

4/10

By its decision of 11 February 2015 in the case no. SJA-1/2015 the Administrative Cases Department of the Supreme Court quashed in part the decision of the Administrative Regional Court that had been adopted in 2006 and sent the case back to that court for a fresh examination. This decision was taken against the background of the ECHR judgment of 29 April 2014 in the case "*L.H. v. Latvia*", application no. 52019/07.

4/11

The Civil Cases Department of the Supreme Court had to examine the question of reopening the proceedings in its decision of 27 March 2015 in the case no. SJC-6/2015. The case came before the Supreme Court in the aftermath of the judgment of the ECHR of 24 June 2014 in the case "*A.K. v. Latvia*", application no, 33011/08.

The Supreme Court found that the petitioner had not substantiated her claim that the judgment of the ECHR required a fresh examination of the case, especially because the ECHR had found a violation of Article 8, and not of Article 6, of the Convention. The ECHR judgment did not contain an indication that it is only possible to achieve the *restitution in integrum* by the way of a new examination of the case. The Supreme Court considered that the losses caused to the petitioner through the violation of Article 8 of the Convention had already been compensated by the Strasbourg Court's award of non-pecuniary damages.

Part Five: I. B. 6. Subjects of International Law – States – Recognition – Non-recognition (including non-recognition of governments) and its effects

5/1

On 16 March 2015 the Ministry of Foreign Affairs issued a statement to mark one year that had passed since the "Crimean referendum".

> On 16 March 2014, an illegal and illegitimate referendum was held on joining Crimea to the Russian Federation. The 18 March decision

of the Russian Federation was the next step in an illegal and illegitimate process of annexation that has followed.

The 18 March 2014 decision was a blatant violation of international law, including international commitments by the Russian Federation. Together with the international community, Latvia has consistently condemned these actions, and together with its partners in the EU and the rest of the world Latvia will be expressing this position also in future thus continuing the policy of non-recognition of the illegal annexation of Crimea. Latvia firmly backs the restoration of Ukraine's territorial integrity and sovereignty.

The illegal annexation of Crimea has sown instability in the region and left a negative impact on the international security environment, as well as leading to rapid deterioration of the human rights situation in Crimea, especially in regard to restrictions and violations of the rights of Crimean Tatars.

Latvia once again emphasises that the annexation of Crimea is an unprecedented case of its kind in the post-war history of Europe; and it is in this light that the international community must invest maximum efforts to see to it that the norms of international law, especially in regard to ensuring territorial integrity and sovereignty of countries are strictly observed.

(Available at the website of the Ministry of Foreign Affairs, <http://www.mfa.gov.lv/en/news/latest-news/45386-one-year-has-passed-since-the-illegal-and-illegitimate-annexation-of-crimea-latvia-will-remain-committed-to-a-policy-of-non-recognition>, visited on 31 July 2017)

5/2
The Crimean annexation was also invoked by the President of Latvia, Mr. Raimonds Vējonis, during his speech at the 70th session of the United Nations General Assembly:

The international community, including the UN General Assembly, supports Ukraine and its territorial integrity. The illegal annexation of Crimea and Sevastopol by Russia will not be recognized. We are particularly concerned about the worsening social, economic and human rights situation in Crimea, especially affecting Crimean Tatars and ethnic Ukrainians.

Together with the rest of the international community, Latvia will continue to support Ukraine's reform process in order to strengthen democracy, economy and good governance.

(Available at the website of the Chancery of the President, <http://www.president.lv/pk/content/?cat_id=603&art_id=23483>, visited on 24 July 2017)

Part Five: II. A. 2. (a) Subjects of International Law –
International organisations – In general – Participation
of States and international organisations in international
organisations and in their activities – Admission

5/3
In 2015 Latvia continued the accession process to the Organisation for Economic Co-operation and Development.

(Available, only in Latvian, at the website of the Ministry of Foreign Affairs, <http://www.mfa.gov.lv/aktualitates/zinas/47923-izverte-latvijas-iestasanas-sarunu-progresu-ekonomiskas-sadarbibas-un-attistibas-organizacija>, visited on 31 July 2017)

Part Five: II. A. 2. (d) Subjects of International Law –
International organisations – In general – Participation
of States and international organisations in international
organisations and in their activities –Representation of
States and international organisations to international
organisations, including privileges and immunities

5/4
During a meeting with representatives of African and Arab countries at the United Nations on 26 May 2015 the Minister of Foreign Affairs, Mr. Edgars Rinkēvičs,

> noted that the UN Security Council was in need of reforms, as the global challenges and the number of member countries in the UN have significantly increased since its establishment, and yet the UN Security Council does not reflect the changes that have taken place in the world. The Minister stressed that serious discussions were needed on the UN Security Council reform to enable the organisation to effectively counter present-day challenges. The use of the veto powers in the event of crimes against humanity should be discussed. The Eastern European Group should also be assigned an additional non-permanent seat

(Available at the website of the Ministry of Foreign Affairs, <http://www.mfa.gov.lv/en/news/latest-news/46695-the-latvian-foreign-minister-highlights-the-need-for-reforming-the-un-security-council>, visited on 31 July 2017)

5/5

The President of Latvia, Mr. Raimonds Vējonis, during his speech at the 70th session of the United Nations General Assembly also invoked the need to reform the UN Security Council:

> It is time to move forward with the UN Security Council reform. We applaud efforts to revive negotiations on this important issue. Latvia supports expansion of the Security Council in both categories of membership. At least one additional non-permanent seat should be ensured to the Eastern European Group of states.
>
> ...
>
> Early action of the UN in situations of concern is crucial. Latvia supports the proposal to voluntarily restrain the use of the veto at the Security Council in situations involving mass atrocity crimes. It also supports a Code of Conduct for any member of the Council not to vote against any action designed to end and prevent mass atrocity crimes.
>
> On several crucial occasions in recent times the Security Council was not able to take timely and decisive action. It has had dire consequences:

The Security Council was blocked from playing a role to stop Russia's aggression against Ukraine and to seek justice for the victims of the flight MH17 in an international tribunal that could establish the truth on who shot down this civilian airplane."

(Available at the website of the Chancery of the President, <http://www.president.lv/pk/content/?cat_id=603&art_id=23483>, visited on 24 July 2017)

Part Six: VIII. C. Human rights and fundamental freedoms – Under Council of Europe treaty system

From the seven judgments adopted in 2015 by the European Court of Human Rights, three highlighted particularly novel aspects of the interplay between the Convention and the Latvian legal system.

6/1

On 13 January 2015 the ECHR adopted a judgment in the case "*Elberte v. Latvia*" (application no. 61243/08), which dealt with the removal of the applicant's deceased husband's tissue without her consent. In its judgment, the ECHR referred to, *inter alia*, documents adopted by the Council of Europe, the European Union and the World Health Organisation. The Court's analysis of the alleged violation of Article 8 of the Convention (namely, of "the applicant's right ... to express consent or refusal in relation to the removal of her husband's tissue", para. 89 of the judgment) hinged on the question of whether the Latvian authorities were required to actively solicit the applicant's consent prior to removing her deceased husband's tissue. As to whether this was required by the Latvian law, the ECHR noted that "the domestic authorities themselves held conflicting views as to the scope of the obligations enshrined in national law" (para. 112 of the judgment). For this reason the Court held that the interference with the applicant's right had not been in accordance with a sufficiently clear law.

Furthermore, the Court noted:

> 115. As to whether the domestic law afforded adequate legal protection against arbitrariness, the Court notes that the removal of tissue in the present case was not an isolated act ... but was carried out under a State-approved agreement with a pharmaceutical com-

pany abroad; removals had been carried out from a large number of people ... In such circumstances it is all the more important that adequate mechanisms are put in place to counterbalance the wide margin of discretion conferred on the experts to carry out removals on their own initiative ... but this was not done ... In response to the Government's argument that nothing had prevented the applicant from expressing her wishes in relation to tissue removal, the Court notes the lack of any administrative or legal regulation in this regard. The applicant was, accordingly, unable to foresee what was expected from her if she wished to exercise that right.

For those reasons the Court found that the interference with the applicant's right to respect for her private life was not in accordance with the law within the meaning of Article 8 § 2 of the Convention and that therefore there had been a violation of Article 8.

The Court furthermore found that the emotional suffering endured by the applicant "on account of the fact that the removal of her husband's tissue had been carried out contrary to domestic law without her prior consent or knowledge and that she had been forced to bury her husband with his legs tied together" (para. 135 of the judgment) amounted to degrading treatment contrary to Article 3 of the Convention.

6/2

On 13 January 2015 the ECHR adopted a judgment in the case "*Petropavlovskis v. Latvia*" (application no. 44230/06). The applicant complained under Articles 10, 11 and 13 of the Convention that the allegedly arbitrary refusal to grant him Latvian citizenship through naturalisation was a punitive measure imposed on him because he had imparted ideas and exercised his right of peaceful assembly in order to criticise the Government's position (para. 3 of the judgment). The crux of the Court's argument was that "under the Convention there is no "right to nationality" similar to that in Article 15 of the Universal Declaration of Human Rights" (para. 81 of the judgment). From that it followed that:

> 84. ... The choice of criteria for the purposes of granting citizenship through naturalisation in accordance with domestic law is linked to the nature of the bond between the State and the individual concerned that each society deems necessary to ensure. In many

jurisdictions, acquisition of citizenship is accompanied by an oath of allegiance whereby the individual pledges loyalty to the State. ...

85. The Court notes that the assessment of loyalty for the purposes of the naturalisation decision in the present case does not refer to loyalty to the government in power, but rather to the State and its Constitution. The Court considers that a democratic State is entitled to require persons who wish to acquire its citizenship to be loyal to the State and, in particular, to the constitutional principles on which it is founded. The applicant did not contest this. The Court agrees with the applicant that, in exercising his freedom of expression and assembly, he is free to disagree with government policies for as long as that critique takes place in accordance with the law; it is also true that the limits of permissible criticism are wider with regard to the government than in relation to a private citizen or even a politician. However, this is an entirely different matter from the issue of the criteria set for naturalisation and its procedure, which are both determined by domestic law. The requirement of loyalty to the State and its Constitution cannot be considered as a punitive measure capable of interfering with the freedom of expression and assembly. Rather, it is a criterion which has to be fulfilled by any person seeking to obtain the Latvian citizenship through naturalisation.

86. The Court does not see in what manner the applicant has been prevented from expressing his disagreement with government policy on the issue of interest to him. Nor can the Court discern any facts which would indicate that he was prevented from participating in any meetings or movements.

87. Consequently, Articles 10 and 11 of the Convention are not applicable in the circumstances of the present case and the Court upholds the Government's objection."

6/3
The ECHR's judgment of 13 January 2015 in the case *"Rubins v. Latvia"* (application no. 79040/12) dealt with a situation in which the applicant had been dismissed from his position of a professor at a state-owned univer-

sity due to an e-mail he had sent to the rector of the university concerning the management and reforms of the institution.

Responding to the applicant's argument that his dismissal for a breach of "good morals" had been based on a provision of law that was insufficiently clear and foreseeable, the Court indicated that

> 73. ... even if the requirement to act in good faith in the context of an employment contract does not imply an absolute duty of loyalty towards the employer or a duty of discretion to the point of subjecting the worker to the employer's interests, certain manifestations of the right to freedom of expression that may be legitimate in other contexts are not legitimate in that of labour relations.

Turning to the question of whether the interference was "necessary in a democratic society", the ECHR pointed out that

> 85. ... the issues invoked by the applicant were of some public interest and that the truthfulness of the information was not challenged by the parties. Nevertheless it is apparent from the appellate court's judgment that these aspects – the public interest and truthfulness of the information – were not assessed at all.

Finally, the Court turned to the severity of the sanction imposed on the applicant:

> 92. Lastly, the Government submitted that the applicant's career had not been affected and that therefore the measure – his dismissal – could not be considered as severe. The Court notes that this was the harshest sanction available and, disregarding the fact that the applicant took up a post in another university soon afterwards, was liable to have a serious chilling effect on other employees of the University and to discourage them from raising criticism ... The Court finds that it is difficult to justify the application of such a severe sanction.

Consequently, a violation of Article 10 of the Convention was found.

Part Seventeen: I. 7. The Law of Armed Conflict and International Humanitarian Law – International armed conflict – International humanitarian law

17/1

During a meeting with representatives of African and Arab countries at the United Nations on 26 May 2015 the Minister of Foreign Affairs, Mr. Edgars Rinkēvičs,

> Referring to the developments in Syria, ... said that the international community should continue efforts to ensure a political solution of the Syrian crisis. Latvia supports UN efforts at seeking a political solution to the crisis in Syria. At the same time, we are concerned over the humanitarian situation in Syria and the region.

(Available at the website of the Ministry of Foreign Affairs, <http://www.mfa.gov.lv/en/news/latest-news/46695-the-latvian-foreign-minister-highlights-the-need-for-reforming-the-un-security-council>, visited on 31 July 2017)

17/2

The President of Latvia, Mr. Raimonds Vējonis, during his speech at the 70th session of the United Nations General Assembly also referred to the humanitarian crisis in Syria:

> The horrific conflict in Syria has entered its fifth year. It has created a humanitarian catastrophe and destabilized the whole region. The international community must not abandon the people of Syria, and must push for a political settlement. Those responsible for the internationally prohibited use of chemical weapons in Syria must be identified and held accountable.
>
> The conflict and fragility of Syria and Iraq have contributed to the rise of ISIL/Daesh and the violent extremism spreading globally. Concerted international action is vital to defeat this evil and is key for achieving lasting peace and stability in Syria, Iraq and the wider region."

(Available at the website of the Chancery of the President, <http://www.president.lv/pk/content/?cat_id=603&art_id=23483>, visited on 24 July 2017)

Part Seventeen: I. 9. The Law of Armed Conflict and International Humanitarian Law – International armed conflict – Conventional, nuclear, bacteriological, and chemical weapons

17/3

During a meeting with representatives of African and Arab countries at the United Nations on 26 May 2015 the Minister of Foreign Affairs, Mr. Edgars Rinkēvičs, stated:

> Latvia supports the efforts to destroy Syria's chemical weapons, and we expect that Syria will continue implementing the UN Security Council Resolutions that set out a special programme for the destruction of chemical weapons in Syria, and do so diligently and in a transparent manner.

(Available at the website of the Ministry of Foreign Affairs, <http://www.mfa.gov.lv/en/news/latest-news/46695-the-latvian-foreign-minister-highlights-the-need-for-reforming-the-un-security-council>, visited on 31 July 2017)

17/4

The President of Latvia, Mr. Raimonds Vējonis, during his speech at the 70th session of the United Nations General Assembly referred to the nuclear program of Iran:

> Latvia welcomes the recent nuclear agreement with Iran. Full and smooth implementation of the Joint Comprehensive Action Plan is now necessary. Only then can a change in the regional dynamics towards more engagement and cooperation, as well as greater stability in the Middle East region become a reality.

(Available at the website of the Chancery of the President, <http://www.president.lv/pk/content/?cat_id=603&art_id=23483>, visited on 24 July 2017)

Part Seventeen: I. 10. The Law of Armed Conflict and
International Humanitarian Law – International armed
conflict – Treaty relations between combatants (cartels,
armistices, etc.)

17/5
The Ministry of Foreign Affairs issued a statement on 12 February 2015, welcoming the conclusion of the Minsk Agreement:

> The Ministry of Foreign Affairs of Latvia evaluates positively the most recent decisions and understandings reached in Minsk for a ceasefire that would take effect as of 15 February, the withdrawal of heavy weapons and other important terms and conditions that should lead to the de-escalation of the crisis and serve as a basis for a sustainable political solution with respect for Ukraine's independence, sovereignty and territorial integrity.
>
> Practical implementation of these agreements will be decisive. Latvia urges all parties, including Russia, to begin conscientiously implementing decisions reached in Minsk without delay, so that human casualties and violence are halted, and further destabilisation of the situation in the region is prevented.

(Available at the website of the Ministry of Foreign Affairs, <http://www.mfa.gov.lv/en/news/latest-news/44821-the-latvian-foreign-ministry-expects-full-implementation-of-the-minsk-agreements>, visited on 1 August 2017)

17/6
However, already on 18 August 2015 the Ministry of Foreign Affairs was forced to issue another statement, reiterating its support for the Minsk Agreement and condemning the re-escalation of violence in Easter Ukraine:

> The Ministry of Foreign Affairs considers that the recent escalation of tension in the conflict zone in Eastern Ukraine is seriously undermining the implementation of the Minsk agreements. The responsibility for the exacerbation of the situation should be assumed by Russia-supported separatists. Particular concern is aroused by the

> growing numbers of civilian casualties and the aggravation of humanitarian situation.
>
> The Ministry of Foreign Affairs is also concerned about the increasing threat to the OSCE Observation Mission and actions against it that considerably interfere with the performance of the mission's tasks. Latvia believes that ensuring unhindered functioning of the OSCE Mission is vital for the fulfilment of the Minsk agreement.
>
> The Ministry of Foreign Affairs calls on all the parties involved, especially the Russian Federation, to make every effort to cease shelling as soon as possible, to withdraw heavy weaponry and restore the ceasefire in the east of Ukraine. The Ministry of Foreign Affairs reasserts that implementing the Minsk Agreement is the main prerequisite for a sustainable political solution to the conflict in Eastern Ukraine, based on respect for Ukraine's independence, sovereignty and territorial integrity.

(Available at the website of the Ministry of Foreign Affairs, <http://www.mfa.gov.lv/en/news/latest-news/47618-statement-from-the-ministry-of-foreign-affairs-on-the-escalation-of-tension-in-the-east-of-ukraine>, visited on 1 August 2017)

17/7

The importance of the Minsk agreements for ceasing the conflict in Ukraine was also underlined by the President of Latvia, Mr. Raimonds Vējonis, during his speech at the 70th session of the United Nations General Assembly:

> The conflict in eastern Ukraine has cost the lives of thousands and led to the suffering of millions of innocent victims. Russia must stop all forms of support to separatists and use its influence to make them adhere to the Minsk agreements. Full implementation of the Minsk agreements by all parties is essential.

(Available at the website of the Chancery of the President, <http://www.president.lv/pk/content/?cat_id=603&art_id=23483>, visited on 24 July 2017)

ANNEX I. A. *Agreements signed by Latvia before 2015 but entered into force in regard to Latvia in 2015 – Bi- and multilateral agreements*

Title	Conclusion	Entry into Force
Agreement between the Government of the Republic of Latvia and the Government of the Republic of Tajikistan on Cooperation in Combating Terrorism, Organised Crime and Illicit Trafficking Narcotic Drugs, Psychotropic Substances and their Precursors	10.06.2014	21.01.2015
European Cooperating State Agreement between the Government of the Republic of Latvia and the European Space Agency	15.03.2013	30.01.2015
Agreement between the Government of the Republic of Tajikistan on Co-operation in the Field of Education and Science	10.06.2014	23.02.2015
Agreement between the Government of the Republic of Latvia and the Government of Mongolia on International Transport by Road	12.06.2014	12.03.2015
Agreement between the Government of the Republic of Latvia and the Government of the Republic of Lithuania on Mutual Protection of Classified Information	03.12.2014	22.05.2015
Agreement between the Government of the Republic of Latvia and the Government of the State of Qatar for the Avoidance of Double Taxation and the Prevention of Fiscal Evasion with Respect to Taxes on Income	26.09.2014	01.06.2015

Title	Conclusion	Entry into Force
Agreement between the Government of the Republic of Latvia and the Government of the Republic of Tajikistan on Cooperation in the Field of Tourism	10.06.2014	13.06.2015
Agreement between the Government of the Republic of Latvia and the Government of the Republic of Belarus on Amendments to the Agreement on International Road Transport of 1 February 1995	06.08.2014	18.06.2015
Air Services Agreement between the Government of the Republic of Latvia and the Government of the United Arab Emirates	25.09.2014	19.06.2015

ANNEX II. *Agreements signed by Latvia in 2015 – Bi- and multilateral agreements*

Title	Conclusion	Entry into Force
Agreement between the Government of the Republic of Latvia and the Government of the Republic of Estonia on Cooperation in the Combating of the Effects of Marine Pollution Incidents	16.01.2015	16.01.2015
Plan for European Cooperating States (PECS) Charter between the Government of the Republic of Latvia and the European Space Agency	30.01.2015	30.01.2015
Memorandum of Cooperation on the National Francophone Initiative for 2015-2018 within the framework of the "French in International Relations" Programme	10.10.2015	10.10.2015

International Road Transport Agreement between the Government of the Republic of Latvia and the Government of Turkmenistan	12.12.2015	07.08.2016
Agreement between the Government of the Republic of Latvia and the Government of the Republic of Cyprus on Mutual Protection of Classified Information	22.06.2015	01.03.2017

Republic of Lithuania Materials on International Law 2015

Edited by Aiste Augustauskaite* and Saulius Katuoka**

[*Editorial Notes:*

1. Republic of Lithuania Materials on International Law 2015 (**RLMIL2015**) are drafted and classified pursuant to Recommendation (97)11 of 12 June 1997 of the Committee of Ministers of the Council of Europe.

2. For the ease of reading a number of abbreviations are used in RLMIL2015, namely ECHR – Convention for Protection of Human Rights and Fundamental Freedoms, 1950; ECtHR – ECtHR; Seimas – Parliament of the Republic of Lithuania; Government – Government of the Republic of Lithuania. Unless explicitly provided for otherwise, references to cases or decisions in RLMIL2015 are references to acts of national courts and institutions. Cases decided by national courts referred to herein are available in Lithuanian free of charge at the following websites: www.lat.lt (Case-law of the Supreme Court), www.lvat.lt (Case-law of the Supreme Administrative Court). Most of the case-law of the Constitutional Court is available on its website http://www.lrkt.lt/index_e.html. Case-law of the European Court of Human Rights is available through the website http://www.echr.coe.int/echr/. Bilateral agreements of Lithuania are mostly available in Lithuanian at the following website: www.lrs.lt. Universal and regional international instruments mentioned in RLMIL2015 do not bear any reference to their source, as may be easily accessed from various pages on the internet. Due to limited scope, the RLMIL2015 does not reproduce entire texts, therefore certain information is omitted and marked as [...].

3. RLMIL2015 consists mainly from translations of texts made by the editors; therefore, translations shall not be regarded as official and shall be used for information purposes only. Documents the translations of which

---

* Lecturer at Mykolas Romeris University (Vilnius); LL.M (Mykolas Romeris University).
** Professor at Mykolas Romeris University (Vilnius).

are provided by national institutions and are available in English on the internet are attached with particular link.

4. A rather technical remark shall be made in regard to ratifications of Seimas and approvals of Government, meaning expression of consent to be bound under national law, rather than meaning of international act, attributed to the notion "ratification" in the Article 2 part 1(b) of the Vienna Convention on the Law of Treaties, 1969.]

Part Four: II. Relationship between International Law and Internal Law – Application and implementation of international law in internal law

4/1

In the ruling No. KT16-N10/2015 *"On the compliance of the provisions of the Republic of Lithuania's law on state assistance for the acquisition or rent of residential properties and for the renovation (modernisation) of blocs of flats and the provisions of the resolution of the government of the republic of Lithuania (no. 670) "on the establishment of the sizes of annual income and property according to which the right to municipal social housing or to the improvement of the existing social housing conditions is established" of 28 may 2003 with the Constitution of the Republic of Lithuania"* of 26 May, 2015, the Constitutional Court of the Republic of Lithuania recognized that the provisions of these Lithuanian legal acts were in conflict with the Constitution of the Republic of Lithuania as well as with the constitutional principle of a state under the rule of law. The relevant parts of the decision are reproduced below:

> 1. Paragraph 1 of Article 11 of the 1966 International Covenant on Economic, Social and Cultural Rights (hereinafter – the Covenant), which came into force for the Republic of Lithuania on 20 February 1992, provides that "the States Parties to the present Covenant recognise the right of everyone to an adequate standard of living for himself and his family, including adequate food, clothing and housing, and to the continuous improvement of living conditions.
>
> In the 2014 Concluding Observations on the Second Periodic Report of Lithuania, the Committee on Economic, Social and Cultural Rights that monitors the implementation of the Covenant by its

States Parties expressed, *inter alia,* its concern at the acute shortage of social housing; Lithuania was urged to ensure that its national housing policy prioritises the needs of marginalised and vulnerable groups who lack access to adequate housing.

While construing the provisions of Paragraph 1 of Article 11 of the Covenant, the Committee on Economic, Social and Cultural Rights has noted that the human right to adequate housing, which is thus derived from the right to an adequate standard of living, is of central importance for the enjoyment of all economic, social and cultural rights. Drawing attention to the fact that, as specified in the preamble to the Covenant, the rights entrenched in the Covenant derive from the inherent dignity of the human person, the said committee emphasised that the right to housing must be understood as the right not just to housing but to adequate housing (General Comment 4: The right to adequate housing (1991) (Paragraph 1 of Article 11 of the Covenant)).

2. The European Social Charter (Revised) (hereinafter – the Charter), which was adopted on 3 May 1996 and came into force (with reservations) for the Republic of Lithuania on 1 August 2001, consolidated the right to social and medical assistance (Article 13) and the right to housing (Article 31). Article 13 of the Charter, *inter alia,* prescribes:

"With a view to ensuring the effective exercise of the right to social and medical assistance, the Parties undertake:

to ensure that any person who is without adequate resources and who is unable to secure such resources either by his own efforts or from other sources, in particular by benefits under a social security scheme, be granted adequate assistance, and, in case of sickness, the care necessitated by his condition;

to ensure that persons receiving such assistance shall not, for that reason, suffer from a diminution of their political or social rights <...>".

Article 31 of the Charter, *inter alia,* prescribes:

"With a view to ensuring the effective exercise of the right to housing, the Parties undertake to take measures designed:

to promote access to housing of an adequate standard;

to prevent and reduce homelessness with a view to its gradual elimination <...>".

The European Committee of Social Rights that monitors the implementation of the Charter by its States Parties, in its 2011 conclusions on the report on the implementation of the Charter submitted by the Republic of Lithuania, noted, *inter alia,* that the situation in Lithuania is not in conformity with Paragraph 1 of Article 31 of the Charter on the grounds that the right to adequate housing is not effectively guaranteed. The same conclusions noted, *inter alia,* that with a view to implementing the provisions of Paragraph 1 of Article 31 of the Charter, the State Parties must pay particular attention to the impact of their policy choices on each category of persons, especially on the most vulnerable groups.

3. Even though the 1950 Convention for the Protection of Human Rights and Fundamental Freedoms (hereinafter – the Convention) does not consolidate the social and economic rights directly, however, in certain cases the social rights of persons (including the right to housing and social assistance) may be defended under the Convention. For example, due to an extremely low size of a pension or social benefit, a question could be raised as to the treatment degrading human dignity within Article 3 of the Convention (see the judgment of 18 June 2009 in the case of *Budina v. Russia,* application No. 45603/05). The European Court of Human Rights also notes that within the meaning of the Convention, the responsibility of the state may also arise in cases where the respective person is in a situation when s/he is completely dependent on state assistance and where such a situation is incompatible with respect for the dignity of the person (see the judgment of 26 June 2001 in the case of *O'Rourke v. the United Kingdom,* application No. 39022/97).

While construing Article 8 of the Convention, the European Court of Human Rights emphasises that this article cannot be interpreted as implying for States a direct positive obligation to provide every person with a home (see the judgment of 18 January 2001 in the case of *Chapman v. the United Kingdom,* application No. 27238/95), however, the duty of States to ensure housing for especially vulnerable persons may be derived from Article 8 of the Convention (see the judgment of 24 April 2012 in the case of *Yordanova and Others v. Bulgaria,* application No. 25446/06, the judgment of 17 October 2013 in the case of *Winterstein and Others v. France,* application No. 27013/07).

4. In this context, a mention should also be made of the Charter of Fundamental Rights of the European Union. Article 1 titled "Human Dignity" of the said charter prescribes: "Human dignity is inviolable. It must be respected and protected", while Paragraph 3 of Article 34 "Social Security and Social Assistance" provides: "In order to combat social exclusion and poverty, the Union recognises and respects the right to social and housing assistance so as to ensure a decent existence for all those who lack sufficient resources, in accordance with the rules laid down by Union law and national laws and practices."

4/2

The Constitutional Court of the Republic of Lithuania, in its ruling "*On the compliance of certain provisions of the rules on the amounts and payment of remuneration to advocates for the provision and coordination of secondary legal aid (wordings of 2 may 2006 and 18 July 2012) as approved by the 22 January 2001 resolution (no. 69) of the government of the republic of Lithuania with the Constitution of the Republic of Lithuania of 9 July 2015*", No. KT20-N13/2015, found that Rules on the Amounts and Payment of Remuneration to Advocates for the Provision and Coordination of Secondary Legal Aid (wording of 2 May 2006; *Valstybės žinios*, 2006, 50-1817) as approved by the Resolution of the Government of the Republic of Lithuania (No. 69) "On the Approval of the Rules on the Amounts and Payment of Remuneration to Advocates for the Provision and Coordination of Secondary Legal Aid" of 22 January 2001 was not in conflict with the Constitution of the Republic of Lithuania. However, certain parts of the decision should be mentioned:

1. In the context of the constitutional justice case at issue, the international obligations of the State of Lithuania assumed under the 1950 Convention for the Protection of Human Rights and Fundamental Freedoms (hereinafter referred to as the Convention), as

well as under the 1966 International Covenant on Civil and Political Rights, are also relevant.

2. Article 6 of the Convention prescribes: "In the determination of his civil rights and obligations or of any criminal charge against him, everyone is entitled to a fair and public hearing within a reasonable time by an independent and impartial tribunal established by law. ... (Paragraph 1);" "Everyone charged with a criminal offence has the following minimum rights: ... (c) to defend himself in person or through legal assistance of his own choosing or, if he has not sufficient means to pay for legal assistance, to be given it free when the interests of justice so require; ..."(Paragraph 3).

3. In its case-law, the European Court of Human Rights (hereinafter referred to as the ECtHR) has clearly emphasised that Paragraph 1 of Article 6 of the Convention secures access to a court for every person wishing to commence an action in order to have his/her civil rights and obligations determined; the right to institute civil proceedings before courts in civil matters constitutes one aspect only; it determines the implementation of this right to the full extent (the judgment of 21 February 1975 in the case of *Golder v. The United Kingdom,* application No. 4451/70, § 36; the Grand Chamber judgment of 19 October 2005 in the case of *Roche v. The United Kingdom,* application No. 32555/96, § 116; the Grand Chamber judgment of 17 January 2012 in the case of *Stanev v. Bulgaria,* application No. 36760/06, §§ 229-235, 241-245). The right of everyone to access a court is also applicable in criminal cases and this rights means that the accused person must be judged for the accusations against him/her before a court where all the guarantees of a fair trial, including the guarantees provided for in Paragraphs 2 and 3 of Article 6 of the Convention, must be applied to him/her (the judgment of 27 February 1980 in the case of *Deweer v. Belgium,* application No. 6903/75, § 56).

In certain cases, the right to efficiently implement the right to access a court may also mean the duty of the state to guarantee legal assistance, including free legal assistance for certain categories of persons. The legal assistance may be necessary when it is obligatory under national law, when it is necessary due to the complexity of the proceedings or case, or when it is necessary due to the importance of the interests of the applicant; additionally, consideration may be taken of the applicant's capacity to represent him/herself effectively (the judgment of 9 October 1979 in the case of *Airey v. Ireland,* application No. 6289/73, § 26; the judgment of 15 February 2005 in the case of *Steel an Morris v. The United Kingdom,* application No. 68416/01, 59–61).

It also needs to be noted that, under the case-law of the ECtHR, the right to legal aid is not absolute; it may be not provided when the claimant has no "reasonable prospects of success" or when the applicant abuses the system of legal aid or law itself (the decision of 18 January 1996 on admissibility in the case of *Sujeeun v. The United Kingdom,* application No. 27788/95). It should also be noted that in the situations where legal aid is necessary to ensure the efficient implementation of the right to access a court, Article 6 of the Convention gives freedom for the states to choose individually the measures for guaranteeing this aid. One of such measures may be the establishment of a legal aid system.

The ECtHR has emphasised that the Convention is intended to guarantee the rights that are practical and effective (the Grand Chamber judgment of 12 July 2001 in the case of *Prince Hans-Adam II of Liechtenstein v. Germany,* application No. 42527/98, § 45); the state must take positive steps to ensure that the person enjoyed effectively the right to legal aid, to which he was entitled; being aware that the appointment of a lawyer does not ensure the effective legal aid, the state authorities must either replace him/her or cause him/her to fulfil his/her obligations (the judgment of 13 May 1980 in the case of *Artico v. Italy,* application No. 6694/74, §§ 33, 36). In the context of a fair trial of Article 6 of the Convention, the principle of appropriate representation of a lawyer appointed by the state was also emphasised in cases against Lithuania (*inter alia,* the judgment of 10 June 2012 in the case of *Slickienė v. Lithuania,* application No. 20496/02, §§ 49–50).

The ECtHR has held on more than one occasion that the opportunity to have a lawyer is one of the conditions for effective implementation of the right to apply to court (the judgment of 8 February 1996 in the case of *John Murray v. The United Kingdom,* application No. 18731/91; the judgment of 9 October 2003 in the case of *Ezeh and Connors v. The United Kingdom,* applications Nos. 39665/98 and 40086/98; the judgment of 12 May 2005 in the case of *Öcalan v. Turkey,* application No. 46221/99, etc.).

The ECtHR has also considered the peculiarities of the legal profession on more than one occasion. In the case of *Bigaeva v. Greece,* when considering the conditions of becoming a lawyer, the ECtHR noted that representatives of the legal profession participate in the process of administration of justice, however, the state enjoys the right to establish the conditions for becoming a lawyer. In addition, the legal profession is a free profession, whose representatives alongside serve the public interest (the judgment of 28 May 2009 in the case of *Bigaeva v. Greece,* application No. 26713/05, §§ 31, 39). Although lawyers have been granted an exclusive right to defend a person in a court, their conduct must be discreet, honest and dignified (the judgment of 24 February 1994 in the case of *Casado Coca v. Spain,* application No. 15450/89, §§ 39, 46).

4. Paragraph 1 of Article 14 of the 1966 International Covenant on Civil and Political Rights also entitles everyone to a fair trial by an independent and impartial tribunal which would determine whether the criminal charge against him/her is reasoned, or would determine the civil rights and obligations impugned by him/her.

Under Paragraph 3 of Article 14 of the said Covenant, in the determination of any criminal charge against him/her, everyone shall be entitled, *inter alia,* to the following minimum guarantees: to have adequate time and facilities for the preparation of his/her defence and to communicate with counsel of his/her own choosing; to be informed, if s/he does not have legal assistance, of this right; and to have legal assistance assigned to him/her, in any case where the interests of justice so require, and without payment by him/her in any such case if s/he does not have sufficient means to pay for it."

4/3

In the case of *Arbačiauskienė v. Lithuania* of 1 March 2016, A*pplication no. 2971/08,* ECHR found a violation of Article 6 § 1 and Article 13 of the Convention. Here are the relevant parts of the decision:

79. The applicant submitted that, in failing to enforce the binding and final court judgment of 5 May 2007, the domestic authorities had infringed her right to a fair hearing within a reasonable time. She contended that she had had the right to acquire two hectares of land from the State since 1995, when this right had been recognised by the local authorities. However, to date she had still not been provided with that land, despite her repeated requests and complaints. Thus, the Supreme Administrative Court's judgment had remained unenforced for eight years and she had been waiting to receive her land for twenty years. ...

82. The Government further argued that any delays in the enforcement had occurred due to reasons outside their control.

83. Lastly, the Government stated that a certain delay in the allocation of a plot of land to the applicant had been caused by her own failure to request such a plot in 1995. They submitted that the applicant had remained inactive and had not petitioned the competent authorities until 2004, thus contributing to the delay.

84. The Court reiterates that the right to a court protected by Article 6 would be illusory if a Contracting State's domestic legal system allowed a final and binding judicial decision to remain inoperative to the detriment of one party. Enforcement of a judgment given by any court must therefore be regarded as an integral part of the "trial" for the purposes of Article 6. An unreasonably long delay in enforcement of a binding judgment may therefore breach the Convention (see *Hornsby v. Greece*, 19 March 1997, § 40, Reports of Judgments and Decisions 1997II, and *Burdov v. Russia (no. 2)*, no. 33509/04, §§ 65-66, ECHR 2009).

85. The Court further reiterates that the reasonableness of such a delay is to be determined having regard in particular to the complexity of the enforcement proceedings, the applicant's own behaviour and that of the competent authorities, as well as the amount and nature of the court award (see *Raylyan v. Russia*, no. 22000/03, § 31, 15 February 2007, and *Rafailović and Stevanović v. Serbia*, nos. 38629/07 and 23718/08, § 78, 16 June 2015). While the Court has due regard to the domestic statutory time-limits set for enforcement proceedings, non-compliance with them does not automatically

amount to a breach of the Convention. Some delay may be justified in particular circumstances but it may not, in any event, be such as to impair the essence of the right protected under Article 6 § 1 (see *Burdov (no. 2)*, cited above, § 67).

98. The Court takes note of the Government's argument that the proceedings in question were complex, as they involved a large area and a high number of applicants with conflicting claims to the land. It has previously held that the enforcement of a judgment concerning allocation of particular property may take a longer time than payment of a sum of money (see *Kopnin and Others v. Russia*, no. 2746/05, § 33, 28 May 2014, and the cases cited therein), and it is certainly aware of the complexity of implementing large-scale land reforms as the one in the present case (see also *Užkurėlienė and Others v. Lithuania*, no. 62988/00, § 35, 7 April 2005). Nonetheless, the Court reiterates that the complexity of the domestic enforcement procedure cannot relieve the State of its obligation under the Convention to guarantee to everyone the right to have a binding judicial decision enforced within a reasonable time, and that it is for the Contracting States to organise their legal systems in such a way that the competent authorities can meet their obligation in this regard (see *Burdov (no. 2)*, cited above, § 70, and the cases cited therein).

108. The Court reiterates that Article 13 gives direct expression to the States' obligation, enshrined in Article 1 of the Convention, to protect human rights first and foremost within their own legal system. It therefore requires that the States provide a domestic remedy to deal with the substance of an "arguable complaint" under the Convention and to grant appropriate relief. The remedy required by Article 13 must be "effective" in practice as well as in law in the sense either of preventing the alleged violation or its continuation, or of providing adequate redress for any violation that has already occurred (see *Kudła v. Poland* [GC], no. 30210/96, §§ 152 and 157, ECHR 2000XI). Accordingly, in cases such as the present one, national legislation should provide the individuals with legal means for ensuring that judgments are timely enforced by the authorities. On the other hand, the Court reiterates that, in any event, in cases concerning non-enforcement of final decisions, where such a decision is delivered in favour of an individual against the State, the former should not, in principle, be compelled to bring separate en-

forcement proceedings (see, *mutatis mutandis*, *Metaxas v. Greece*, no. 8415/02, § 19, 27 May 2004).

110. With regard to the Government's argument that the applicant should have lodged a civil claim for damages, the Court recalls, *mutatis mutandis*, its judgment in *Nekvedavičius* (cited above, § 45, and see the cases cited therein), where it held that while compensation may sometimes be deemed a sufficient remedy for the State's failure to enforce a judgment, it could not be considered a proper alternative to the measures that the domestic legal system should have afforded the applicant in order to obtain the restoration of his ownership rights. In the light of all the essential elements of the present case, the Court is of the view that a civil claim for damages could not be considered an effective remedy against the lengthy non-enforcement of a judgment granting the applicant the right to acquire property."

4/4
In the case of *Buterlevičiūtė v. Lithuania* of 12 January 2016, Application no. 42139/08, ECHR found a violation of Article 6 § 1 of the Convention. Here are the relevant parts of the decision:

48. The applicant complained that the domestic courts had decided on her suspension from her post without holding oral hearings, and where such hearings were held, she had not been duly informed of them and thus could not participate. In particular, the applicant claimed that she had not received any notification of the hearings held before the appellate court on 27 December 2007, 21 March, 26 May, 18 June and 6 August 2008. She contended that her absence from those hearings had prevented her from submitting arguments to the courts, requesting the removal of judges, and otherwise defending her rights. ...

55. The Court firstly reiterates that Article 6 § 1 of the Convention does not guarantee the right to be present before the court in cases which do not concern a determination of a criminal charge, but rather a more general right to present one's case effectively before the court and to enjoy equality of arms with the opposing side. Article 6 § 1 leaves to the State a free choice of the means to be used in guaranteeing litigants these rights (see *Steel and Morris v. the United*

Kingdom, no. 68416/01, §§ 59-60, ECHR 2005II, and *Artyomov v. Russia*, no. 14146/02, § 201, 27 May 2010).

56. The Court also reiterates that the Convention is intended to guarantee not rights that are theoretical or illusory but rights that are practical and effective (see, among many other authorities, *Cudak v. Lithuania* [GC], no. 15869/02, § 58, ECHR 2010). It considers that the right to a public hearing would be devoid of substance if a party to the case were not apprised of the hearing in such a way as to have an opportunity to attend it, should he or she decide to exercise the right to appear established in the domestic law (see *Yakovlev v. Russia*, no. 72701/01, § 21, 15 March 2005). ...

58. The Court further reiterates that Article 6 § 1 cannot be construed as conferring on litigants a right to obtain a specific form of service of court documents, such as by registered post (see *Perihan and Mezopotamya Basın Yayın A.Ş. v. Turkey*, no. 21377/03, § 39, 21 January 2014, and *Kolegovy v. Russia*, no. 15226/05, § 40, 1 March 2012). Nonetheless, the Court considers that in the interests of the administration of justice a litigant should be notified of a court hearing in such a way as to not only have knowledge of the date and the place of the hearing, but also to have enough time to prepare his or her case and to attend the court hearing. A formal dispatch of a notification letter without any confidence that it will reach the applicant in good time cannot be considered by the Court as proper notification (see *Kolegovy*, cited above § 40, and the cases cited therein). ...

61. The Court further notes the Government's argument that all the notification letters were sent to the same address and therefore it must be presumed that the applicant had received all of them. The Court observes that the only time when the authorities could be confident that the applicant had received the notification was when the letter had been delivered to the applicant in person and not by post. ...

63. In this connection, the Court reiterates that when determining whether Article 6 § 1 of the Convention has been complied with, it must take account of the proceedings as a whole (see, among other authorities, *Perihan and Mezopotamya Basın Yayın A.Ş.*, cited above,

§ 40). In the present case, the Court notes that the appellate court was the only instance at which an oral hearing in the proceedings concerning the applicant's suspension from her post was held. The judgments of the appellate court were final and not subject to any further appeal. Moreover, on one of the five above-mentioned occasions, the prosecutor was present at the hearing and made oral submissions in favour of the applicant's suspension from her post. As a result, the applicant did not have an opportunity to effectively defend herself and to respond to the prosecutor's submissions in an oral hearing (see, *mutatis mutandis*, Švenčionienė, cited above, §§ 2728).

67. The applicant complained under Article 1 of Protocol No. 1 to the Convention and Article 6 § 1 of the Convention that suspension from her post left her without any source of income for more than one year, causing her grave financial difficulties, especially as she was the sole provider for her young daughter. The Court considers that this complaint falls to be examined solely under Article 1 of Protocol No. 1 [..]. ...

69. The Court reiterates that the applicant may allege a violation of Article 1 of Protocol No. 1 only in so far as the impugned decision relates to her "possessions" within the meaning of that provision. Article 1 of Protocol No. 1 does not guarantee the right to acquire property (see *Kopecký v. Slovakia* [GC], no. 44912/98, § 35 (b), ECHR 2004IX) and future income constitutes a "possession" only if the income has been earned or where an enforceable claim to it exists (see *Wendenburg and Others v. Germany* (dec.), no. 71630/01, 6 February 2003, and the cases cited therein).

4/5

In the case of *Kardišauskas v. Lithuania* of 7 July 2015, *Application no. 62304/12*, ECHR found no violation of Article 3. Here are the relevant parts of the decision:

64. The Court reiterates that where an individual raises an arguable claim that he has been seriously ill-treated in breach of Article 3, that provision, read in conjunction with the State's general duty under Article 1 of the Convention to "secure to everyone within their jurisdiction the rights and freedoms defined in ... [the] Convention",

requires by implication that there should be an effective official investigation (see, *mutatis mutandis, Assenov and Others v. Bulgaria*, 28 October 1998, § 102, *Reports of Judgments and Decisions* 1998VIII, and *Cucu v. Romania*, no. 22362/06, § 89, 13 November 2012). This obligation arises even where ill-treatment is inflicted by one detainee on another (see *Tautkus v. Lithuania*, no. 29474/09, § 59, 27 November 2012). The standard against which the investigation's effectiveness is to be assessed may be less exacting in cases such as the present one in which the ill-treatment has not been caused by use of force or similar direct official action. However, even in such situations, those concerned are entitled to an independent and impartial official investigation procedure that satisfies certain minimum standards as to its effectiveness (see, *mutatis mutandis*, *Česnulevičius*, cited above, § 93).

65. The Court has also held that an obligation to investigate "is not an obligation of result, but of means": not every investigation should necessarily be successful or come to a conclusion which coincides with the claimant's account of events; however, it should in principle be capable of leading to the establishment of the facts of the case and, if the allegations prove to be true, to the identification and punishment of those responsible. Thus, the investigation into serious allegations of ill-treatment must be thorough. That means that the authorities must always make a serious attempt to find out what happened and should not rely on hasty or ill-founded conclusions to close their investigation or as the basis of their decisions. They must take all reasonable steps available to them to secure the evidence concerning the incident, including, *inter alia*, eyewitness testimony, forensic evidence, and so on. Any deficiency in the investigation which undermines its ability to establish the cause of injuries or the identity of the persons responsible will risk falling foul of this standard (see *Chember v. Russia*, no. 7188/03, § 61, ECHR 2008).

Concurring opinion by Judge Kūris

Not long ago, in 2012, in *Česnulevičius v. Lithuania* (no. 13462/06, 10 January 2012), the Court found a violation of Article 2 § 1 of the Convention under its procedural aspect (under the substantive head, too). The events mentioned in *Česnulevičius* and *Kardišauskas* had taken place in the same prison, except that *Česnulevičius* was an Article 2 case because the inmate died.

The *Česnulevičius* judgment reads (§ 99) (emphasis added):

"... However, in the instant case, the Court finds that anonymous witnesses do not appear to have been the only source of evidence. Although it is not the Court's role to assess the probative value of each piece of evidence, it cannot fail to note that on 4 April 2000 a metal bar and masks with holes were found at the crime scene and that, according to the applicant, the guards apprehended three identified prisoners nearby. Lastly, *the Court also gives substantial weight to the Kaunas Regional Prosecutor's suggestion that the anonymous witnesses could have been questioned once they had finished serving their sentences ... . Given that more than eleven years have passed since the death of the applicant's son, it is not unreasonable to assume that at least some of those witnesses are at large by now. Nonetheless, the Government have not provided any information as to whether those witnesses, except for one of them ..., have been questioned by the prosecutors again with a view to compelling them to testify.*"

And § 73 of the present judgment states:

"The Court further observes that since December 2003 the actions taken by the investigators have been less frequent. Additional operational measures were ordered and performed in May-July 2005 and in 2007, which, however, did not produce any leads to pursue (see paragraphs 21-24 and 28 above)."

Full stop.

We are now in the year 2015, eight years after the last "operational measure". In *Česnulevičius*, "substantial weight" was attached to a period of eleven years. In the present case, a time-lapse of eight years was deemed to merit not even one line of comment.

There are several outstanding differences pertaining to the procedure of investigating the crime (i.e. the procedural aspect either of Article 3 or Article 2 § 1 of the Convention) between *Kardišauskas* and *Česnulevičius* (see in particular § 96 of the latter judgment). First of all, unlike in *Česnulevičius*, the investigation in *Kardišauskas* had not been frequently closed and reopened. Secondly, unlike in *Česnulevičius*, in the present case the authorities did not fail to order proper expert examinations. Thirdly, unlike in *Česnulevičius*, there is nothing in this case to suggest that the investigation was not carried out by competent, qualified and impartial experts. Fourthly, unlike in that earlier case, where there was obvious inaction on the part of the investigating authorities, in *Kardišauskas* the investigation is continuing, albeit slowly and with no success as yet.

But even given all these differences, the "eleven years" argument had been of special importance in *Česnulevičius*, a pinnacle of its line of reasoning. Therefore, it would have been logical for the Court in this case to reach a conclusion similar to that in *Česnulevičius*. Instead, the "eight years" circumstance was not even addressed, and the opposite conclusion was reached, namely no violation.

Why did the Court make a different finding? It has provided no explanation. This omission might be interpreted as tacitly setting a "threshold" for the "permissible" protraction of an investigation: eight years might be all well and good, but eleven years would constitute a violation of the procedural head of Article 2.

Such an interpretation would be utterly wrong. The Court should not have left any possibility for it.

The possibility of such speculation could have been eliminated (or at least minimised) had the Court explicitly stated what transpires from the case file, namely: (i) that the timing of "additional operational measures" was dependent on the possibilities for the investigators to question potential witnesses who had been inmates of the prison in May 2003 and who had already finished serving their sentences; (ii) that that was the strategy pursued by the investigators; and (iii) that such a strategy was neither unreasonable nor belated.

3. One further aspect has been passed over in silence. The judgment does not mention that, as it (also) transpires from the case file, the applicant's conduct in prison was far from commendable. True, in 2003-2011 he was commended six times for good behaviour; but he

was also warned or received disciplinary penalties on sixteen occasions for breaching prison rules, namely for being intoxicated and (*sic!*) using physical force against another prisoner. Given this record of disciplinary violations, the applicant could hardly be considered a genuinely vulnerable type of prisoner.

Nor could he be considered credible. He had misled the investigation on several counts, including the weapon and the nature of the attack on him, as well as the personality of the alleged attacker (see, respectively, paragraphs 17, 21 and 74, 17-19 and 71 of the judgment). The authorities showed leniency by refraining from investigating the manner in which the deliberate false accusation, by the applicant, of an uninvolved person of having committed a serious offence were dealt with under criminal legislation.

Against this whole background, one might wish that more weight had been given in the judgment to the Government's submission that "the applicant was not willing to cooperate with the investigation authorities and to secure a positive outcome to the investigation" (§ 63 of the judgment). *Curantes iura iuvant*, and, I believe, vice versa.

4/5
In the case of *Kudrevičius and Others v. Lithuania* of 15 October 2015, *Application no. 37553/05*, ECHR found no violation under Article 11. However, the relevant parts of the decision should be mentioned:

82. The applicants complained that their criminal conviction had violated their rights to freedom of expression and freedom of peaceful assembly, guaranteed by Articles 10 and 11 of the Convention respectively. ...

91. The Court must first determine whether the facts of the present case fall within the ambit of Article 11 of the Convention. It reiterates that the right to freedom of assembly is a fundamental right in a democratic society and, like the right to freedom of expression, is one of the foundations of such a society. Thus, it should not be interpreted restrictively (see *Taranenko v. Russia*, no. 19554/05, § 65, 15 May 2014). As such this right covers both private meetings and meetings in public places, whether static or in the form of a pro-

cession; in addition, it can be exercised by individual participants and by the persons organising the gathering (see *Djavit An v. Turkey*, no. 20652/92, § 56, ECHR 2003-III; *Ziliberberg v. Moldova* (dec.), no. 61821/00, 4 May 2004; and *Barraco v. France*, no. 31684/05, § 41, 5 March 2009).

92. Article 11 of the Convention only protects the right to "peaceful assembly", a notion which does not cover a demonstration where the organisers and participants have violent intentions (see *Stankov and the United Macedonian Organization Ilinden v. Bulgaria*, nos. 29221/95 and 29225/95, § 77, ECHR 2001-IX). The guarantees of Article 11 therefore apply to all gatherings except those where the organisers and participants have such intentions, incite violence or otherwise reject the foundations of a democratic society (see *Sergey Kuznetsov v. Russia*, no. 10877/04, § 45, 23 October 2008; *Alekseyev v. Russia*, nos. 4916/07, 25924/08 and 14599/09, § 80, 21 October 2010; *Fáber*, cited above, § 37; *Gün and Others v. Turkey*, no. 8029/07, § 49, 18 June 2013; and *Taranenko*, cited above, § 66). ...

94. In this connection, it is not without interest to note that an individual does not cease to enjoy the right to freedom of peaceful assembly as a result of sporadic violence or other punishable acts committed by others in the course of the demonstration if the individual in question remains peaceful in his or her own intentions or behaviour (see *Ziliberberg*, decision cited above). The possibility of persons with violent intentions, not members of the organising association, joining the demonstration cannot as such take away that right (see *Primov and Others*, cited above, § 155). Even if there is a real risk that a public demonstration might result in disorder as a result of developments outside the control of those organising it, such a demonstration does not as such fall outside the scope of Article 11 § 1, and any restriction placed thereon must be in conformity with the terms of paragraph 2 of that provision (see *Schwabe and M.G.*, cited above, § 103, and *Taranenko*, cited above, § 66). ...

108. The Court reiterates its case-law to the effect that the expressions "prescribed by law" and "in accordance with the law" in Articles 8 to 11 of the Convention not only requires that the impugned measure should have a legal basis in domestic law, but also refers to the quality of the law in question, which should be accessible to

the person concerned and foreseeable as to its effects (see, among other authorities, *Rotaru v. Romania* [GC], no. 28341/95, § 52, ECHR 2000-V; *VgT Verein gegen Tierfabriken v. Switzerland*, no. 24699/94, § 52, ECHR 2001-VI; *Gawęda v. Poland*, no. 26229/95, § 39, ECHR 2002-II; *Maestri v. Italy* [GC], no. 39748/98, § 30, ECHR 2004-I; *Vyerentsov*, cited above, § 52; *Gorzelik and Others v. Poland* [GC], no. 44158/98, §§ 64-65, ECHR 2004-I; and *Sindicatul "Păstorul cel Bun" v. Romania* [GC], no. 2330/09, § 153, ECHR 2013 (extracts)). ...

142. The right to freedom of assembly, one of the foundations of a democratic society, is subject to a number of exceptions which must be narrowly interpreted and the necessity for any restrictions must be convincingly established. When examining whether restrictions on the rights and freedoms guaranteed by the Convention can be considered "necessary in a democratic society" the Contracting States enjoy a certain but not unlimited margin of appreciation (see *Barraco*, cited above, § 42). It is, in any event, for the Court to give a final ruling on the restriction's compatibility with the Convention and this is to be done by assessing the circumstances of a particular case (see *Rufi Osmani and Others v. the former Yugoslav Republic of Macedonia* (dec.), no. 50841/99, ECHR 2001-X, and *Galstyan*, cited above, § 114).

143. When the Court carries out its scrutiny, its task is not to substitute its own view for that of the relevant national authorities but rather to review under Article 11 the decisions they took. This does not mean that it has to confine itself to ascertaining whether the State exercised its discretion reasonably, carefully and in good faith; it must look at the interference complained of in the light of the case as a whole and determine, after having established that it pursued a "legitimate aim", whether it answered a "pressing social need" and, in particular, whether it was proportionate to that aim and whether the reasons adduced by the national authorities to justify it were "relevant and sufficient" (see *Coster v. the United Kingdom* [GC], no. 24876/94, § 104, 18 January 2001; *Ashughyan v. Armenia*, no. 33268/03, § 89, 17 July 2008; *S. and Marper v. the United Kingdom* [GC], nos. 30562/04 and 30566/04, § 101, ECHR 2008; *Barraco*, cited above, § 42; and *Kasparov and Others*, cited above, § 86). In so doing, the Court has to satisfy itself that the national authorities applied standards which were in conformity with the principles embodied

in Article 11 and, moreover, that they based their decisions on an acceptable assessment of the relevant facts (see *Rai and Evans*, decision cited above, and *Gün and Others*, cited above, § 75; see also *United Communist Party of Turkey and Others v. Turkey*, 30 January 1998, § 47, Reports 1998-I, and *Gerger v. Turkey* [GC], no. 24919/94, § 46, 8 July 1999).

146. The nature and severity of the penalties imposed are also factors to be taken into account when assessing the proportionality of an interference in relation to the aim pursued (see *Öztürk v. Turkey* [GC], no. 22479/93, § 70, ECHR 1999-VI; *Rufi Osmani and Others*, decision cited above; and *Gün and Others*, cited above, § 82). Where the sanctions imposed on the demonstrators are criminal in nature, they require particular justification (see *Rai and Evans*, decision cited above). A peaceful demonstration should not, in principle, be rendered subject to the threat of a criminal sanction (see *Akgöl and Göl v. Turkey*, nos. 28495/06 and 28516/06, § 43, 17 May 2011), and notably to deprivation of liberty (see *Gün and Others*, cited above, § 83). Thus, the Court must examine with particular scrutiny the cases where sanctions imposed by the national authorities for non-violent conduct involve a prison sentence (see *Taranenko*, cited above, § 87).

(β) *The requirement of prior authorisation*

147. It is not, in principle, contrary to the spirit of Article 11 if, for reasons of public order and national security a High Contracting Party requires that the holding of meetings be subject to authorisation (see *Oya Ataman*, cited above, § 37; *Bukta and Others v. Hungary*, no. 25691/04, § 35, ECHR 2007-III; *Balçık and Others v. Turkey*, no. 25/02, § 49, 29 November 2007; *Nurettin Aldemir and Others v. Turkey*, nos. 32124/02, 32126/02, 32129/02, 32132/02, 32133/02, 32137/02 and 32138/02, § 42, 18 December 2007; *Éva Molnár*, cited above, § 35; *Karatepe and Others v. Turkey*, nos. 33112/04, 36110/04, 40190/04, 41469/04 and 41471/04, § 46, 7 April 2009; *Skiba*, decision cited above; *Çelik v. Turkey (no. 3)*, no. 36487/07, § 90, 15 November 2012; and *Gün and Others*, cited above, §§ 73 and 80). Indeed, the Court has previously considered that notification, and even authorisation procedures, for a public event do not normally encroach upon the essence of the right under Article 11 of the Convention as long as the

purpose of the procedure is to allow the authorities to take reasonable and appropriate measures in order to guarantee the smooth conduct of any assembly, meeting or other gathering (see *Sergey Kuznetsov*, cited above, § 42, and *Rai and Evans*, decision cited above). Organisers of public gatherings should abide by the rules governing that process by complying with the regulations in force (see *Primov and Others*, cited above, § 117).

148. Prior notification serves not only the aim of reconciling the right of assembly with the rights and lawful interests (including the freedom of movement) of others, but also the aim of preventing disorder or crime. In order to balance these conflicting interests, the institution of preliminary administrative procedures appears to be common practice in member States when a public demonstration is to be organised (see *Éva Molnár*, cited above, § 37, and *Berladir and Others v. Russia*, no. 34202/06, § 42, 10 July 2012). However, regulations of this nature should not represent a hidden obstacle to freedom of peaceful assembly as protected by the Convention (see *Samüt Karabulut v. Turk*ey, no. 16999/04, § 35, 27 January 2009, and *Berladir and Others*, cited above, § 39).

149. Since States have the right to require authorisation, they must be able to impose sanctions on those who participate in demonstrations that do not comply with such requirement (see *Ziliberberg*, decision cited above; *Rai and Evans*, decision cited above; *Berladir and Others*, cited above, § 41; and *Primov and Others*, cited above, § 118). At the same time, the freedom to take part in a peaceful assembly is of such importance that a person cannot be subject to a sanction – even one at the lower end of the scale of disciplinary penalties – for participation in a demonstration which has not been prohibited, so long as that person does not himself commit any reprehensible act on such an occasion (see *Ezelin*, cited above, § 53; *Galstyan*, cited above, § 115; and *Barraco*, cited above, § 44). This is true also when the demonstration results in damage or other disorder (see *Taranenko*, cited above, § 88).

150. An unlawful situation, such as the staging of a demonstration without prior authorisation, does not necessarily justify an interference with a person's right to freedom of assembly (see *Cisse v. France*, no. 51346/99, § 50, ECHR 2002-III; *Oya Ataman*, cited above,

§ 39; *Barraco*, cited above, § 45; and *Skiba*, decision cited above). While rules governing public assemblies, such as the system of prior notification, are essential for the smooth conduct of public demonstrations, since they allow the authorities to minimise the disruption to traffic and take other safety measures, their enforcement cannot become an end in itself (see *Primov and Others*, cited above, § 118). In particular, where demonstrators do not engage in acts of violence it is important for the public authorities to show a certain degree of tolerance towards peaceful gatherings if the freedom of assembly guaranteed by Article 11 of the Convention is not to be deprived of all substance (see *Oya Ataman*, cited above, § 42; *Bukta and Others*, cited above, § 37; *Nurettin Aldemir and Others*, cited above, § 46; *Ashughyan*, cited above, § 90; *Éva Molnár*, cited above, § 36; *Barraco*, cited above, § 43; *Berladir and Others*, cited above, § 38; *Fáber*, cited above, § 47; İzci v. Turkey, no. 42606/05, § 89, 23 July 2013; and *Kasparov and Others*, cited above, § 91).

151. The absence of prior authorisation and the ensuing "unlawfulness" of the action do not give *carte blanche* to the authorities; they are still restricted by the proportionality requirement of Article 11. Thus, it should be established why the demonstration was not authorised in the first place, what the public interest at stake was, and what risks were represented by the demonstration. The method used by the police for discouraging the protesters, containing them in a particular place or dispersing the demonstration is also an important factor in assessing the proportionality of the interference (see *Primov and Others*, cited above, § 119). Thus, the use by the police of pepper spray to disperse an authorised demonstration was found to be disproportionate, even though the Court acknowledged that the event could have disrupted the flow of traffic (see *Oya Ataman*, cited above, §§ 38-44). ...

153. The Court has also clarified that the principle established in the case of *Bukta and Others* cannot be extended to the point where the absence of prior notification of a spontaneous demonstration can never be a legitimate basis for crowd dispersal. The right to hold spontaneous demonstrations may override the obligation to give prior notification of public assemblies only in special circumstances, namely if an immediate response to a current event is warranted in the form of a demonstration. In particular, such derogation from

the general rule may be justified if a delay would have rendered that response obsolete (see *Éva Molnár*, cited above, §§ 37-38, and *Skiba*, decision cited above).

(γ) *Demonstrations and disruption to ordinary life*

155. Any demonstration in a public place may cause a certain level of disruption to ordinary life, including disruption of traffic (see *Barraco*, cited above, § 43; *Disk and Kesk v. Turkey*, no. 38676/08, § 29, 27 November 2012; and *İzci*, cited above, § 89). This fact in itself does not justify an interference with the right to freedom of assembly (see *Berladir and Others*, cited above, § 38, and *Gün and Others*, cited above, § 74), as it is important for the public authorities to show a certain degree of tolerance (see *Ashughyan*, cited above, § 90). The appropriate "degree of tolerance" cannot be defined *in abstracto*: the Court must look at the particular circumstances of the case and particularly at the extent of the "disruption to ordinary life" (see *Primov and Others*, cited above, § 145). This being so, it is important for associations and others organising demonstrations, as actors in the democratic process, to abide by the rules governing that process by complying with the regulations in force (see *Oya Ataman*, cited above, § 38; *Balçık and Others*, cited above, § 49; *Éva Molnár*, cited above, § 41; *Barraco*, cited above, § 44; and *Skiba*, decision cited above).

156. The intentional failure by the organisers to abide by these rules and the structuring of a demonstration, or of part of it, in such a way as to cause disruption to ordinary life and other activities to a degree exceeding that which is inevitable in the circumstances constitutes conduct which cannot enjoy the same privileged protection under the Convention as political speech or debate on questions of public interest or the peaceful manifestation of opinions on such matters. On the contrary, the Court considers that the Contracting States enjoy a wide margin of appreciation in their assessment of the necessity in taking measures to restrict such conduct.

157. Restrictions on freedom of peaceful assembly in public places may serve to protect the rights of others with a view to preventing disorder and maintaining an orderly flow of traffic (see *Éva Molnár*, cited above, § 34). Since overcrowding during a public event

is fraught with danger, it is not uncommon for State authorities in various countries to impose restrictions on the location, date, time, form or manner of conduct of a planned public gathering (see *Primov and Others*, cited above, § 130).

(δ) *The State's positive obligations under Article 11 of the Convention*

158. States must not only refrain from applying unreasonable indirect restrictions upon the right to assemble peacefully but also safeguard that right. Although the essential object of Article 11 is to protect the individual against arbitrary interference by public authorities with the exercise of the rights protected (see *Associated Society of Locomotive Engineers and Firemen (ASLEF) v. the United Kingdom*, no. 11002/05, § 37, 27 February 2007, and *Nemtsov*, cited above, § 72), there may in addition be positive obligations to secure the effective enjoyment of these rights (see *Djavit An*, cited above, § 57; *Oya Ataman*, cited above, § 36; and *Gün and Others*, cited above, § 72).

159. The authorities have a duty to take appropriate measures with regard to lawful demonstrations in order to ensure their peaceful conduct and the safety of all citizens (see *Oya Ataman*, cited above, § 35; *Makhmoudov v. Russia*, no. 35082/04, §§ 63-65, 26 July 2007; *Skiba*, decision cited above; and *Gün and Others*, cited above, § 69). However, they cannot guarantee this absolutely and they have a wide discretion in the choice of the means to be used (see *Protopapa v. Turkey*, no. 16084/90, § 108, 24 February 2009). In this area the obligation they enter into under Article 11 of the Convention is an obligation as to measures to be taken and not as to results to be achieved (see *Plattform "Ärzte für das Leben" v. Austria*, 21 June 1988, § 34, Series A no. 139, and *Fáber*, cited above, § 39).

160. In particular, the Court has stressed the importance of taking preventive security measures such as, for example, ensuring the presence of first-aid services at the site of demonstrations, in order to guarantee the smooth conduct of any event, meeting or other gathering, be it political, cultural or of another nature (*Oya Ataman*, cited above, § 39)

170. As already pointed out, the disruption to ordinary life and traffic was not a side-effect of a demonstration held in a public place. As long as the demonstrations took place in the designated locations, the flow of traffic was not affected. The decision of the farmers to move onto the highways and to use the tractors could not but be an attempt to block or reduce the passage of vehicles and create chaos in order to draw attention to the farmers' needs. The intentional roadblocks could not but have been aimed at pressuring the government to accept the farmers' demands, as shown by the fact that they were lifted as soon as the demonstrators had been informed of the successful outcome of the negotiations. This feature distinguishes the present case from those in which the Court has observed that demonstrations may cause a certain level of disruption to ordinary life, including disruption to traffic.

171. The Court has already been called upon to examine situations where demonstrators had tried to prevent or alter the exercise of an activity carried out by others. In *Steel and Others* (cited above) the first and second applicants had obstructed a hunt and had impeded engineering work for the construction of a motorway, respectively. In *Drieman and Others* (decision cited above), *Greenpeace* activists had manoeuvred dinghies in such a manner as to physically obstruct whaling, forcing the whalers to abandon their lawful exploitation of the living resources in Norway's exclusive economic zone. In these two cases, the Court considered that the inflicting of sanctions (in *Steel and Others*, forty-four hours' detention pending trial and sentencing to twenty-eight days' imprisonment for the obstruction of the hunt and seventeen hours' detention pending trial and sentencing to seven days' imprisonment for the protest against the construction of the motorway; in *Drieman and Others*, two days' detention on remand, fines convertible into imprisonment in case of default on payment and confiscation of a dinghy) was a reaction proportionate to, *inter alia*, the legitimate aim of protecting the rights and freedoms of others. The Court considers that the same conclusion should *a fortiori* be reached in the present case, where the actions of the demonstrators had not been directly aimed at an activity of which they disapproved, but at the physical blocking of another activity (the use of highways by carriers of goods and private cars) which had no direct connection with the object of their

protest, namely the government's alleged lack of action *vis-à-vis* the decrease in the prices of some agricultural products.

174. The Court considers that even though the applicants had neither performed acts of violence nor incited others to engage in such acts (contrast *Osmani and Others*, decision cited above; *Protopapa*, cited above; and *Primov and Others*, cited above), the almost complete obstruction of three major highways in blatant disregard of police orders and of the needs and rights of the road users constituted conduct which, even though less serious than recourse to physical violence, can be described as "reprehensible".

(γ) *The authorities' conduct during the demonstrations*

176. As to the conduct of the authorities, the Court notes that as requested by the farmers, they had issued permits to hold peaceful assemblies at specific locations and that they did not interfere with the meetings until the demonstrators moved onto different locations, namely the highways. From that moment on, the police confined themselves to ordering the applicants to remove the roadblocks and to warning them about their possible liability. Even when the applicants refused to obey these lawful orders, the police chose not to disperse the gatherings. The farmers only decided to stop demonstrating when their demands had been met by the government. Moreover, when tensions arose between the farmers and the truck drivers, the police urged the parties to the conflict to calm down in order to avoid serious confrontations. Finally, the authorities tried to re-direct the traffic onto secondary, neighbouring roads with a view to reducing the traffic jams.

177. In the light of the above, the Court considers that, despite the serious disruptions caused by the applicants' conduct the authorities showed a high degree of tolerance (see, *mutatis mutandis*, *Éva Molnár*, cited above, § 43; *Barraco*, cited above, § 47; and *Skiba*, decision cited above; see also, by contrast, *Primov and Others*, cited above). Moreover, they had attempted to balance the interests of the demonstrators with those of the users of the highways, in order to ensure the peaceful conduct of the gathering and the safety of all citizens, thus satisfying any positive obligation that they might be considered to have had.

180. In addition, the Court considers that due account should be taken of the width of the margin of appreciation enjoyed by the State in relation to the subject matter in the particular circumstances of the present case. In this regard, it is noteworthy that according to the comparative law material available to the Court, there is no uniform approach amongst the member States as to the legal characterisation of the obstruction of traffic on a public highway, which is treated as a criminal offence in some States and as an administrative matter in others. Therefore, a wide discretion should be given to the domestic authorities as to the characterisation of the conduct attributed to the applicants. Thus, the domestic authorities did not overstep the limits of their wide margin of appreciation by holding the applicants criminally liable for their conduct. ...

185. The applicants further alleged that they had been convicted in breach of Article 7 of the Convention. ...

193. The Court observes that it has held that the interference with the applicants' freedom of peaceful assembly was "prescribed by law" within the meaning of Article 11 § 2 of the Convention, including that it was foreseeable for the applicants. It also reiterates that when speaking of "law" Article 7 alludes to the very same concept as that to which the Convention refers elsewhere when using that term, a concept which comprises statute law together with case-law and implies qualitative requirements, notably those of accessibility and foreseeability (see the restatement of relevant principles in *Rohlena v. the Czech Republic* [GC], no. 59552/08, § 50, ECHR 2015). The Court further notes that in their observations before the Grand Chamber, the applicants did not specifically address the complaint that they had raised before the Chamber under Article 7 of the Convention. That being so, the Court considers that it is not necessary to carry out a separate examination of whether there has been a violation of Article 7 of the Convention.

Concurring opinion of Judge Wojtyczek (translation)

4. <...> I would note in this connection that in a democratic State – member of the Council of Europe – citizens necessarily have various means by which they can express their opinions collec-

tively and defend their interests without directly and intentionally undermining the freedom of movement and legitimate economic interests of others. At the same time, the fact that the applicants had the possibility of defending their interests through complaints to administrative courts does not seem to me to be pertinent for the legal characterisation of their actions. Even if, for various reasons, the economic interests defended by demonstrators cannot be protected effectively by the courts and their claims are not justiciable, that does not justify causing prejudice to the legitimate interests and rights of others. Conversely, the justiciability of claims expressed during a peaceful gathering cannot reduce the extent of the protection afforded to demonstrators under Article 11.

5. Whatever the answer to the question of the applicability of Article 11 in the present case, the finding that the Lithuanian authorities had complied with the Convention seemed to impose itself as self-evident. Given the particular circumstances of the case, as presented in detail in the judgment's reasoning, the application could even have been declared manifestly ill-founded.

4/6

In the case of *Mironovas and Others v. Lithuania* of 8 December 2015, Applications nos. 40828/12, 29292/12, 69598/12, 40163/13, 66281/13, 70048/13 and 70065/13, ECHR found violation of Article 3 of the Convention. Here are the relevant parts of the decision:

> 71. All seven applicants complained that the conditions of their detention in the various correctional facilities in which they had been held had fallen short of standards compatible with Article 3 of the Convention. ...

> 115. The Court reiterates that Article 3 of the Convention enshrines one of the most fundamental values of a democratic society. It prohibits in absolute terms torture or inhuman or degrading treatment or punishment, irrespective of the circumstances and the victim's behaviour (see, for example, *Labita v. Italy* [GC], no. 26772/95, § 119, ECHR 2000-IV). Ill-treatment must attain a minimum level of severity if it is to fall within the scope of Article 3. The assessment of this minimum is relative; it depends on all the circumstances of the case, such as the duration of the treatment, its physical and mental

effects and, in some cases, the sex, age and state of health of the victim (see, among other authorities, *Ireland v. the United Kingdom*, 18 January 1978, § 162, Series A no. 25). ...

117. In the context of deprivation of liberty the Court has consistently stressed that, to fall under Article 3, the suffering and humiliation involved must in any event go beyond that inevitable element of suffering and humiliation connected with detention. The State must ensure that a person is detained in conditions which are compatible with respect for human dignity, that the manner and method of the execution of the measure do not subject him to distress or hardship of an intensity exceeding the unavoidable level of suffering inherent in detention and that, given the practical demands of imprisonment, his health and well-being are adequately secured (see *Kudła,* cited above, §§ 92-94; and *Popov v. Russia*, no. 26853/04, § 208, 13 July 2006). ...

119. Extreme lack of space in a prison cell weighs heavily as a 'central factor' to be taken into account for the purpose of establishing whether the impugned detention conditions were "degrading" from the point of view of Article 3 (see *Karalevičius v. Lithuania*, no. 53254/99, §§ 36 and 39, 7 April 2005; and, more recently, *Vladimir Belyayev v. Russia*, no. 9967/06, § 30, 17 October 2013). ...

121. However, the Court has so far refrained from determining how much space should be allocated to a detainee in terms of the Convention, having considered that a number of other relevant factors, such as the duration of detention, the possibilities for outdoor exercise, the physical and mental condition of the detainee and so forth, play an important part in deciding whether the detention conditions complied with the guarantees of Article 3 of the Convention (see *Trepashkin v. Russia*, no. 36898/03, § 92, 19 July 2007, and *Torreggiani and Others,* cited above, § 69). Furthermore, when assessing the issue of overcrowding in post-trial detention facilities such as correctional colonies, as opposed to pre-trial detention facilities and high-security prisons where inmates are confined to their cell for most of the day, the Court has held that the personal space in the dormitory should be viewed in the context of the applicable regime, as detainees in correctional colonies enjoy a wider freedom of movement during the daytime, which may ensure that they have

unobstructed access to natural light and air (see *Insanov v. Azerbaijan*, no. 16133/08, § 120, 14 March 2013).

122. Applying this approach, the Court has found that the strong presumption that the conditions of detention amounted to degrading treatment in breach of Article 3 on account of a lack of personal space were refuted by the cumulative effect of the conditions of detention. These included the brevity of the applicant's incarceration (see, for example, *Fetisov and Others v. Russia*, nos. 43710/07, 6023/08, 11248/08, 27668/08, 31242/08 and 52133/08, § 138, 17 January 2012, and *Dmitriy Rozhin v. Russia*, no. 4265/06, § 53, 23 October 2012) or the freedom of movement afforded to inmates and their unobstructed access to natural light and air (see, for example, *Shkurenko v. Russia* (dec.), no. 15010/04, 10 September 2009).

123. On the other hand, even in cases where the inmates appeared to have sufficient personal space at their disposal and where a larger prison cell was at issue – measuring in the range of three to four square metres per inmate – the Court noted other aspects of physical conditions of detention as being relevant for the assessment of compliance with Article 3. It found a violation of that provision since the space factor was coupled with an established lack of ventilation and lighting (see, for example, *Vlasov v. Russia*, no. 78146/01, §§ 81 and 84, 12 June 2008) and a lack of outdoor exercise (see *Longin v. Croatia*, no. 49268/10, §§ 60-61, 6 November 2012). ...

130. The Court has already held, albeit as regards prison cells, that when the space allocated to a detainee is below 3 square metres, it can hardly be compensated by other factors and is in principle considered to be so severe as to justify of itself a finding a violation of Article 3. Thus, such a scarce allocation of space, if established, creates a strong indication (see *Olszewski v. Poland*, no. 21880/03, § 98, 2 April 2013) or, as noted in *Ananyev and Others*, a strong presumption (see § 148 of that judgment; also see, *a contrario*, *Vladimir Belyayev*, cited above, §§ 33-36) that Article 3 of the Convention has been violated. ...

135. The Court recalls that the Committee for the Prevention of Torture expressed strong concern and objections to the very principle of dormitory-type accommodation arrangements frequently

encountered in Central and Eastern European prisons, because the dormitories in question had been found to hold prisoners in extremely cramped and insalubrious conditions. The Committee also noted that such accommodation inevitably implied a lack of privacy for prisoners in their everyday lives (see point 29 of the 11th General Report, cited in paragraph 63 above). ...

148. <...> the Court has also held that other aspects of detention, while not in themselves capable of justifying the notion of "degrading" treatment, are relevant – in addition to the focal factor of overcrowding – in demonstrating that the conditions of detention went beyond the threshold tolerated by Article 3 (see *Novoselov v. Russia*, no. 66460/01, § 44, 2 June 2005). Even if overcrowding is not so serious as to amount in itself to a breach of Article 3 of the Convention, it can still give rise to a breach of that provision if, combined with other factors – such as lack of privacy when using the toilet, poor ventilation, lack of access to natural light and fresh air, lack of proper heating or lack of basic hygiene – it results in a level of suffering that exceeds that inherent in detention (see *Torreggiani and Others*, cited above, § 69).

Partly dissenting opinion of Judge Pinto de Albuquerque

On 15 January, the European Court of Human Rights gave a judgment in the case of *Rummi v. Estonia*, where the applicant complained that her right of access to court had been violated (Article 6 § 1), she had been deprived of the possessions which had belonged to her husband and which had become her possessions through succession (Article 1 of Protocol No. 1), that the length of the proceedings in which her civil rights were determined had been excessive (Article 6 § 1), and had had no effective remedy in respect of her complaint of excessive length of civil proceedings (Article 13). The Chamber found the following:

14. The criteria for determining the amount of the compensation do not fall within the discretion of the national authorities. There are three basic principles that any compensatory remedy must adhere to. Firstly, the individualisation principle, i.e., the amount of the compensation must correspond to the concrete situation of

each prisoner; secondly, the holistic principle, i.e., the amount of the compensation must take into account the "aggravating cumulative effect" of deficient material prison conditions, such as a lack of personal sleeping space, lack of access to natural light during the day and electric lighting at night, lack of ventilation and heating, improper hygiene conditions or inadequate food or health care;[1] and thirdly, the resocialisation principle, i.e., the amount of the compensation must take into account the existence and degree of implementation of the individual sentence plan.[2] ...

18. Consideration of the country's economic situation is an intrinsic limitation of monetary compensation. While an economic crisis in itself does not justify Article 3 violations – the Contracting Parties to the Convention having the obligation to comply with its requirements even in hard times – it is understandable for the amounts awarded to the victims of these violations to be reasonably aligned with the living standard of the country.[3] In any event, economic difficulties do not relieve them of their obligation to organise the

---

1 The ground-breaking text of the CPT on the "detrimental cumulative effect" of prison conditions in overcrowded facilities is paragraph 50 of the Second General report (CPT/Inf (91) 3): "The CPT would add that it is particularly concerned when it finds a combination of overcrowding, poor regime activities and inadequate access to toilet/washing facilities in the same establishment. The cumulative effect of such conditions can prove extremely detrimental to prisoners". The Court has accepted this test since *Dougoz v. Greece* (no. 40907/98, § 46, ECHR 2001-II) and has repeatedly held that overcrowding may be aggravated by other prison conditions (for example, *Orchowski*, cited above, §§ 132-135, *Ananyev and Others*, cited above, §§ 142 and 151, *Vasilescu*, cited above, §§ 101-104, *Neshkov and Others*, cited above, § 235, and *Varga and Others*, cited above, §§ 72, 78, 89-92).

2 The cornerstone of a penal policy aimed at resocialising prisoners is the individualised sentence plan, under which the prisoner's risk and needs in terms of health care, activities, work, exercise, education and contacts with the family and outside world should be assessed (Rule 103.8 of the 2006 European Prison Rules and the commentary to Rule 103 in the relevant Explanatory Report; and see also the opinions joined to *Valiuniene v. Lithuania*, no. 33234/07, 26 March 2013, and *Khoroshenko v. Russia (GC)*, no. 41418/04, 30 June 2014).

3 That does not mean that I can accept the highly speculative argument of the Government that large compensation amounts could risk encouraging people to commit criminal offences in order to be kept in inadequate prisons and afterwards secure the desired compensation (paragraph 77 of the judgment).

penal system in such a way as to ensure respect for the dignity of prisoners.[4] ...

19. Finally, compensatory remedies are not the sole possible satisfaction for prison overcrowding. Although not mentioned in the present case, the reduction of a sentence may be an appropriate way of remedying the Convention breach.[5]

4/7

In the case of *Noreikienė and Noreika v. Lithuania* of 24 November 2015, Application no. 17285/08, ECHR found a violation of Article 1 of Protocol No. 1 to the Convention. Here are the relevant parts of the decision:

14. The applicants complained that the State had unlawfully deprived them of their property and had not provided them with adequate compensation. They relied on Article 1 of Protocol No. 1 to the Convention, which reads as follows:

"Every natural or legal person is entitled to the peaceful enjoyment of his possessions. No one shall be deprived of his possessions except in the public interest and subject to the conditions provided for by law and by the general principles of international law ..."

28. The Court reiterates that any interference with property must, in addition to being lawful and having a legitimate aim, also satisfy the requirement of proportionality. A fair balance must be struck between the demands of the general interest of the community and the requirements of the protection of the individual's fundamental rights, the search for such a fair balance being inherent in the whole of the Convention. The requisite balance will not be struck where

---

[4] According to *Ananyev and Others*, cited above, § 117, the scarcity of means available to the State should not be accepted as mitigating its liability and was thus irrelevant in assessing damages under the compensatory remedy. Here again, the position of the Court is much more tolerant in *Stella and Others* (dec.), cited above, § 62.

[5] A reduced prison sentence may offer adequate redress for deficient material conditions of detention, provided the reduction is carried out in an express and measurable way. In spite of the doubts raised by *Ananyev and Others*, cited above, § 222-226, the Court has accepted this practice in *Stella and Others* (dec.), cited above, §§ 60-63, *Neshkov and Others*, cited above, § 287, and *Varga and Others*, cited above, § 109.

the person concerned bears an individual and excessive burden (see *Sporrong and Lönnroth v. Sweden*, 23 September 1982, §§ 69-74, Series A no. 52; *Brumărescu v. Romania* [GC], no. 28342/95, § 78, ECHR 1999-VII; and *Anthony Aquilina v. Malta*, no. 3851/12, §§ 58-59, 11 December 2014, and the cases cited therein).

29. On several occasions in similar cases which, as in the present case, concerned the correction of mistakes made by the State authorities in the process of restitution, the Court has emphasised the necessity of ensuring that the remedying of old injuries does not create disproportionate new wrongs (see *Velikovi and Others v. Bulgaria*, nos. 43278/98, 45437/99, 48014/99, 48380/99, 51362/99, 53367/99, 60036/00, 73465/01 and 194/02, § 178, 15 March 2007). To that end, the legislation should make it possible to take into account the particular circumstances of each case, so that individuals who have acquired their possessions in good faith are not made to bear the burden of responsibility, which is rightfully that of the State which confiscated those possessions. In other words, the risk of any mistake made by the State authority must be borne by the State, and errors must not be remedied at the expense of the individual concerned (see *Gladysheva v. Russia*, no. 7097/10, § 80, 6 December 2011, and *Pyrantienė*, cited above, § 70). ...

34. In this context, the Court reiterates the particular importance of the principle of good governance, which requires that where an issue pertaining to the general interest is at stake – especially when it affects fundamental human rights, including property rights – the public authorities must act promptly and in an appropriate and consistent manner (see *Beyeler v. Italy* [GC], no. 33202/96, § 120, ECHR 2000-I; *Rysovskyy v. Ukraine*, no. 29979/04, § 71, 20 October 2011; and *Pyrantienė*, cited above, § 55). ...

38. The Court reiterates that the taking of property without payment of an amount reasonably related to its value will normally fail to respect the requisite fair balance between the demands of the general interest of the community and the requirements of the protection of the individual's fundamental rights and will constitute a disproportionate burden on the applicant (see *The Holy Monasteries v. Greece*, 9 December 1994, § 71, Series A no. 301-A, and *Former King of Greece and Others v. Greece* [GC], no. 25701/94, § 89, ECHR

2000-XII). In line with the Court's case-law in similar cases concerning expropriation of property, the balance mentioned above is generally achieved where compensation paid to the person whose property has been taken reasonably relates to its "market" value as determined at the time of expropriation (see *Pincová and Pinc v. the Czech Republic*, no. 36548/97, § 53, ECHR 2002VIII; *Vistiņš and Perepjolkins*, cited above, § 111; and *Guiso-Gallisay v. Italy (just satisfaction)* [GC], no. 58858/00, § 103, 22 December 2009). It follows that the amount of compensation for the applicants' loss of title to the land must be calculated using the value of the property on the date ownership was lost.

4/8

In the case of *Paliutis v. Lithuania* of 24 November 2015, Application no. 34085/09, ECHR found a violation of Article 6 § 1 of the Convention. Here are the relevant parts of the decision:

> 38. The Court reiterates that Article 6 § 1 secures to everyone the right to have any claim relating to his or her civil rights and obligations brought before a court or tribunal. In this way the Article embodies the "right to a court", of which the right of access, that is, the right to institute proceedings before courts in civil matters, constitutes one aspect only (see, among many other authorities, *Golder v. the United Kingdom*, 21 February 1975, § 36, Series A no. 18, and *Prince Hans-Adam II of Liechtenstein v. Germany* [GC], no. 42527/98, § 43, ECHR 2001VIII). ...
>
> 40. The Court reaffirms, moreover, that while Article 6 § 1 obliges the courts to give reasons for their judgments, it cannot be understood as requiring a detailed answer to every argument put forward by the parties. The extent to which this duty to give reasons applies may vary according to the nature of the decision. It is moreover necessary to take into account, *inter alia*, the diversity of the submissions that a litigant may bring before the courts and the differences existing between the Contracting States with regard to statutory provisions, customary rules, judicial opinion and the presentation and drafting of judgments. That is why the question as to whether a court has failed to fulfil the obligation to state reasons, deriving from Article 6 of the Convention, can only be determined in the light of the circumstances of the case (see, among many other au-

thorities, *Ruiz Torija v. Spain*, 9 December 1994, § 29, Series A no. 303A, and *Wagner and J.M.W.L. v. Luxembourg*, no. 76240/01, § 90, 28 June 2007). ...

45. However, even assuming that the domestic courts had compelling reasons not to examine the applicant's request, the Court notes that no such reasons were provided in any of the judgments delivered in the case. In this connection the Court reiterates that, even though the courts cannot be required to state the reasons for rejecting each argument of a party, they are nonetheless not relieved of the obligation to undertake a proper examination of, and to respond to, the main pleas put forward by that party (see *Wagner and J.M.W.L.*, cited above, § 96). One of the functions of a reasoned decision is to demonstrate to the parties that they have been heard, while it also affords a party the possibility to appeal against the decision and have it reviewed by an appellate body (see *Suominen v. Finland*, no. 37801/97, § 37, 1 July 2003, and *Kuznetsov and Others v. Russia*, no. 184/02, § 83, 11 January 2007). While an appellate court may, in principle, simply endorse the reasons for a lower court's decision, this will not suffice in those cases where the lower court did not provide such reasons as to enable the parties to make effective use of their right of appeal (see *Jokela v. Finland*, no. 28856/95, § 73, ECHR 2002IV, and *Boldea v. Romania*, no. 19997/02, § 33, 15 February 2007). ...

47. The Court further notes that the applicant repeatedly raised his request to order the TCA to approve the plan in all his appeals to the domestic courts, and that the request was formulated in a sufficiently clear and precise manner (see *Ruiz Torija*, cited above, § 30; *Pronina v. Ukraine*, no. 63566/00, § 25, 18 July 2006; and *Kuznetsov and Others*, cited above, § 84). While it is not the Court's task to examine whether the applicant's claim was well-founded, it nonetheless observes that by failing to examine it without giving sufficient reasons, the domestic courts denied the applicant the right to have a final determination on a matter submitted to a court (see *Ruiz Torija*, cited above, § 30; *Pronina*, cited above, § 25; and, *mutatis mutandis, Marini v. Albania*, no. 3738/02, § 120, 18 December 2007).

4/9

In the case of *Paukštis v. Lithuania* of 24 November 2015, Application no. 17467/07, ECHR found a violation of Article 1 of Protocol No. 1. Here are the most relevant parts of the decision:

> 51. The applicant complained under Article 1 of Protocol No. 1 to the Convention that the State authorities had breached his rights by not restoring his title to his father's land *in natura* or by failing to grant a fair compensation for that land. He was also dissatisfied with the overall length of the restitution process in his case. ...
>
> 67. The Court has consistently held that the Convention does not guarantee, as such, the right to restitution of property. "Possessions" within the meaning of Article 1 of Protocol No. 1 can be either "existing possessions" or legal situations where an applicant can argue that he or she has at least a legitimate expectation that a specific action will be undertaken in his or her favor. The hope that a long-extinguished right to a property may be revived cannot be regarded as a "possession" within the meaning of Article 1 of Protocol No. 1; nor can a conditional claim which has lapsed as a result of the failure to fulfil the condition (see, *mutatis mutandis, Jasiūnienė v. Lithuania*, no. 41510/98, § 40, 6 March 2003). ...
>
> 70. The Court has held that the first and most important requirement of Article 1 of Protocol No. 1 is that any interference by a public authority with the peaceful enjoyment of possessions should be lawful: the second sentence of the first paragraph authorises a deprivation of possessions only "subject to the conditions provided for by law" and the second paragraph recognises that States have the right to control the use of property by enforcing "laws". Moreover, the rule of law, one of the fundamental principles of a democratic society, is inherent in all the Articles of the Convention (see *Former King of Greece and Others v. Greece* [GC], no. 25701/94, § 79, ECHR 2000-XII). ...
>
> 73. Lastly, the Court has held that both an interference with the peaceful enjoyment of possessions and an abstention from action must strike a fair balance between the demands of the general interest of the community and the requirements of the protection of the individual's fundamental rights (see, among other authorities,

Sporrong and Lönnroth v. Sweden, 23 September 1982, § 69, Series A no. 52). In each case involving an alleged violation of Article 1 of Protocol No. 1 the Court must, therefore, ascertain whether by reason of the State's action or inaction the person concerned had to bear a disproportionate and excessive burden (see *Aleksa v. Lithuania*, no. 27576/05, § 85, 21 July 2009, with further references).

74. <...>The Court is also cautious to note that in regulating the restitution process the Contracting States have a wide discretion, including over the rules of how compensation for long-extinguished property rights should be assessed (see *Jantner v. Slovakia*, no. 39050/97, § 34, 4 March 2003, and *Bergauer and Others v. the Czech Republic* (dec.), no. 17120/04, 13 December 2005). Even so, on numerous occasions in the context of revocation of property titles granted erroneously, the Court has emphasised that the principle of good governance may not only impose on the authorities an obligation to act promptly to correct their mistake (see *Moskal v. Poland*, no. 10373/05, § 69, 15 September 2009), but may also necessitate the payment of adequate compensation or another type of appropriate reparation to a *bona fide* former holder (see *Pincová and Pinc v. the Czech Republic*, no. 36548/97, § 53, ECHR 2002-VIII, and *Toşcuţă and Others v. Romania*, no. 36900/03, § 38, 25 November 2008). In other words, the terms of compensation are material to the assessment of whether the contested measure respects the requisite fair balance and, notably, whether it imposes a disproportionate burden on the applicant (see *Albergas and Arlauskas v. Lithuania*, no. 17978/05, § 73, 27 May 2014). ...

77. To the extent that the applicant complained about his inability to recover the remaining part of his father's land *in natura*, or to obtain market-value compensation for it following the re-establishment of the Lithuanian State, the Court reiterates that Article 1 of Protocol No. 1 to the Convention does not guarantee, as such, the right to restitution of property. Nor can it be interpreted as creating any general obligation on the Contracting States to restore rights to property which had been expropriated before they ratified the Convention, or as imposing any restrictions on their freedom to determine the scope and conditions of any property restitution to former owners (see *Igarienė and Petrauskienė v. Lithuania*, no. 26892/05, § 53, 21 July 2009, and the case-law cited therein).

78. To be compatible with Article 1 of Protocol No. 1, an interference must fulfil three basic conditions: it must be carried out "subject to the conditions provided for by law", which excludes any arbitrary action on the part of the national authorities; it must be "in the public interest"; and it must strike a fair balance between the owner's rights and the interests of the community (see, *mutatis mutandis, Vistiņš and Perepjolkins v. Latvia* [GC], no. 71243/01, § 94, 25 October 2012).

4/10

In the case of *Sidabras and Others v. Lithuania* of 23 June 2015, Applications nos. *50421/08 and 56213/08,* ECHR found a violation of Article 14 of the Convention, taken in conjunction with Article 8. Here are the relevant parts of the decision:

74. Relying on Article 46 of the Convention, the applicants complained that Lithuania's failure to repeal the legislative provision banning former KGB employees from working in certain spheres of the private sector, notwithstanding the Court's judgments of 27 July 2004 and 7 April 2005, was not consistent with the Court's findings of a violation of Article 14 of the Convention, taken in conjunction with Article 8. The applicants also referred to Article 13 of the Convention; however, the Court considers that that complaint is absorbed by the principal complaint. ...

102. As to the three applicants' reference to Article 46 of the Convention, the Court observes that in its previous judgments of *Sidabras and Džiautas* and *Rainys and Gasparavičius* (cited above), the Court did not provide for any individual or general measures to be taken by the Government in its operative part or its reasoning. Furthermore, the Court has previously held, both in the reasoning and in the operative part, that there had been a violation of a substantive provision of the Convention – in that instance Article 8 – taken together with Article 46, in a follow-up case after the Court had previously found a violation in the same applicant's case (see *Emre v. Switzerland (no. 2)*). As in the present case, the solution adopted in *Emre (no. 2)* was in line with the Court's Grand Chamber judgment in *Verein gegen Tierfabriken Schweiz (VgT) v. Switzerland (no. 2)* (cited above), in so far as the Court found that it had jurisdiction to examine whether a decision delivered by a domestic court following the finding of a violation in Strasbourg satisfied the require-

ments of Article 46. However, it went further, since in the *Verein gegen Tierfabriken Schweiz (VgT)* case, the Grand Chamber did not formally find a violation of Article 46. The findings of the Court in *Emre (no. 2)* were made within the context of new proceedings at domestic level which directly confronted the national courts with interpreting and applying the Court's previous judgment in the applicant's case. The Court thus considered that "the most natural execution of its judgment, and that which would best correspond to the principle of *restitutio in integrum,* would have been to annul purely and simply, with immediate effect, the exclusion measure ordered against the applicant" (see *Emre (no. 2),* cited above, § 75).

103. <...> Although the Court can examine whether measures taken by a respondent State in execution of one of its judgments are compatible with the substantive clauses of the Convention (see *Verein gegen Tierfabriken Schweiz (VgT) (no. 2),* cited above, §§ 6168 and 7898), it has consistently ruled that it does not have jurisdiction to verify, by reference to Article 46 § 1, whether a Contracting Party has complied with the obligations imposed on it by one of the Court's judgments (see *Akdivar and Others v. Turkey* (Article 50), 1 April 1998, § 44, Reports of Judgments and Decisions 1998II; *Mehemi (no. 2),* cited above, § 43; *Haase and Others v. Germany* (dec.), no. 34499/04, 7 February 2008; *Wasserman v. Russia (no. 2),* no. 21071/05, § 31 *in fine,* 10 April 2008; *Burdov v. Russia (no. 2),* no. 33509/04, § 121, ECHR 2009; and *Kafkaris v. Cyprus* (dec.), no. 9644/09, § 74, 21 June 2011). So did the former Commission (see *Times Newspapers Ltd. and Others v. the United Kingdom,* no. 10243/83, Commission decision of 6 March 1985, Decisions and Reports (DR) 41, p. 123; *RuizMateos and Others v. Spain,* no. 24469/94, Commission decision of 2 December 1994, DR 79B, p. 141; and *Oberschlick v. Austria,* nos. 19255/92 and 21655/93, Commission decision of 16 May 1995, DR 81A, p. 5). The new paragraphs 4 and 5, added to Article 46 by Article 16 of Protocol No. 14, seem to confirm that as well.

Concurring opinion of Judge Keller

10. <...> it is not asserted that Article 46 of the Convention confers an ascertainable, freestanding right on individuals that may be in-

voked separately before the Court. However, where an admissible claim of a fresh or continuing violation of a substantive provision of the Convention is closely linked to non-compliance with a previous judgment of the Court, there are good reasons why the Court should be in a position to assess the applicants' complaints also under Article 46 and to make an incidental finding thereunder. Whilst such an approach may neither correspond to the traditional "Convention wisdom" nor to the interpretation offered by my concurring colleagues, it is in line with the evolving role of the Court under Article 46 of the Convention and the current trend of interpreting implementation as a shared responsibility.

Joint concurring opinion of Judges Spano and Kjolbro

4. The judgment attempts to reconcile diverging case-law of the Court in this area, in particular *Emre v. Switzerland (no. 2)*, no. 5056/10, 11 October 2011, and *The United Macedonian Organisation Ilinden – PIRIN and Others v. Bulgaria (no. 2)*, nos. 41561/07 and 20972/08, 18 October 2011. In both cases the applicants had invoked Article 46, but the Court adopted different approaches in determining whether to apply that Article to the facts.

5. In the judgment in the present case, the Court solves the problem of this divergence of case-law by distinguishing this case from *Emre* and following the approach adopted in *Ilinden*. However, in our view, the Court should rather have stated clearly that Article 46 does not confer assertable rights on individuals that may be invoked before the Court in an individual application. For the reasons explained below, such reasoning would in our view have been more in accordance with the wording and purpose of Article 46 of the Convention and the Court's case-law.

8. <...> the role of the Committee of Ministers in the sphere of execution of the Court's judgments does not prevent the Court from examining a fresh application concerning measures taken by a respondent State in execution of a judgment if that application contains relevant new information relating to issues undecided by the initial judgment (see *Bochan*, cited above, § 33). Thus, the Court may, for example, entertain a complaint that a retrial at domestic

level by way of implementation of one of its judgments gave rise to a new breach of the Convention (see *Verein gegen Tierfabriken Schweiz (VgT) v. Switzerland (no. 2)* [GC], no. 32772/02, § 62, ECHR 2009).

9. The fact that the Court may deal, in the context of a fresh application, with relevant new information that is capable of giving rise to a fresh violation of the Convention does not alter the fact that the Court cannot, as mentioned, deal with a complaint alleging failure to execute one of its judgments or to redress a violation already found by it.

10. This interpretation of the Court's jurisdiction in individual applications is also supported by Article 46 § 4 of the Convention, enacted by Protocol No. 14, which provides that the Committee of Ministers, under certain conditions, may institute infringement proceedings in the Court against a State that, in the view of the Committee of Ministers, refuses to abide by a final judgment in a case to which it is a party. In such cases it is for the Court to decide whether the State has failed to fulfil its obligations resulting from the judgment finding a violation of the Convention. As stated by the Court in *Bochan* (cited above, § 33), "[t]he question of compliance by the High Contracting Parties with the Court's judgments falls outside its jurisdiction if it is not raised in the context of the 'infringement procedure' provided for in Article 46 §§ 4 and 5 of the Convention". ...

13. Therefore, and to conclude, the Court should, in our view, have stated clearly that Article 46 of the Convention does not confer assertable rights on individuals that may be invoked before the Court in an individual application. We admit that this would entail a departure from *Emre*, but it would, in our view, be in accordance with the wording and purpose of Article 46 of the Convention and the Court's case-law.

Joint dissenting opinion of Sajo, Vučinic and Garlicki

2. The position of the majority is based on the finding that neither the first nor the second applicant "plausibly demonstrate[d] that

a discriminatory act [had] occurred" (paragraph 107). Only after such a "plausible demonstration" has been successfully made by an alleged victim, and only then, will the burden of proof shift to the Government. The majority refer here to paragraph 36 of the *Rainys and Gasparavicius v. Lithuania* judgment (nos. 70665/01 and 74345/01, 7 April 2005), but it should be noted that the term "plausibly demonstrated" is absent from that paragraph.

We are not convinced that the "plausible demonstration" requirement can be applied in the present case. Both of the applicants in question claimed to be victims of the continuing existence of the KGB Act. As the Court has held on several occasions (starting with the *Klaas*,[6] *Marckx*[7] and *Dudgeon*[8] cases), the mere existence of legislation permitting interference with a Convention right may be sufficient to confirm the standing of all those who are affected by it. Therefore, a practical attempt to circumvent such legislation cannot necessarily be required. This would be particularly problematic in situations where such an attempt could expose the applicant (or any cooperating persons) to a criminal or administrative penalty. In such situations, applicants can only be required to demonstrate that they fall within the scope of the disputed legislation. ...

5. Therefore, a violation of Article 14 in conjunction with Article 8 should have been found in the present case. In our opinion, the mistake of the majority was to apply the "plausible demonstration" requirement to a case in which legislation constituted the direct source of interference. This mistake is, at least in part, due to the lack of clearly established criteria on "victim status" and "practical attempts" in such cases. As the present judgment may contribute to further confusion, it may be time for the Grand Chamber to clarify the issue.

---

6 *Klaas v. Germany*, 22 September 1993, Series A no. 269.
7 *Marckx v. Belgium*, 13 June 1979, Series A no. 31.
8 *Dudgeon v. the United Kingdom*, 22 October 1981, Series A no. 45.

4/11

In the case of *Tunaitis v. Lithuania* of 24 November 2015, Application no. 42927/08, ECHR found a violation of Article 1 of Protocol No. 1 to the Convention. Here are the relevant parts of the decision:

> 16. The applicant complained that the State had unlawfully deprived him of his property and had not provided him with adequate compensation. He relied on Article 1 of Protocol No. 1 to the Convention. ...
>
> 26. The Government argued that any errors made by the domestic authorities had occurred in the context of land reform, which was linked to the process of restoration of former owners' rights to property that had been previously nationalised by the Soviet regime. According to the Court's caselaw in the context of central and eastern European States, the circumstances concerning the transition from a totalitarian regime to a democracy and the specific circumstances of each case therefore had to be taken into account. ...
>
> 33. In order to assess the burden borne by the applicant, the Court must examine the particular circumstances of each case, such as the conditions under which the disputed property was acquired and the compensation that was received by the applicant in exchange for the property, as well as his or her personal and social situation (see *Pyrantienė*, cited above, § 51). ...
>
> 36. The applicant's title to the land was invalidated after the former owners lodged a civil claim, which was then allowed by the domestic courts. It was established that the local authorities had not been entitled to transfer the disputed property to the applicant before the question of restoration of the former owners' rights had been resolved. The Government argued that the errors made by the domestic authorities had occurred in the context of land reform, which was linked to the complex process of restoration of former owners' property rights in Lithuania. In the Court's view, although it is true that States face complex legal and factual issues when resolving such matters, in the present case the hindrance to the peaceful enjoyment of the property is attributable exclusively to the respondent State, and the existence of any justifying exceptional circumstances has not been demonstrated by the Government (see

Nekvedavičius v. Lithuania, no. 1471/05, § 88, 10 December 2013, and *Albergas and Arlauskas*, cited above, § 62).

4/12
In the case of *Vasiliauskas v. Lithuania* of 20 October 2015, *Application no. 35343/05*, ECHR found violation of Article 7 of the Convention. Here are the relevant parts:

> 114. The applicant complained that the wide interpretation of the crime of genocide, as adopted by the Lithuanian courts, did not have a basis in the wording of that offence as laid down in public international law. He claimed that his conviction for genocide therefore amounted to a breach of Article 7 of the Convention. ...

> 131. The Government submitted that to understand this case it was of paramount importance to comprehend the Soviet repressive policy in Lithuania. They noted that the crimes against Lithuanians were a part of a targeted and systematic totalitarian policy pursued by the USSR. The repressions against Lithuanians were not coincidental or chaotic. They sought to exterminate the former social and political structure of the State, which was the very basis of the political nation of Lithuania. They were directed against the most active political and social groups, namely resistance members and their supporters, civil servants and officials of the State of Lithuania, Lithuanian public figures, intellectuals, academics, farmers, priests, and members of the families of those groups. ...

> 153. The Court reiterates that the guarantee enshrined in Article 7, which is an essential element of the rule of law, occupies a prominent place in the Convention system of protection, as is underlined by the fact that no derogation from it is permissible under Article 15 in time of war or other public emergency. It should be construed and applied, as follows from its object and purpose, in such a way as to provide effective safeguards against arbitrary prosecution, conviction and punishment (see *Kononov*, cited above, § 185; *Del Rio Prada v. Spain* [GC], no. 42750/09, § 77, ECHR 2013).

> 154. Accordingly, Article 7 is not confined to prohibiting the retrospective application of the criminal law to an accused's disadvantage: it also embodies, more generally, the principle that only the

law can define a crime and prescribe a penalty (*nullum crimen, nulla poena sine lege*) and the principle that the criminal law must not be extensively construed to an accused's detriment, for instance by analogy. It follows from these principles that an offence must be clearly defined in the law, be it national or international. This requirement is satisfied where the individual can know from the wording of the relevant provision – and, if need be, with the assistance of the courts' interpretation of it and with informed legal advice – what acts and omissions will make him criminally liable. The Court has thus indicated that when speaking of "law" Article 7 alludes to the very same concept as that to which the Convention refers elsewhere when using that term, a concept which comprises written as well as unwritten law and implies qualitative requirements, notably those of accessibility and foreseeability (see *Korbely v. Hungary* [GC], no. 9174/02, § 70, ECHR 2008; *Kononov*, cited above, §§ 185 and 196; *Del Río Prada*, cited above, § 91).

155. The Court reiterates that however clearly drafted a legal provision may be, in any system of law, including criminal law, there is an inevitable element of judicial interpretation. There will always be a need for elucidation of doubtful points and for adaptation to changing circumstances. Indeed, in the Convention States, the progressive development of the criminal law through judicial interpretation is a well-entrenched and necessary part of legal tradition. Article 7 of the Convention cannot be read as outlawing the gradual clarification of the rules of criminal liability through judicial interpretation from case to case, provided that the resultant development is consistent with the essence of the offence and could reasonably be foreseen (see *S.W. v. the United Kingdom*, 22 November 1995, § 36, Series A no. 335B; *C.R. v. the United Kingdom*, 22 November 1995, § 34, Series A no. 335C; *Streletz, Kessler and Krenz v. Germany* [GC], nos. 34044/96, 35532/97 and 44801/98, § 50, ECHR 2001II; *K.H.W. v. Germany*, cited above, § 45; *Jorgic v. Germany*, no. 74613/01, § 101, ECHR 2007III; and *Kononov*, cited above, § 185). ...

158. According to the general principles of law, defendants are not entitled to justify the conduct which has given rise to their conviction simply by showing that such conduct did in fact take place and therefore formed a practice. Whilst this defence was not raised specifically by the applicant, the Court nevertheless considers it

important to reiterate its previous finding in *K.-H.W.* (cited above, § 75) to the effect that even a private soldier could not show total, blind obedience to orders which flagrantly infringed internationally recognised human rights, in particular the right to life, which is the supreme value in the hierarchy of human rights. A State practice of tolerating or encouraging certain acts that have been deemed criminal offences under national or international legal instruments and the sense of impunity which such a practice instils in the perpetrators of such acts does not prevent their being brought to justice and punished (see *Streletz, Kessler and Krenz*, cited above, §§ 74, 77-79).

159. The Court reiterates that in the event of a change of State sovereignty over a territory or a change of political regime on a national territory, it is entirely legitimate for a State governed by the rule of law to bring criminal proceedings against those who have committed crimes under a former regime. The courts of such a State, having taken the place of those which existed previously, cannot be criticised for applying and interpreting the legal provisions in force at the material time in the light of the principles governing a State subject to the rule of law (see *Streletz, Kessler and Krenz*, cited above, § 81, and *Kononov*, cited above, § 241). As well as the obligation on a State to prosecute drawn from the laws and customs of war, Article 2 of the Convention also enjoins the States to take appropriate steps to safeguard the lives of those within their jurisdiction and implies a primary duty to secure the right to life by putting in place effective criminal-law provisions to deter the commission of offences which endanger life (see *Kononov*, cited above, § 241). ...

166. The Court therefore considers it clear that the applicant's conviction was based upon legal provisions that were not in force in 1953 and that such provisions were therefore applied retroactively. Accordingly, this would constitute a violation of Article 7 of the Convention unless it can be established that his conviction was based upon international law as it stood at the relevant time. The applicant's conviction, in the Court's view, must therefore be examined from that perspective (see, by converse implication, *K.-H.W. v. Germany*, cited above, § 50).

170. The Court begins by noting that the crime of genocide prohibited by Article II of the 1948 Convention lists four protected groups of

persons: national, ethnical, racial or religious. That provision does not refer to social or political groups. Furthermore, the *travaux préparatoires* disclose an intention by the drafters not to include political groups in the list of those protected by the 1948 Convention. The ICJ, when examining the drafting history of Article II of the 1948 Convention in the *Bosnia and Herzegovina v. Serbia and Montenegro* case, observed that the drafters of the Convention "gave close attention to the positive identification of groups with specific distinguishing characteristics in deciding which groups they would include and which (such as political groups) they would exclude" (see paragraph 105 above). The Court finds no convincing arguments for departing from the treaty definition of genocide as established in 1948, including the list of the four protected groups referred to therein. On the contrary, all references to the crime of genocide in subsequent international law instruments – the Convention on the Non-Applicability of Statutory Limitations to War Crimes and Crimes Against Humanity of 1968, the ICTY Statute of 1993, the ICTR Statute of 1994 as well as in the most recent international law instrument – the ICC Statute of 1998 – describe that crime in similar, if not identical, terms. In particular, genocide is defined as acts committed to destroy a national, ethnical, racial or religious group, without reference to political groups (see paragraphs 83, 85, 86 and 87 above). In the Court's view, the fact that certain States decided later to criminalise genocide of a political group in their domestic laws (see paragraphs 36 and 38 above) does not, as such, alter the reality that the text of the 1948 Convention did not do so.

178. the Court finds that in 1953 international treaty law did not include a "political group" in the definition of genocide, nor can it be established with sufficient clarity that customary international law provided for a broader definition of genocide than that set out in Article II of the 1948 Genocide Convention. ...

181. The Court accepts that the domestic authorities have discretion to interpret the definition of genocide more broadly than that contained in 1948 Genocide Convention. However, such discretion does not permit domestic tribunals to convict persons accused under that broader definition retrospectively. ...

183. The Court also notes that, in accordance with Article 31 § 1 of the Vienna Convention on the Law of Treaties, the ordinary meaning is to be given to the terms of the treaty. In this regard, it is not immediately obvious that the ordinary meaning of the terms "national" or "ethnic" in the Genocide Convention can be extended to cover partisans. Thus, the Court considers that the domestic courts' conclusion that victims came within the definition of genocide as part of a protected group was an interpretation by analogy, to the applicant's detriment, which rendered his conviction unforeseeable (see *Kokkinakis v. Greece*, 25 May 1993, § 52, Series A no. 260 A; also see *Korbely*, cited above, § 70).

184. On this last point, the Court also gives weight to the applicant's argument that the definition of the crime of genocide in Lithuanian law not only had no basis in the wording of that offence as expressed in the 1948 Genocide Convention, but had also been gradually enlarged during the years of Lithuania's independence, thus further aggravating his situation (see paragraphs 51–53 and 123 above). It has been pointed out by the Lithuanian Constitutional Court that to prosecute retroactively for genocide of persons belonging to a political or social group, if the events took place before those two groups were added to the Lithuanian Criminal Code, would be against the rule of law and in breach of Lithuania's obligations under international law (see paragraph 60 above). The Court cannot accept the argument by the Lithuanian Supreme Court that the 1998 amendments to the Criminal Code, expanding the definition of genocide to include "political groups", could be justified on the basis of Article V of the Genocide Convention. While Article V of the Genocide Convention does not prohibit expanding the definition of genocide, it does not authorise the application of a broader definition of genocide retroactively (see *Scoppola v. Italy (no. 2)* [GC], no. 10249/03, § 93, 17 September 2009; *Maktouf and Damjanović v. Bosnia and Herzegovina* [GC], nos. 2312/08 and 34179/08, § 66, ECHR 2013 (extracts)).

Joint dissenting opinion of Judges Villinger, Power-Forde, Pinto de Albuquerque and Kūris

We cannot accept that a protected group (a nation) which defends itself against the destruction of its very fabric though the mobilisation of a resistance movement suddenly, by that act of resistance, transforms itself solely into a 'political group', thus placing itself outside the terms of the Genocide Convention. This would be to interpret both the Genocide Convention and Convention's provisions in an overly formalistic manner and in a spirit inconsistent with their purpose.

In our view, the national authorities based their decisions on an acceptable assessment of the relevant facts, and did not reach arbitrary conclusions (see, *mutatis mutandis, Chauvy and Others v. France*, no. 64915/01, § 69, ECHR 2004VI; also see *Ždanoka v. Latvia* [GC], no. 58278/00, § 96, ECHR 2006IV). We therefore do not depart from the Constitutional Court's assessment of the role of the partisans, and accept that because of their "prominence" and "emblematic" character (see *Prosecutor v. Krstić* and *Croatia v. Serbia*, paragraphs 101 and 108 of the judgment respectively) the Lithuanian partisans may be considered as a significant "part of" the national group. In this regard we note the finding of the Constitutional Court to the effect that "in consideration of the international and historical context, it should be noted that, in the course of the qualification of the actions against the participants of the resistance against the Soviet occupation as a political group, one should take into account the significance of this group for the entire respective national group (the Lithuanian nation) which said group is covered by the definition of genocide according to the universally recognised norms of international law" (see paragraph 63 of the judgment).

Having regard to the factors outlined above, we find that the Lithuanian partisans must be considered as a substantial part of the national group, the latter being a group protected under Article II of the Genocide Convention. We therefore conclude that the Court of Appeal, whose decision was not overruled by the Supreme Court, interpreted the term "in part", as referred to in Article II Genocide Convention, in a manner consistent with its interpretation in international law, having regard to the particular social and political context prevailing in Lithuania at the relevant time.

It remains to be examined whether such an interpretation of Article II of the Genocide Convention was foreseeable by the applicant in 1953. ...

33. On this point, we observe that under Article I of the Genocide Convention, genocide is a crime under international law, whether committed in time of peace or in time of war. It may also be noted that the presence of those actively involved in a conflict, including when the victims bore arms, has not been an obstacle for the international courts in finding their killing to be a crime against humanity (see *Prosecutor v. Kupreškić and Others* in paragraph 111 of the judgment; see also, *mutatis mutandis*, *Croatia v. Serbia* in paragraph 108 of the judgment). This reasoning applies with greater force where the crime of genocide is at issue. On this point we note that, under Article II of the Genocide Convention, genocide is not defined as a crime directed against a civilian population only. In our view, to interpret the Genocide Convention as not applying to those who took up arms to defend themselves would not be in conformity with the underlying purpose of that Convention.

34. We further reiterate the Constitutional Court's conclusion that the Soviet authorities regarded the Lithuanian partisans as illegal rebels. No combatant status, or that of prisoner of war, was ever granted to them during Soviet times. On the contrary, as noted by the Constitutional Court, Lithuanian partisans were portrayed by the Soviet authorities, including the MGB unit in which the applicant served, as "bandits", "terrorists", and "bourgeois nationalists". Special "extermination" squads were established and these were used in the fight against the Lithuanian partisans and their supporters (see paragraphs 18, 19 and 63 of the judgment).

35. Accordingly, the fact that the brothers J.A. and A.A. were armed partisans who had been targeted on account of their membership of and significance within a protected group (the nation) does not preclude charging the applicant with genocide (see, by converse implication and *mutatis mutandis*, *Korbely v. Hungary* [GC], no. 9174/02, §§ 86-94, ECHR 2008).

Conclusion

36. In the light of the above considerations, we find that, within the general context of large-scale and systematic actions against the Lithuanian population, the applicant's participation in the 2 January 1953 operation to capture and/or kill partisan brothers J.A. and A.A., viewed within the framework of the Soviet authorities' operations to eradicate the Lithuanian partisans as a significant part of the nation in 1944-53 with the intent of destroying the fabric of the nation of Lithuania, could reasonably be regarded as falling within the ambit of the offence of genocide under Article II of the Genocide Convention. The interpretation by the domestic courts could thus reasonably have been foreseen by the applicant at the material time. In view of the foregoing, we are satisfied that the requirements to convict the applicant for the crime of genocide have been met in the instant case. We also reiterate the ICJ conclusion that "where those requirements are satisfied... the law must not shy away from referring to the crime committed by its proper name" (see paragraph 112 of the judgment).

38. We conclude that the applicant's conviction for genocide was not in breach of Article 7 § 1 of the Convention. Lastly, these requirements of Article 7 § 1 being met, it is not therefore necessary to examine the case under Article 7 § 2 of the Convention <...>

39. Our disagreement with the majority does not pertain to the facts as these have been established – it pertains to their interpretation. The majority has likewise accepted that the acts in respect of which the applicant was charged and convicted were indeed committed by him. Having been shielded by the occupant regime for many years, the applicant could nurture an expectation that his impunity would outlive him. For a while, it seemed that the termination of Lithuania's occupation had put an end to such an expectation. Now, by the judgment of this Court, that expectation has been revived. This is a matter of regret."

Dissenting opinion of Judge Ziemele

26. The Court is confronted with a historically and legally complex case. It is true that some of the reasoning given by the domestic courts could have been clearer. However, the Court has given and should give a margin for the development of national case-law and for some differences in the domestic courts' reasoning. The Court's role is not to form a different view on the scope of the provisions of the 1948 Convention from that of the primary interpreters of the Convention in the international legal system.

27. More broadly, while it is true that the Court has in recent years paid particular attention to Article 7 principles and cases, major questions remain. In the present case, the Court is not only dealing yet again with the rights of the applicant, but also finds itself at the centre of a complex social process in a society seeking to establish the truth about the past and its painful events. The United Nations has worked on the issue of mass human-rights violations, and has come up with a set of principles which are indispensable for peace in any society going through complex historical transitions (see the Report of the Independent Expert, E/CN.4/2005/102/Add.1). While maintaining the rule-of-law standard that Article 7 provides, it is particularly important that this Court, at the level of the presentation of facts and the choice of methodology and issues, is guided by these broader principles regarding the right to truth and prohibition of impunity.

Dissenting opinion of Judge Power-Forde

<...>The four constitutive requirements of the offence of genocide under international law were met – (i) an *intention* (ii) to *destroy* (iii) *part of* (iv) a *protected group*. That he could find himself charged with and convicted of genocide – must be regarded as having been foreseeable by the applicant (in the event of a regime change, of course!) given that genocide was recognized, clearly, as a crime, under international law at the time of his participation in the deaths of the partisans.

The Court was presented with an opportunity to refer to what happened in the Soviet era – and in which the applicant was a wilful participant – by its proper name. Through this case law, it has shied away from so doing, preferring instead to conclude that the applicant was wronged for having been convicted of genocide by the Lithuanian courts."

Dissenting opinion of Judge Kūris

In the present case, the Court has dealt with facts which are self-evident. It is obvious that the occupied Lithuanian nation did not joyfully embrace the occupation with open arms. It is obvious that the repressions of Lithuanians by the occupying regime were on a massive scale. It is obvious that the resistance against occupation was nation-wide. It is obvious that the partisans were the spearhead of this resistance. It is obvious that they enjoyed, at least until the resistance was suppressed, wide support from the population. It is obvious that their main goal – an independent Lithuania – was also the main goal of the Lithuanian nation. And it is obvious that by performing the function of defenders of independence, however unrealistic their prospects of success at that time, the partisan movement represented the body and the spirit of the Lithuanian nation. As such, the partisans were a substantive and emblematic part of that nation.

4/13

In the case of *Žilinskienė v. Lithuania* of 1 December 2015, Application no. 57675/09, ECHR found a violation of Article 1 of Protocol No. 1 to the Convention. Here are the relevant parts of the decision:

> 30. The applicant submitted that she had acquired the plot of land in good faith and that her interests therefore had to be protected. She argued that any losses on the part of the State should be covered by those individuals who had acted unlawfully and not by confiscating the land from the applicant, who was a *bona fide* owner. ...
>
> 35. The Court reiterates that Article 1 of Protocol No. 1 to the Convention, which guarantees in substance the right to property, comprises three distinct rules. The first rule, which is expressed in the

first sentence of the first paragraph and is of a general nature, lays down the principle of the peaceful enjoyment of property. The second rule, in the second sentence of the same paragraph, covers deprivation of possessions and makes it subject to certain conditions. The third rule, contained in the second paragraph, recognises that the Contracting States are entitled, among other things, to control the use of property in accordance with the general interest. The second and third rules, which are concerned with particular instances of interference with the right to the peaceful enjoyment of property, must be construed in the light of the general principle laid down in the first rule (see, among many authorities, *Immobiliare Saffi v. Italy* [GC], no. 22774/93, § 44, ECHR 1999-V, and *Broniowski v. Poland* [GC], no. 31443/96, § 134, ECHR 2004-V). ...

37. The Court's constant approach has been that confiscation, while it involves the deprivation of possessions, also constitutes control of the use of property within the meaning of the second paragraph of Article 1 of Protocol No. 1 (see *Sun v. Russia*, no. 31004/02, § 25, 5 February 2009; *C.M. v. France* (dec.), no. 28078/95, 26 June 2001; and *Air Canada v. the United Kingdom*, 5 May 1995, § 34, Series A no. 316-A). ...

43. The Court reiterates that because of their direct knowledge of society and its needs, the national authorities are in principle better placed than the international judge to appreciate what is "in the public interest". Under the system of protection established by the Convention, it is thus for the national authorities to make an initial assessment as to the existence of a problem of public concern warranting measures of deprivation of property. Here, as in other fields to which the safeguards of the Convention extend, the national authorities accordingly enjoy a certain margin of appreciation (see, among other authorities, *Pincová and Pinc v. the Czech Republic*, no. 36548/97, § 47, ECHR 2002-VIII, and *Velikovi and Others v. Bulgaria*, nos. 43278/98, 45437/99, 48014/99, 48380/99, 51362/99, 53367/99, 60036/00, 73465/01 and 194/02, § 168, 15 March 2007). ...

47. Within the context of revoking ownership of a property transferred erroneously, the good governance principle may not only impose on the authorities an obligation to act promptly in correcting their mistake, but may also necessitate the payment of adequate

compensation or another type of appropriate reparation to the former *bona fide* holder of the property (see *Romankevič v. Lithuania*, no. 25747/07, § 37, 2 December 2014, and the cases cited therein). ...

50. The Court considers that at the time of the acquisition, the applicant did not have any reason to doubt the validity of L.S.G.'s property rights, which had been recognised by the State authorities. She was also entitled to rely on the fact that the administrative acts of 2000 and 2001, on the basis of which she had acquired the property, would not be retrospectively invalidated to her detriment (see *Kopecký v. Slovakia* [GC], no. 44912/98, §§ 45-47, ECHR 2004-IX, and *Pyrantienė*, cited above, § 61). The Court also reiterates that for the purpose of acquiring a proprietary interest it is immaterial whether the applicant acquired the land for free or for a monetary payment (see *Vistiņš and Perepjolkins v. Latvia* [GC], no. 71243/01, § 121, 25 October 2012).

51. <...> the domestic courts which examined the case did not consider that the applicant had acted in bad faith, and the Court sees no reason to doubt their conclusion (see, *mutatis mutandis*, *Vistiņš and Perepjolkins*, cited above, § 120). Therefore, the Court is satisfied that the applicant was a *bona fide* owner, as found by the domestic courts, and that her proprietary interest in the enjoyment of the land had been sufficiently established (see *Pyrantienė*, cited above, § 60, and *Albergas and Arlauskas*, cited above, §§ 68-69). As a result, the Court finds that the applicant had a "legitimate expectation" of being able to continue to enjoy that possession.

4/14

The Constitutional Court of the Republic of Lithuania in its ruling "*On the interpretation of certain provisions of the ruling of the constitutional court of the republic of Lithuania of 29 June 2010*" *of 14 January 2015, No KT1-S1/2015*" stated that when the legislature reorganises the system of the state pensions of judges, no regulation which would reduce the statutory level of the social (material) guarantees of judges may be established. The relevant parts of the ruling are provided below:

1. In this context, it should be noted that the Constitutional Court's ruling of 29 June 2010, the interpretation of which is requested, mentions that the social (material) guarantees of the principle of

the independence of judges which stem from the Constitution are also consolidated in the law of other democratic states as well as in various international acts.

2. In its ruling of 12 July 2001, the Constitutional Court noted that, by its resolution of 13 December 1985, the General Assembly of the United Nations endorsed the Basic Principles on the Independence of the Judiciary; on 13 October 1994, the Committee of Ministers of the Council of Europe, in response to the said document, adopted the Recommendation on the Independence, Efficiency and Role of Judges addressed to the Member States of the Council of Europe; Item 1.1 of the European Charter on the Statute for Judges, which was approved, on the initiative of the Council of Europe, on 10 July 1998, consolidates that its provisions aim at raising the level of guarantees of competence, independence and impartiality of judges in the various European States, and that the provisions of the Charter cannot justify modifications in national statutes tending to decrease the level of guarantees already achieved.

In its ruling of 22 October 2007, the Constitutional Court noted that Item 6 of the European Charter on the Statute for Judges, which was approved on the Initiative of the Council of Europe on 10 July 1998, provides that "judges exercising judicial functions in a professional capacity are entitled to remuneration, the level of which is fixed so as to shield them from pressures aimed at influencing their decisions and more generally their behaviour within their jurisdiction, thereby impairing their independence and impartiality", that "remuneration may vary depending on length of service, the nature of the duties which judges are assigned to discharge in a professional capacity, and the importance of the tasks which are imposed on them, assessed under transparent conditions", that "the statute provides a guarantee for judges acting in a professional capacity against social risks linked with illness, maternity, invalidity, old age and death", and also that "in particular the statute ensures that judges who have reached the legal age of judicial retirement, having performed their judicial duties for a fixed period, are paid a retirement pension, the level of which must be as close as possible to the level of their final salary as a judge".

3. In the context of this decision, it should be noted that Item 54 of the Recommendation CM/Rec(2010)12 of the Committee of Ministers of the European Council to member states on judges: independence, efficiency and responsibilities, *inter alia,* states that guarantees for judges should exist for maintaining a reasonable remuneration in case of illness, maternity or paternity leave, as well as for the payment of a retirement pension, which should be in a reasonable relationship to their level of remuneration when working.

4. In the context of this decision, the judgment of the Supreme Court of Estonia of 26 June 2014 in case No. 3-4-1-1-14 should also be mentioned. <...> The court noted that the right of the person to a pension, which can be assessed in money, falls within the scope of property rights and should be categorised as one of fundamental human rights, i.e. the right to property; in this regard, the principle of the legitimate expectations, which stems from the Constitution, means that everyone has the right to have a reasonable expectation that the established legal regulation will remain in force <...>

4/16

In the 26 May 2015 case No. 2K-276-976/2015 the Supreme Court Criminal Law Division ruled on the application of the Code of Criminal Procedure (CCP) of the Republic of Lithuania art. 276 and 301 in relation to the evidence.

The panel of judges also drew attention to the fact that based on the practice of the European Court of Human Rights in the application of Article 6, paragraph 3 of the Convention which sets out the principle according to which, before the conviction of the accused person, all of its inculpatory evidence should normally be disclosed in its presence at a public hearing in order to ensure the adversarial file reading. Exceptions to this principle are possible, but they must respect the right of the defence, which normally requires that the defendant has to be given an adequate and proper opportunity to challenge evidence of the witness and to provide questions to the witness, either at the time when he provides evidences, or at a later stage. It is possible to use the evidence in the case that was given by witness earlier, even if the defence at any stage of the proceedings could not examine it in accordance with these requirements.

Lithuanian Supreme Court noted that in the case of the witness death, his testimony during the investigation, can be used as evidence, but the defence right to submit questions to the witness was never realised. In such a case the court has an obligation to determine whether the witness testimony is crucial and if recognised as such – to ensure a fair and proper assessment of witness credibility. In the case law of the European Court of Human Rights evidence is described as decisive (the concept is understood in the strict sense) if the meaning or importance of the evidence can determines the outcome of the case. In the case of the witness testimony is corroborated by other evidence, the assessment of whether such evidence is decisive depends on the evidence supporting the probative value of the testimony. The stronger the supporting evidence, the less likely that evidence of the witness who is not participating in the court proceedings will be treated as decisive.

4/17

In the 28 April, 2015 case No. 2K-7-124-648 / 2015 the Supreme Court Criminal Law Division of the Republic of Lithuania ruled on the Code of Criminal Procedure of the Republic of Lithuania ar. 58 para 2(2) application to the criminal case.

On the impartiality of the court, determining when the judge in the pre-trial stage, has adopted the same crime-related decision, the Court of Cassation indicated that the interpretation of the Code of Criminal Procedure art. 58 para. 2(2) and the prohibition contained in the scope of its application, is relevant to the ECHR jurisprudence on the interpretation of the art. 6 para. 1, according to which the fact that the trial judge at the pre-trial stage, has adopted the same crime-related decisions can not in itself be regarded as a circumstance justifying fears for his lack of impartiality. In cases before the judge in criminal proceedings when he has adopted only formal procedural decisions, the adoption of which is not evidence based and the position on the guilt of the accused (merits) is not expressed, the lack of impartiality problem does not arise.

The Supreme Court noted that there is no doubt that when ensuring the individual's right to a fair trial, a judge cannot participate in the proceedings if he dealt with issues of punitive measures application (or its time expansion) or considered complaints of the punitive measures justifications. In each case, the judge must first evaluate the merits of the allegations and the supporting data adequacy. The investigating judge within its competence during the investigation has to also carry out other activities (i.e. questioning of witnesses, victims, suspects), deals with other types of complaints (i.e. On the prosecutor's decision to suspend defence (CPC Article 49), on the prosecutor's decision to refuse the access of the investigation data (CPC Article 181)) etc. Therefore when considering the question of impartiality of the judge it is necessary to assess the nature of the decisions taken in each case separately. In the present case, the Court of Cassation did not find the judge of impartiality infringement in the objective aspect. The judge that dealt with the criminal case only considered the pre-trial investigation prosecutor's decision to refuse access to the data of the investigation.

4/18

On 16 June, 2015 case No. 2K-305-788 / 2015 the Supreme Court of the Criminal Law Division ruled a case concerning the application of the Criminal Code (CC) of the Republic of Lithuania art. 235 para. 1 in relation to the giving of false testimony.

In this particular case Mrs. D. P. has been accused according to CC art. 235 para. 1, that is, she was giving false testimony while repeatedly being questioned as a witness during the investigation.

The Court stated that the aggrieved party or witness shall not be liable for false testimony provided by the law if she, according to the law, had the right to refuse to testify, but was not familiarised with this right before the questioning (CC art. 235, paragraph 4). The Code of Criminal Procedure of the Republic of Lithuania art. 80, paragraph 1 provides that a witness cannot be questioned by a person who can testify about their own possible involvement in the criminal offence, unless he agrees to give such evidence (CCP art. 82 para 3). Moreover, the domestic law recognises that the provision must be interpreted in a broader context, taking into account both the Constitution of the Republic of Lithuania and ECHR judgments. According to the ECHR case law, testifying against oneself is a violation of the fair trial principle, enshrined in European Convention on Human Rights (hereinafter – the Convention) Article 6, paragraph 1. The obligation to answer questions or testify within the meaning of Article 6 of the Convention, is in line with the right to remain silent and not to incriminate oneself, which is an integral part of the concept of a fair trial if a person exercises it voluntarily. This principle also applies in cases when the mentioned obligation is applied in a different process than the one in which the indictment has been issued. Article 31 paragraph 3 of the Constitution of the Republic of Lithuania prohibits giving evidence against oneself, his family members or close relatives. In the constitutional jurisprudence, this principle is interpreted with the meaning that an individual may refuse to give evidence based on which he, his family member or close relative could be subject to not only criminal, but any other type of liability if the penalty according to their nature and size (strictness) would amount to criminal punishment. On the other hand, Article 31, paragraph 3 of the Constitution its legal regulation does not mean that the individual cannot give the evidence voluntarily. The panel of judges drew attention to the fact that a person cannot be questioned as a witness about any circumstances, which could be the basis for future allegations not only under present investigation in a criminal case, but also in any other "punitive" action. If there are no formal allegations, one cannot categorically state that a person's right to refuse to give evidence against oneself was inapplicable. Therefore, in determining whether such right was applicable, it is necessary to take into account not only whether the allegations were raised in the procedural sense and were investigated in a criminal case, but it is necessary to assess all the factual details of the case. In this case, Mrs. D. P., as a witness, although warned of criminal liability for false testimony, had a real reason to believe that she was questioned not as a neutral witness, but as a potential suspect, since before her first official questioning her apartment was searched, accounting and other types of documents were seized, and immediately after the questioning her mobile phone was also seized. Mrs. D. P. gave testimony to the fact that informally, under the cover of a business license issued on her behalf, other persons worked against whom criminal proceedings were commenced. The panel of judges considered that D. P. had good reasons to fear legal liability, i.e., for aiding an abetting other people to carry out criminal activities, or for the same actions in the sense of an administrative punishment.

In view of the fact that during the questioning there was a condition set out in the CCP art. 80, paragraph 1, the panel of judges found that Mrs. D. P., as a witness, could be questioned only in circumstances where there was her consent, the right to have an attorney was clarified, if she demanded to be recognised as a suspect or she wouldn't have been notified of the liability for giving, refusing or avoiding to give false testimony (CCP art. 82, paragraph 3). This was not done. The Court came to a conclusion that Mrs. D. P. is not to be held responsible for her false testimony.

4/19

In 16 June 2015 case No. 3K-3-430-415/2015 the Supreme Court ruled a case concerning the implementation of the right to privacy in relation to the giving of false testimony.

The applicant requested the co-owner of the land to remove surveillance cameras, which were installed without her consent in the total residential area. The Court of First Instance dismissed the claim and the appellate court satisfied the claim.

The Court of Cassation stated that the legality of installing surveillance cameras have to be considered by taking into account both the applicant's right to respect for private life (it may be limited if limitation comply with the principle of proportionality) and the true interests of both parties (interests of the the dispute parties have to be balanced according to judicial proceedings). The Court of Cassation noted that residential area is not a public place. Defendant equipped it with surveillance systems with the purpose to protect property – as he says, the need arose after the property has been spoiled. The restriction of the applicant's private life has a legitimate purpose under the Convention – the defendant has a right to protect it's property (Article 1 of Protocol No. 1 (protection of property). Having recognised that the restriction of the applicant's private life had a legitimate objective, the Court of Cassation assessed the proportionality of limiting the applicant's private life. The courts found that the defendant's camera was filming not only the defendant's owned part of the house, but also part of the shared land, courtyard, as well as all persons living in the house, and the people who are coming to the house. There is no evidence in the case that it is not possible to install cameras in such a way that they are filming only the defendant owned and protected objects. The Court of Cassation did conclude that the defendant has the possibility to narrow the monitored area reaching the same legitimate aim, as well as avoiding the restriction of the applicant's private life or, if it is objectively impossible, making them proportionate to the aim pursued. The Court of Cassation held that the defendant wrongly limited the applicant's right to respect for private life, installation of surveillance cameras contravened the fair balance of interests of the parties in principle, the right to privacy provided in the Convention was not guaranteed.

The Court of Cassation also pointed out that the applicant has no practical control over the use of data obtained, storage, deletion. Video surveillance has a legitimate objective, but it does not comply with the Article 19 paragraph 1 of Personal Data Protection Law. Therefore, the defendant was obliged to remove all cameras from the residential home. However, the Court of Cassation noted that this does not detract from the defendant's right to use video surveillance for a legitimate purpose and conditions conforming to the Personal Data Protection Law.

4/20

In the 27 October, 2015 case No. 2K-418-699/2015, the Supreme Court Criminal Law Division ruled on the court's duty to provide its reason. The case considered art. 320 para. 3 and art. 332 para. 2, 5 of the Code of Criminal Procedure of the Republic of Lithuania and the application of art. 6 para. 1 of the Convention.

The Court of Cassation stated that in cases where the appellant provides the objections to the judgment on the lack of legitimacy and legality, the court of appeal in its decision must clarify why such a decision was made. When the court of appeal ruling is based on general statements, without specific arguments and circumstances related to the appeal case, the judgment cannot be concluded. So that the validity and legitimacy of the judgment was ensured and the substantive issues raised by the appeal needed a response.

The court noted that in the case law of the ECtHR the right to a fair trial as guaranteed by the Convention Article 6, paragraph 1, includes the parties right to submit to the court any, in their view, important arguments. Since the objective of the Convention is to guarantee not theoretical or illusory, but real and effective rights, this right can only be effective if the arguments are actually "heard", i.e. they have to be properly examined by the court. One of the functions of a reasoned decision – show to the parties that they have been heard.

Thus, the right to be heard includes not only an opportunity to present arguments in court, but also the court is obliged to present the reasons for which the arguments were accepted or rejected in the motivated decision. According to consistent ECHR case law related to Article 6, paragraph 1, which among other things requires the court to properly consider explanations, arguments and evidence, though not impose on assessment or value judgment. The ECHR does not examine whether the arguments are answered correctly in substance to or to the required detail because the court might believe that there is no need to reply to the arguments that are clearly irrelevant, unfounded, given improperly or are not acceptable for other reasons, according to the clear provisions of the law or case law. Although Article 6 paragraph 1 obliges courts to provide reasons for their decisions, it cannot be understood as requiring a detailed answer to every argument, but the decision has to be made clear. It should be noted that in the ECHR decisions, including those relied on by the appellate court in this case, attention is drawn to the fact that it is necessary to take into account, among other things, the arguments of the parties, the diversity of the Contracting Parties in their law provisions, customary rules (traditions), doctrine and judicial decisions. That is why the question of whether the court has fulfilled its duty to state reasons, stemming from Article 6 paragraph 1, can be resolved only in the light of the circumstances of the case. ECHR case indicates the fact that the reasoned decision given to the parties help review of the decision before a higher court, but the lower court which does not provide specific reasons for its decision, deprives a person of the opportunity to effectively challenge it.

Part Six: I. The Position of the Individual (including the Corporation) in International Law – Nationality

On 26 March 2015, administrative case A-1424-602/2015, the Supreme Administrative Court adopted a decision on the deadline to take the oath to the Republic of Lithuania, when a person is granted Lithuanian citizenship by Presidential Decree and the application of the principle of *Lex retro non agit*.

On 28 March 2007 the applicant submitted an application for citizenship of the Republic of Lithuania. President of the Republic of Lithuania in 8 August 2007 with a decree granted Lithuanian citizenship for the applicant T. Y. The decree came into force in 15 August 2007. In 7 February 2013 the applicant lost citizenship of another state. The Law of Citizenship, adopted on 17 September 2002, did not provide a timeframe within which the person, who has been granted citizenship of the Republic of Lithuania, has to take the oath. Since 22 July 2008 the previously mentioned regulation has been changed, with the introduction of a two-year term, during which a person, who has been granted citizenship of the Republic of Lithuania, has to take the oath. On 29 August 2013 the applicant appealed to the Migration Department with a request for the oath to the Republic of Lithuania. On 4 October 2013 the Migration Department refused to accept the request of the applicant, because the applicant missed the statutory period to take the oath of the Republic of Lithuania and the Law of Citizenship does not provide the possibility to renew the term, regardless of the reason for the missed deadline.

In the case the parties, the applicant and the administrative authority, differently interpreted the question of the change of the regulatory provisions on the requirement to take the oath to the Republic of Lithuania when citizenship was granted by decree of the President of the Republic of Lithuania. The applicant argued that he should be subject to the requirements that have been set when the decree was adopted. The defendant argues that should apply the standards which are in force at the time the applicant expressed his request to take the oath and the deadline to take the oath to the Republic of Lithuania was 2 years after the decree comes into force.

College of judges firstly noted that the granting of citizenship is a process which involves several stages – adoption of the presidential decree and the entry into force of the oath to the Republic of Lithuania, but it is a continuum. The panel of judges stated that the fact that the oath to the Republic of Lithuania is related to the Republic of Lithuania citizen's rights and duties, so appearance tons. y. substantive entitlement, assessed as a factor that determines the requirements for the oath is also a substantive law. As a result, the Court of First Instance wrongly decided that the law, which was introduced by the oath of the term, or the term itself is of a procedural nature, the applicable law (and the term), current application for the oath at the time. It is therefore concluded that the applicant's request for citizenship be examined under the rules in force in the applicant requesting the granting of citizenship, because the legislature did not identify any other specific rules on the substantive rules, the validity of time, t. y. the legislator has never been established that the new requirement of the term also applies to persons who have applied for citizenship or for which the decree to grant citizenship to the entry into force of the Citizenship Act 2008. Applicant applying for citizenship has been observed in the period during which it was possible to take the oath. As a result of the Migration Department in addition to the legal basis of the applicant has applied legislation, which did not identify material legal relations at the time, and was wrong to conclude that the applicant missed the deadline to take the oath to the Republic of Lithuania. Thus, the applicant has correctly pointed out that the public administration in breach of the *lex retro non agit* principle that legislative power is directed to the future and allowed the legislation take effect retroactively.

Part Six: III. The Position of the Individual (including the Corporation) in International Law – Aliens

6/1

Decision in the administrative case No A-1798-624/2015 dated 12 February 2015 dealt with the legality of alien detention, where he applies for asylum immediately after his detention and where he illegally travelled through the territories of other countries before being detained.

It was established in the case that M. I. left his country of origin on 28 September 2010, he had gone to Lebanon, Algeria, Argentina, Brazil, Spain, Turkey, Bulgaria, Romania, Greece, Germany, Poland, Lithuania and Latvia. On 4 November 2014 he was detained in Poland while travelling by car from Latvia to Germany and on 5 November 2014 he was returned to the Republic of Lithuania where on 5 November 2014 he was detained after having determined that his stay in the Republic of Lithuania is unlawful. Based on the Judgement of the District Court of Lazdijai Region dated 7 November 2014 and in accordance with Article 113 (1)(2) and Article 114(4) of the Law on the Legal Status of Aliens (hereinafter referred to as 'the Law'), M. I. was detained at the Foreigners' Registration Centre until his legal status in the Republic of Lithuania is established, but not longer than 7 May 2014, on the grounds that his entry and stay in the Republic of Lithuania is unlawful. By the Judgement No (15/6-7) 15PR-354 of 5 December 2014 the Migration Department decided to examine M. I.'s application for asylum on its merits to grant him temporary territorial asylum in the Republic of Lithuania and issue an alien registration certificate.

The Supreme Administrative Court of Lithuania noted that the fact that the applicant lodged an application for asylum in the Republic of Lithuania immediately after being detained and transferred by the Polish officers to the Republic of Lithuania, which he entered while travelling to Germany, does not, in itself, form the grounds for stating the existence of the basis referred to in Article 113(2) of the Law. <...>. In the case in question, as was evident from the data presented in the case, the Migration Department, having conducted examination under M. I.'s application for asylum, failed to establish that it was manifestly unfounded; the fact that M. I. did not applied for asylum in Germany and Latvia or failed to do so immediately after his arrival to the Republic of Lithuania, i.e. that he unlawfully travelled within the EU countries prior to acquiring the status of an asylum seeker, also does not, in itself, constitute the basis for the presence of grounds for detention as referred to in Article 113(2) of the Law, because unlawful entry and stay in the Republic of Lithuania forms the basis for detention of the person under the grounds provided for in Article 113(1)(2) of the Law; however, the absence of other data (departure from the other country prior to the decision-making, etc.) does not, in itself, constitute grounds to conclude that the person hinders the Migration Department from adopting or enforcing the decision, and that he may abscond avoiding the return, expulsion or transfer.

6/2

In the administrative case, the alien has been detained in the Foreigners Registration Centre from 14th of January, 2015, i.e., longer than four months, and accommodation in the Foreigners Registration Centre was provided for his family (wife and children) from 12 February 2015 without any restrictions of freedom of movement. According to the alien, he has very limited possibilities to see his family, to take care his children, and to contribute to their upbringing. He emphasized that he wants to be with his wife and children, who do not feel safe without him, and he does not plan to go out of Lithuania illegally once again.

The panel of judges of the Supreme Administrative Court noted that although, objectively, the circumstance that the asylum seeker, ignoring the clear prohibitions, tried to go out from the Republic of Lithuania without the valid travel document could be the basis to restrict his movement of freedom in the Republic of Lithuania, and to impose detention, continuance of this measure to the person, who must care of under-age children, in this case should be considered as inappropriate measure, disproportionately restricting his rights, and according to the panel of judges of the Supreme Administrative Court, there were no circumstances, which could be considered as special within the scope of the Law on Legal Status of Alien, and could be the reason to continue detention of the applicant in the Foreigners Registration Centre.

The panel of judges of the Supreme Administrative Court decided that Švenčionys District Area Court, considering the provisions of paragraph 3 of article 114 of the Law on Legal Status of Alien and the determined circumstances, was wrong to decide that no alternative detention measures were possible. The panel of judges of the Supreme Administrative Court stated that the measure, specified in paragraph 5 of article 115 of the Law on Legal Status of Alien, i.e., accommodation of the alien in Foreigners Registration Centre without restriction of movement of freedom, which may be imposed for asylum seeker (paragraph 5 of article 115 of the Law), is sufficient and appropriate measure, therefore, applicable.

6/3

In the decision in administrative case No. A-2621-662/2015, dated 20th of May, 2015, regarding possible breach of procedure of temporal leave from the Foreigners Registration Centre, the Foreigners Registration Centre indicated that the alien planned to go out from the Republic of Lithuania, and was found in the car, driven by the citizen of the Republic of Lithuania, together with other four citizens, in one of municipalities of Lithuania, on 21st of January, 2015.

The panel of judges of the Supreme Administrative Court noted that the Foreigners Registration Centre failed to specify in detail how these actions violated the procedure of temporal leave from the Foreigners Registration Centre. According to the panel of judges, considering the provisions of paragraph 5 of article 114 and article 113, there are no reasons to make unambiguous conclusion that detention of the alien, which significantly limits the freedom of movement and other rights, was required. Therefore, the decision of the court of the first instance is annulled, and a new decision, whereby the proposal, regarding detention of the appellant, of Foreigners Registration Centre of the State Board Guard Service under the Ministry of the Interior of the Republic of Lithuania is rejected.

6/4

In the decision in administrative case No. A-2622-858/2015, dated 26th of May, 2015 regarding the duty of Migration Department to explain the asylum seeker what legal consequences will be caused by cancellation of asylum application processing , there was a dispute over legality and validity of decision of the Migration Department to cancel the asylum application processing. According to the applicant, he submitted the request to cancel its asylum processing procedure and to return his personal documents without understanding the future legal consequences because he was misled by employees of the Migration Department. The applicant stated that no decision was made on asylum application longer than 4 months. The employees of the Migration Department advised that he must address for permit to temporarily reside in the Republic of Lithuania on the basis of family unification, however, failed to explain that if the Migration Department cancels the asylum application processing procedure, he will lose the legal status of asylum seeker and temporary territorial asylum in the Republic of Lithuania.

The panel of judges of the Supreme Administrative Court noted that the Law on Legal Status of Alien does not directly specify the duty of the Migration Department to explain the consequences of cancelling the application processing procedure for the alien (asylum seeker), who wishes to cancel his asylum application processing. However, it should be considered that the asylum seeker is the citizen of the foreign country, who, as it is usual, does not understand the national language and does not know the legal system of the Republic of Lithuania, and the European Union, therefore, it is more difficult for him to understand the legal consequences of the actions, related with asylum application. The principle of good administration should also be considered, whereby it is requested that the state institutions, passing administrative decisions, would act thoroughly and carefully, in order to ensure that all legislation would be followed in the administrative procedure. This principle also implies that the subject of public administration has the duty to provide objective and accurate information on the given question for the interested person (see, e.g., the ruling of extended panel of judges of the Supreme Administrative Court of Lithuania, dated 4th of October, 2012, in administrative case No. A502-134/2012; ruling, dated 26th of March, 2013, in administrative case mNo.A756-708/2013; ruling, dated 14th of May, 2015, in administrative case No. A-1316-756/2015). Thus, as it was stated by the panel of judges of the Supreme Administrative Court of Lithuania, before accepting the request of asylum seeker to cancel the asylum application processing, the Migration Department must make sure that as an asylum seeker understands the legal consequences of cancellation of asylum application processing, and that precisely these circumstances are what he seeks for. There were no data that the consequences of cancellation of asylum application processing were explained to asylum seeker. Considering the arguments of complaint and appeal of the applicant, it should be considered that he, submitting the request to cancel his asylum application processing, did not want to lose his asylum seeker status and temporary asylum of the Republic of Lithuania.

6/5

In the decision in administrative case No. eA-2142-624/2015, dated 26th of May, 2015 the Supreme Administrative Court of Lithuania noted certain principles regarding the imposition of alternative detention remedies for asylum seeker to whom there is valid restriction to enter the Republic of Lithuania and whose underaged wife is pregnant.

In the relevant case there was an issue regarding the part of the decision of the court of first instance. By this part, the court of the first instance, did not satisfy the application of applicant, regarding Ignalina's district court decision and regarding the imposition of alternative detention measures legality and validity.

On 14th of April of 2015, Migration department under Ministry of Internal Affairs took the decision to accept the application of the applicant for asylum. They granted to him temporary territorial asylum and accommodated in Foreigners' Registration Center. However, applicant together with his wife, violated the rules of accommodation in Foreigners' Registration Center. They did not arrive to the Center on time and on 13th of May 2015 the were returned to Lithuania from Republic of Latvia.

Furthermore, on 15th August of 2012 applicant resubmitted the application where he was asking for the asylum in the Republic of Lithuania. However, he did not wait for the final decision and left the Foreigners' Registration Center, where he was accommodated, later he was returned to Lithuania from the UK. The submitted new application where he was asking for the asylum in the Republic of Lithuania, however later he rejected the application. There is a restriction for the applicant to enter the Republic of Lithuania till the end of 20th May of 2016.

The panel of judges of the Supreme Administrative Court have noted, the vulnerable persons and families, with under-aged children, can be detained only in special cases, taking into account the child's and vulnerable persons' best interests. In this case, the Law of Legal Status of Aliens, regarding the legislation of "On the legal status of foreigners", wasn't understood as special cases, in the evaluation by the board of judges. However, the objective circumstances, that applicant personal identification wasn't approved officially. Although the asylum seeker (applicant), rudely ignored the clear prohibitions, and tried to leave the Republic of Lithuania without the travel document. This could be one of the reasons and remedies to restrict his movement in the Republic of Lithuania and to apply the detention measure for the applicant, who has to take care of his under-aged, pregnant and special needs required wife (family member), her living condition has an impact on applicant detention, however detention could be made only in special cases (a threat to national security etc.), if there is no other alternative (person violated the alternative remedy etc.) (example in the case of Supreme Administrative Court of Lithuania, February 15th 2015, case number Nr. A-1797-756/2015). In this case, detention in the Foreigners Registration Centre was assessed as an inappropriate and disproportionate measure and the circumstances as special.

The panel of judges of the Supreme Administrative Court of Lithuania, decided that the Law of Legal Status of Aliens, article 115, part 1, point 5, provided the foreigner's accommodation at the Foreigners Registration Center, without restricting freedom of movement. In this case this was sufficient and appropriate.

Part Six: VIII. D. The Position of the Individual (including the Corporation) in International Law – Human rights and fundamental freedoms – Other aspects of human rights and fundamental freedoms

6/6

In the 28 April 2015 case No. 2K-7-130-699 / 2015, the Supreme Court ruled on the unlawful property seizure. The case conserned art. 72 para. 2 and art. 199 para. 1 of the Criminal Code of the Republic of Lithuania. The court considered that the seizure, which is applicable to the obligation to declare cash to customs officials, is part of a common control system, designed to deal with serious financial offences. Seizures are designed to meet the general public interest, but in this case, a punitive measure was applied to the convict – the seizure of all of the cash that was carried by him. This, according to the circumstances is disproportionate (inadequate) in view of the violation and was imposed regardless of the ECHR evolving jurisprudence in these cases, and without clear arguments, which would justify such strict measures.

The panel of judges noted that it was not established that the cash was of an illegal origin, that is the income from criminal offence or obtained illegally. It has not been established that the money, without declaring them, was transported for the purpose to use it in an illegal manner. The panel of judges drew attention to the fact that the amount of money that can be legally transported across the border of the Republic of Lithuania, is not limited; if one carries a certain amount of cash, there is no obligation to pay any tax, one just has to declare if the amount exceeds 10 000 EUR. Thus, the State did not suffer and could not suffer any financial damage. The convict has not been tried in the past, any negative characteristics about the person do not exist, the majority of the transported money is owned by a company (that is, by a third party), which has not been accused or suspected of dishonesty, illegally conducting its business or sought to conceal imported money. The seized amount of money is significant to the convict, as it was her honestly earned savings. The money that the company lost is regarded, as the debt of the company, whose recovery options, depending on the financial status of the aggrieved party, is limited. The only illegal offences that have been committed by the convict was the declaration failure of the transported money across the border. ECHR jurisprudence emphasised that the restriction of property rights, according to the circumstances, must comply with the infringement, that is, failure to comply with declaration requirements, gravity, rather than the breach which is presumed (i.e. such as money laundering, tax evasion), but in practice has not been determined. The panel of judges found that the sentence imposed (9412 EUR. fine) is sufficiently effective and punitive, therefore an additional measure – seizure of undeclared money, was disproportionate and caused her undue financial burden.

Information for Authors

1. All contributions are refereed. The editors reserve the right to suggest modifications and/or additions to submitted contributions, and further reserve the right to reject or to revoke acceptance.
2. Languages: Contributions must be submitted in English. Authors should ensure that their contribution is reviewed by a person who is competent in English, and edited as necessary. Contributions accepted for publication may, at the discretion of the editors, be linguistically revised. Contributions in German and French may be considered for publication.
3. Proofs: The authors may receive proofs for correction. Authors are requested to keep corrections to a minimum, with the exception of taking into account important material or references not previously available, or development of notes. Substantial modifications other than those described are permitted at the discretion of the editors.
4. Manuscripts should not exceed 25 pages. They should be typed, double-spaced with wide margins, and presented in Microsoft Word format.
5. Manuscripts should be submitted via e-mail attachment. Always keep a copy of the submission.
6. Authors should check for errors before submitting their work. They are responsible for providing complete and correct references, for accuracy and quotations, and for obtaining any permission necessary for quoting another author's work.
7. Manuscripts must adhere to guidelines on format, spelling and style available from the editors, especially: UK English must be the language selected in Microsoft Word.
8. Book reviews: The editor will accept reviews of books published internationally and locally and in languages other than English. Book reviews should not exceed five pages. They should be submitted to Kristine.Zubkane@satv.tiesa.gov.lv.
9. Copyright and Permissions: Copyright is established in the name of Koninklijke Brill NV, which incorporates the imprints Brill, Brill Nijhoff, and Hotei Publishing. Submission of a paper for publication implies that the copyright reverts to the publisher from the author and that the article has not been published elsewhere, and is not being considered for publication elsewhere. Consent to Publish and

Transfer of Copyright forms will be sent to authors whose work has been accepted for publication.

10. Fees: Authors will not receive a fee, but will be presented with a copy of the Yearbook and and an e-offprint of each article free of charge. Ordering information for additional offprints will be sent to each author as publication nears.

Submissions should be addressed to Kristine Zubkane at Kristine.Zubkane@satv.tiesa.gov.lv by the 15th of March of each year for publication the same year.

Authors are request to follow the guidelines below when preparing their manuscripts:

Elements of Style

1. British English spelling should be used.
2. The preferred reference source is the Oxford English Dictionary.
3. The preferred font and size for text and footnotes are Times New Roman 12 pt and Times New Roman 10 pt, respectively.
4. Do not use bold or underline formats to emphasise a word or sentence. Words should only be emphasised using italics, sparingly.
5. When beginning a new section the first paragraph should not be indented, however, subsequent paragraphs should be indented.

Punctuation

1. One space after each punctuation mark is sufficient. That is, after a full stop (.) there should only be one space.

Figures and Numerals

1. Spell out the numbers from one to ten (except in pages, legislation, dates and other similar references); use numerals for numbers 11 and higher. Also use numerals throughout for dates and times.
2. For percentages spell out the word per cent. For example, eight per cent, not 8%.
3. Spell out fractions. For example, two-thirds or three-quarters.
4. Page ranges should be separated by an en dash. For example, pp. 26-46.

Foreign and Latin Words

1. Foreign and Latin words should be italicised.

Italicising

1. Italics are used for emphasis. Do not use bold or underline formatting for emphasis.
2. Italics should be used sparingly. If they are used too often the emphasis will be weakened.
3. Foreign and Latin words should be italicised.
4. All case names should be italicised, however, the word case and the v. should not be italicised.
   For example, *Hermes* v. *FHT Marketing* case.
5. All signals should be italicised in footnotes. Such signals include *see, see also, cf., contra, but see, but cf., see generally, et seq.*, and *e.g.*

Monetary Amounts

1. Do not use dollar signs, use USD (US dollars), SEK (Swedish Kronor), EUR (Euro), etc. This abbreviation should be placed directly before the amount it refers to. For example, EUR 100.

Dates and Time

1. For dates including day, month and year use the following format, 1 January 2003.
2. If only month and year is included use the following format, January 2003.
3. If only month and day is used use the following format, 1 January.
4. Years should be separated by an en-dash. For example, 1980–1986.

Headings

1. Authors are asked to use only three levels of headings, although four can be accommodated. They should be numbered consecutively and formatted as in the example. The first letter of all words should be *capitalised*, except prepositions and articles.

Example:

1. Democracy within States
   1.1. Key Principles and Institutions
      1.1.1. Civil and Political Rights

Quotations

1. *Direct* quotations should be enclosed in double quotation marks (" ") and run on in the text.

2. Single quotation marks (' ') are used to distinguish words, concepts or short phrases under discussion.
3. For larger sections of quoted text (*i.e.*, anything over five lines) use block quotes: set these off from other text by adding a blank line above and below the section, and indent the block of text on the left and right by five points. Reduce type size to 10 pt. These larger sections, or 'block quotes', should be enclosed in quotation marks.
4. Quotation marks should come before all punctuation, except where the whole sentence is a quotation.

Example:
He said "I agree with you". "Don't do it."

5. Where the quoted material begins with a capital but is being placed in the middle of a sentence and the letter should grammatically be lower case, place the letter in square brackets and change to lower case.

Example:
As explicitly stated in Article 20 "[a]ny propaganda for war shall be prohibited by law".

6. Omission points
    a. Use to designate that the quoted material has omitted information (usually only in a sentence).
    b. Should be styled as three spaced points (full stops), with a space before the first point and a space after the last point.
    c. When used within quotations, omit all punctuation (including full stops) immediately prior to the omission points.
    d. It is *unnecessary* to include omission points at the beginning of a quote if the first letter of the quoted material is in lower case. The lower case letter denotes that the quote comes from the middle of a sentence.

Example:
Article 6 also states that the right to life "shall be protected by law".
Article 50 states that the "... Covenant shall extend to all parts of federal States without any limitations or exceptions".

INFORMATION FOR AUTHORS

Citations

1. When citing the following general guidelines should be observed:
2. When in doubt, provide all information – it is easier and faster to cut than to hunt down minutiae.
3. If there is one footnote in a sentence the footnote should follow all punctuation. However, when there is more than one footnote the footnotes should be placed after the idea, quote, article, etc, *except* for the last footnote, which should follow all punctuation.

Examples:

Article 6 can be said to predate the Covenant by many years.[12]
Both case law[13] and customary practice illustrate this point.[14]

4. Do not use endnotes; use footnotes (bottom of page).
5. All footnotes should end with a full stop.
6. Footnotes should be in Times New Roman 10 pt.
7. Do not make reference within the text to other parts of the text using page numbers. Use section headings, numbers/letters, or a prose description of the part of the text you wish to refer to.
8. The following abbreviations should be used:

pp. = pages; p. = page; para. = paragraph; paras. = paragraphs

Example:

pp. 25-27.

9. *et seq.* is preferred to ff.
10. All signals should be italicised in footnotes. Signals (for example: *see, see also, cf., but see,* etc.) should not be separated from the rest of the citation by a comma, except for *e.g.*

Examples:

See Rispoli v. *Italy,* 30 October 2003 ...
E.g., J. Klabbers, 'The Concept of Treaty ...

References and Cross References

1. When referring to a previously cited work use the following format: author's surname, *supra* note ... and give the number of the footnote in which the work was first cited.

Example:
Bogdan, *supra* note 8.

2. When referring to a previously cited case use the following format: case name, *supra* note ... and give the number of the footnote in which the case was first cited. Note: long case names should be shortened appropriately.

Example:
Lockerbie case, *supra* note 2.

3. When referring to a previously cited work or case but referring to a different page or paragraph than what was originally cited indicate the page or paragraph referred to.

Examples:
Crawford, s*upra* note 10, p. 25.
Rispoli v. *Italy*, *supra* note 6, para. 18.

4. When referring to a work cited *immediately above* the citation in question, and with the same page number, use the following: *Ibid.* Remember: use *ibid.* only for immediately preceding references, otherwise, use *supra* note.
5. In cases such as no. 4 above, but with a different page number indicate the page referred to.

Example:
Ibid., p. 4.

References: Examples

References should adhere to the specifications below, in accordance with the publisher's requirements. Most importantly, our ability to furnish missing bibliographic information on sources is limited by time constraints. The guidelines below have been simplified greatly with respect to the publisher's guidebook in order to facilitate adherence.

1. Website/Internet references

For journal articles, books, case law, newspaper articles, and other documents accessed via the Internet simply cite as normal adding the URL (website address) in angle brackets (omitting http://) and the date the material was accessed *to the end of the citation.*

For example:
Legality of the Threat or Use of Nuclear Weapons, 8 July 1996, ICJ, Advisory Opinion, paras. 61–63, <www.icj-cij.org/icjwww/icases/iunan/iunan-frame.htm>, visited on 29 October 2003.

If the material does not lend itself to the above mentioned citation format provide the following information in this order:
a. The capitalised initial of the author's first name and middle name (if applicable), followed by the author's surname (If relevant) *and/or* issuing institution, group, etc. (if relevant).
b. Title of document in italics.
c. URL (website address) in angle brackets omitting http://.
d. Date that the material was accessed.

2. Articles in journals
The following information should be contained in this order:
a. The capitalised initial of the author's first name and middle name (if applicable), followed by the author's surname.
b. The name of the article enclosed in single quotation marks.
c. The volume number.
d. The name of the journal in italics.
e. The year in parentheses.
f. Page(s)/paragraph(s) directly referred to or the page range of the article.

Examples:
R. O'Keefe, 'The Admission to the United Nations of the Ex-Soviet and Ex-Yugoslav States', 1 *Baltic Yearbook of International Law* (2001) p. 170.
O. Spiermann, 'Humanitarian Intervention as a Necessity and the Threat or Use of *Jus Cogens*', 71:4 *Nordic Journal of International Law* (2002) pp. 530–534.

3. Books
The following information should be contained in this order:
a. The capitalised initial of the author's first name and middle name (if applicable), followed by the author's surname. If an article has two authors their names should be separated by the word and. If an

article has more than two authors, list only the first author, followed by *et al.*
b. The title of the book in italics.
c. The publisher, the place of publication and the year of publication in parentheses.
d. Editor and editors should be specified as: (ed.) and (eds.) respectively.
e. Page(s) or paragraph(s) referred to (if applicable).

Example:

L. Holmström (ed.), *Concluding Observations of the UN Committee on the Elimination of Racial Discrimination* (Kluwer Law International, The Hague, 2002) pp. 77-79.

4. Chapters in books

The page reference at which the cited chapter begins should always be specified *or* specify the specific page(s) referred to.

Example:

A. Eide, 'Cultural Rights and Minorities: Essay in Honour of Erica-Irene Daes', in G. Alfredsson and M. Stavropoulou (eds.), *Justice Pending: Indigenous Peoples and Other Good Causes* (Kluwer Law International, The Hague, 2002) p. 83.

5. Case law

The following information should be contained in this order:
a. Case name in italics, excluding 'v.' which should be in roman.
b. Parties to the case if *not* included in case name, in parentheses.
c. Date of judgement.
d. Issuing court, this can be abbreviated if the court is well known internationally. For example, ECHR, ICJ, etc.
e. In the absence of any indication to the contrary the cited case is a judgement on the merits. Any variation from that should be stated. For example, advisory opinion, a dissenting opinion, provisional measures or if it has some other unique characteristic.
f. Reference or application number (if applicable).
g. Source (however if accessed by Internet cite appropriately, see above).
h. Page(s) or paragraph(s) referred to (if applicable).

Examples:

International Court of Justice:
Arrest Warrant of 11 April 2000 (Democratic Republic of the Congo v. Belgium), 8 December 2000, ICJ, Provisional Measures, *I.C.J. Reports 2000*, p. 182.

Legality of the Threat or Use of Nuclear Weapons, 8 July 1996, ICJ, Advisory Opinion, paras. 61-63, <www.icj-cij.org/icjwww/icases/iunan/iunanframe.htm>, visited on 29 October 2003.

European Court of Human Rights:
Rispoli v. Italy, 30 October 2003, ECHR, no. 00055388/00, para. 26, <hudoc.echr.coe.int/hudoc/ViewRoot.asp?Item=1&Action=Html&X=1030183728&Notice=0&Noticemode=&RelatedMode=1>, visited on 29 October 2003.

Velikova v. Bulgaria, 18 May 2000, ECHR, no. 41488/98, *Reports of Judgments and Decisions 2000-VI*, para. 92.

Inter-American Court of Human Rights:
The Case of the Mayagna (Sumo) Awas Tingni Community v. Nicaragua, 31 August 2001, Inter-American Court of Human Rights, Series C No. 79, para. 164, <www.corteidh.or.cr/seriecing/serie_c_79_ing.doc>, visited on 29 October 2003.

6. UN documents, publications, and resolutions

The following information should be contained in this order:
a. Author/agency/body (if necessary).
b. Title in italics (if necessary).
c. Document symbol or publication sales number in parentheses.
d. Specific page(s) or paragraph(s) referred to (if applicable).

7. Newspaper articles

The following information should be contained in this order:
a. The capitalised initial of the author's first name and middle name (if applicable), followed by the author's surname.
b. Title of article.
c. Newspaper.
d. Date.
e. Page or section.

Example:

S. Kishkovsky, 'The Most Dangerous Place in Europe for Journalists', *The International Herald Tribune*, 24 October 2003, p. 2.

Printed in the United States
By Bookmasters